DAY OF PERDITION

We Almost Stopped Him

Kaelyn Hart

ZERUBBABEL MEDIA

Published by Zerubbabel Media

ISBN: 978-0-615-26423-3

THEREFORE SEEING WE HAVE THIS MINISTRY, AS WE HAVE RECEIVED MERCY, WE FAINT NOT;

FOR WE PREACH NOT OURSELVES, BUT CHRIST JESUS THE LORD; AND OURSELVES YOUR SERVANTS FOR JESUS' SAKE.

WE ARE TROUBLED ON EVERY SIDE, YET NOT DISTRESSED; WE ARE PERPLEXED, BUT NOT IN DESPAIR;

PERSECUTED, BUT NOT FORSAKEN; CAST DOWN, BUT NOT DESTROYED;

KNOWING THAT HE WHICH RAISED UP THE LORD JESUS SHALL RAISE UP US ALSO BY JESUS, AND SHALL PRESENT US WITH YOU.

FOR ALL THINGS ARE FOR YOUR SAKES, THAT THE ABUNDANT GRACE MIGHT THROUGH THE THANKSGIVING OF MANY REDOUND TO THE GLORY OF GOD.

FOR WHICH CAUSE WE FAINT NOT; BUT THOUGH OUR OUTWARD MAN PERISH, YET THE INWARD MAN IS RENEWED DAY BY DAY.

FOR OUR LIGHT AFFLICTION, WHICH IS BUT FOR A MOMENT, WORKETH FOR US A FAR MORE EXCEEDING AND ETERNAL WEIGHT OF GLORY;

WHILE WE LOOK NOT AT THE THINGS WHICH ARE SEEN, BUT AT THE THINGS WHICH ARE NOT SEEN: FOR THE THINGS WHICH ARE SEEN ARE TEMPORAL; BUT THE THINGS WHICH ARE NOT SEEN ARE ETERNAL.

2 CORINTHIANS 4:1,5,8-9,16-18

CONTENTS

PREFACE

He is a study in contradictions. It is he, who has caused this American housewife to go beyond the normal confines of grocery stores, soccer fields and playdates.

There is something about him, that causes the hair to stand up on the back of my neck and gives me cause to shudder when he looks directly through the camera at us, the "American people" to make a point.

We have been dared to ask questions. The anger and audacity is seeping out at the rallies. You can see the frustration in the eyes of the people who realize just how far we have slipped away from the days when we knew we had every right to ask any and every question that might be pertinent to the well-being of our nation.

It is he, and his minions, who tell us that what we see, is not really what we see. Who he associates with, says nothing about who is. What he said in his own words, in his own book, gives us no cause for concern. Documents that state his religion aren't true. Housing deals and money allocated to specific non-profits while he was in office, if there is any impropriety in their transactions, don't have anything to do with his character or lack of judgement. No. None of that matters or is to be questioned.

It is he, but it is also them.

My precious brood, the children that God has blessed me with, they also are the impetus driving me to learn and study subjects that I have never had more than a perfunctory knowledge of…such as: black liberation theology, socialism, communism, economic history, conspiracy theories and many more areas that require thought-provoking contemplation.

Hey, what does a mom know? What good can a mom do? We'll see. At least, I'll give it a shot. For them. For Him.

Yes, for Him. The Lord Jesus Christ.

Who am I to think that I am worthy to do anything of any significance. I am nothing, but He is everything. And through him, I can do ANYTHING!

> And he said unto me, My grace is sufficient for thee: for my strength is made perfect in weakness. Most gladly therefore will I rather glory in my infirmities, that the power of Christ may rest upon me.
>
> Therefore I take pleasure in infirmities, in reproaches, in necessities, in persecutions, in distresses for Christ's sake: for when I am weak, then am I strong.
> 2 Corinthians 12:9-10

So, for these reasons…I will take on the task at hand. I can't begin to reveal everything that there is to be revealed or even a fraction of it, the mountain of information to sift through is enormous. But I can tell you what I've learned and then it's up to you.

> "There are some truths which are so obvious that, for this very reason, they are not seen or at least not recognized by ordinary people. They sometimes pass by such truisms as though blind, and are most astonished when someone suddenly discovers what everyone really ought to know."
>
> **- Adolf Hitler, Mein Kampf (1925)**

What woke me up out of my idyllic life? Necessity. All of sudden, I realized that my children would be the ones to suffer for my being asleep at the wheel. It was only then, as I began to look at things a bit more closely, that I discovered that for the most part, we are all asleep at the wheel. At least a good, 96% of us.

And they count on it. I can hear you saying, "Who counts on it?" Well, after all the research and words of wisdom taken from some of our former Presidents, Congressmen and people in-the-know, I can tell you that there are groups of people, who count on us to stay in the dark and go about our daily tasks without delving in too deep. Who are they? The answer to that question is the basis for numerous conspiracy theories and you can find the subject being debated all over the internet. Even Glenn Beck, on a recent program was questioning whether we were in the middle of some vast conspiracy.

Who specifically is involved is not the most important question. Why we are being moved like pawns and what we do about it is the greater issue. At what point will we choose to become an active player in this game?

This is an election like no other. That is very clear. Our time is running out How did we get to the place in America where someone with so many questionable acquaintances, alliances, and experiences could have the chance to be in the most important position in our land? When did we first let our guard down to allow the media to take the truth and regurgitate it back in our lap in the form of something unrecognizable?

If we question anything, we will be labeled: racist, bigot, fanatical, out of touch, and old-fashioned. We are told that we must be politically correct or be charged with a hate crime. Our pastors may not voice an opinion from the pulpit or they risk losing their non-profit status. Churches teach prosperity, purpose-driven lives instead of preaching the Bible from beginning to end, the love, fear and judgement of God.

Where did our backbone go? Where are the men and women who will fight, if need be, to take back what we gave up so freely.

The men and women who are serving our country in Iraq deserve no less than our full attention and our resolve to do what we can here at home.

FUTURE GENERATIONS DESERVE NO LESS!

INTRODUCTION

It was never supposed to turn out like this. Precautions were taken to fight the enemy.

BUT...they trusted the wrong people to give them their knowledge. They allowed their world to be turned completely upside down and not only did they let it happen, they invited the evil in.

Could it have been prevented? Could they have stopped him? Somewhere deep inside, they know the truth.

The passion was on the other side, the wrong side. Call it what you will, liberal, left-wing...now is not the time to be politically correct. Using the power of their vote, their influence within their circle of family, friends and acquaintances - they should've done more. How did they become casual, disinterested observers of their lives, instead of passionate participants? Why didn't they teach their children from an early age, how important it was to learn about the history of this great country. About our Founding Fathers, our laws, our Constitution, the great privilege to vote after extensive research of the issues and candidates. Above all, how did they allow the degradation of society to creep in to their own families?

Now they will face the repercussions of their complacency.

Now...they must explain to these precious children how the unthinkable had occurred on their watch.

Letters To The Children

Dear Emma and Jake:

Memaw had to write this letter to you today, although it will probably be one of the hardest things I've ever had to do.

You are the heart of your grandma. When you were born you brought back a sparkle to my life that had been missing for awhile.

We have been so proud of the way your momma and daddy have been bringing you up. They have read all the books and know alot more about parenting than we did. But I think we did pretty well. There may not have been much money, but there was always plenty to eat and plenty of love in our house.

You may not know this, but your momma had your names picked out from the time she was a little girl. She always dreamed about the day she would have her kids and she felt so blessed to have two healthy children.

I know how much it hurts her now to see what you've got facing you growing up in this world. It's not going to be easy. It never was, but this is a whole new way of life. Not anything like we were used to.

The day he got into office, I knew it was a day of "change." Just not the good kind of "change." Sure, we all had our misgivings and we felt like we would do our part to stop him from being elected, but now we know - it wasn't enough.

We should've been screaming from the rooftops, telling it to everyone that would listen, that we wouldn't allow this to happen. But we really didn't realize what exactly the stakes were.

By ignoring the obvious danger, we played with our future. And now you suffer. There's nothing more I can say, except...

I'm so sorry, my babies. If I could do it over, I promise, I would.

I'd do anything to change what you now face.

Dear Emma and Jake:

This doesn't come easy
for me. That last time
I put pen to paper for a
letter was back when I
was trying to win your
grandma's fancy. Those
were the days, although
you couldn't have told
me that then.

We had been looking forward to our "retirement" years, slowing down, grandkids spending the summer with us and just enjoying watching the sun go down over the garden every evening. Those were our dreams. Not very exciting, but that's all we wanted. A simple peace as we grew older.

I'm sorry to say, it won't be that way for us. The end of my life has turned out much different than I had hoped.

The worst part of it all, is that you won't even get to live your life in the kind of country I was privileged to have. You'll never know what it's like not to worry every day about what's coming next to take away your basic freedoms.

My generation was all about "God and Country." We knew if anyone threatened our peace, we would take the fight to them. What we didn't know is that for years, they had been bringing the fight right up to our doorstep and we turned away, too busy to notice or care.

We took our country for granted. We figured what always was, would always be.

We took care of our bills, our retirement plan, made sure we had life insurance, but we never even took the time to see how they were changing our laws. We never took it upon ourselves to see how much could change just with the wrong one being nominated, much less elected.

I'm sorry kids, it's not enough, but it's all I have.

If I could do it over, I promise, I would.

Dear Emma and Jake:

Please understand, I did the best I could.

Every night as I lay under the Iraqi stars, I dreamed of coming home to my blue-eyed little boy and my little girl with the blonde bouncy curls.

I thought as long as I did my part, the American people would do their part. When I was home on leave, I saw all the yellow "Support the Troops" magnets. I had people stop me in the airport, when they saw me in uniform and they would hug me and give me high fives. I was so confident from the outpouring of love that I saw, that it meant they really did care about what we were fighting for and for America's future.

When I think about why I joined, it still makes me cry. I left my job, your mother and my babies to go and fight against the devastation of what the terrorists left us on 9/11.

Now, I am just angry. All we needed were a few good men and women on the homefront to really and truly mean it when they pledged allegiance to the flag, or hold their hand over their heart when the National Anthem is played. Was it all just meaningless words? Could they not at least care enough to find out the truth about him and act on it?

I don't know what more I could have done. I was busy enough fighting to stay alive.

The ones who professed to have morality, just gave up. They figured that the few questionable things they heard about him were just rumors and they really didn't have the time with their busy lives to do more than listen to what the media fed them. They figured they would do what they were required, go vote and whoever won, well, it was just like any other election.

Boy, were they wrong. It changed everything. I know if they had only had a glimpse into what one election would do to the world, they would have fought like hell and the outcome would've been different.

The war I fought doesn't compare to the one were are in now. Who could've ever guessed that the war brewing within our country would have far more casualties than any we've ever been through.

I'm sorry for what we've left you to deal with. Maybe I should've rallied the people back home to at least honor my service with their promise to be an activist in their own lives for the sake of all our children.

If I could do it over, I promise, I would.

I'd fight again for you, for your future. Anything.

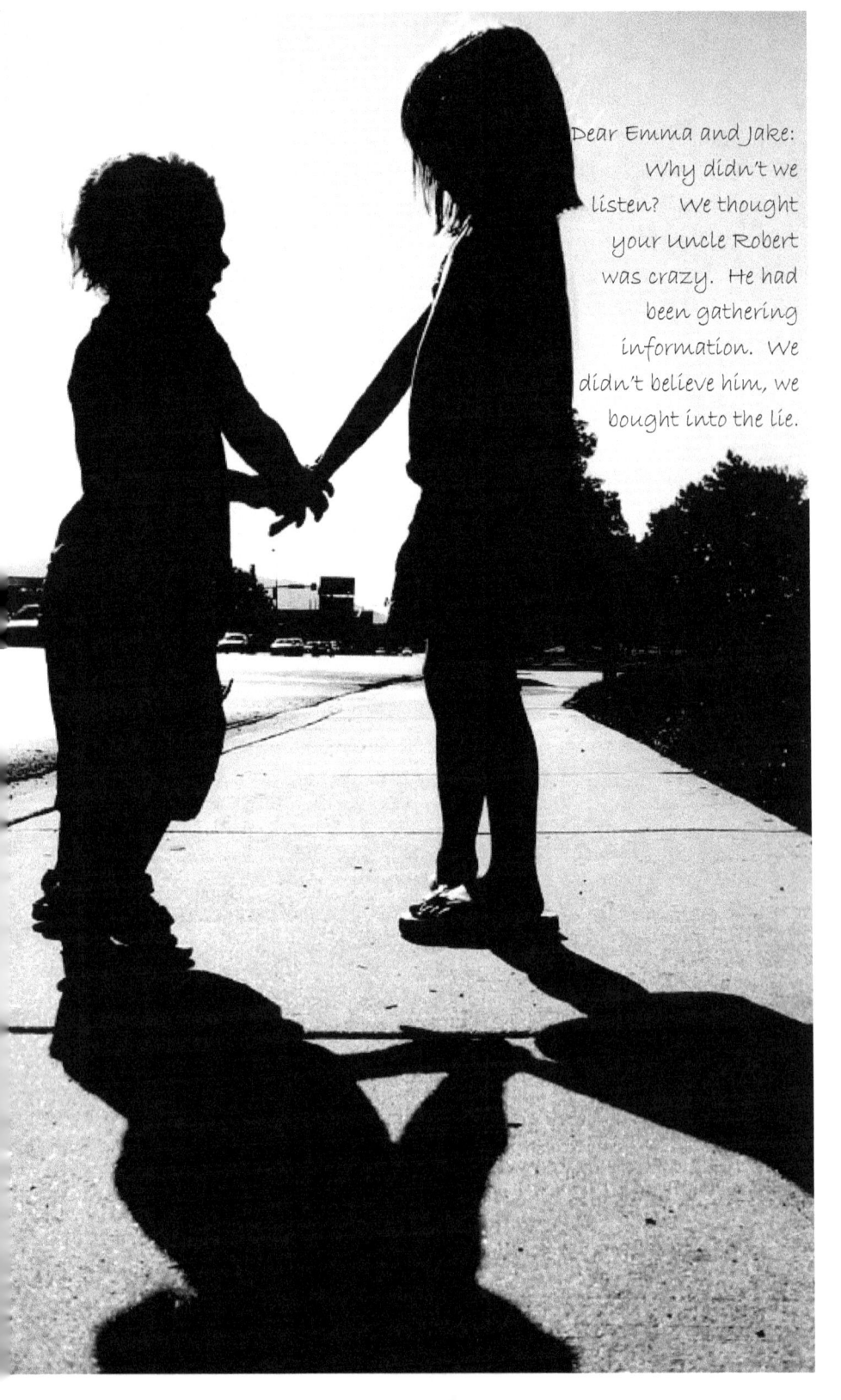

Dear Emma and Jake: Why didn't we listen? We thought your Uncle Robert was crazy. He had been gathering information. We didn't believe him, we bought into the lie.

Words can't express the sadness I feel over what your mommy needs to tell you. The life you have enjoyed for such a brief period of time, is no more.

I've put together the findings of Uncle Robert and gathered these letters for you, so that someday you will understand what it was like then. Still, it's no excuse.

The world around us has changed and in some way if America makes it through this catastrophe, maybe you can learn from our mistakes and pick up the pieces again.

I'm sorry. I'm sorry for allowing the mundane everyday tasks of our lives, to keep me from being vigilant about the decisions being made far away that would ulitmately have great impact on your life.

From the time you were placed in my arms, I swore with my being that I would protect you and do everything within my power to give you a wonderful life.

Your father and I planned for your college, prayed for your future and did all the things that good parents do.

But as it turns out, we didn't do enough.

While I was busy packing lunches and checking homework, your world was changing.

If we had paid more attention to the signs, surely, we would have done something. Anything.

We were mainly worried about what every struggling family was preoccupied with: The Economy.

Meanwhile, I let the lions in and they have ravaged my home. I didn't see the danger.

I pray to God that he will have mercy on us. Can you forgive me?

Can it ever go back to the way it was? It wasn't perfect, but we still had our freedoms and the American way of life. So much has changed.

If I could do it over, I promise, I would.

I'd do anything to take twenty years back. What would I do? I'd be on my knees everyday asking God to show me how to begin to tell the world what we would face. Just like in Noah's day...they'd probably laugh at me...but if I could get just one, then one more...then maybe God would've blessed the effort and today would be a different day for you.

But, too late.

Please take this information and try to understand.

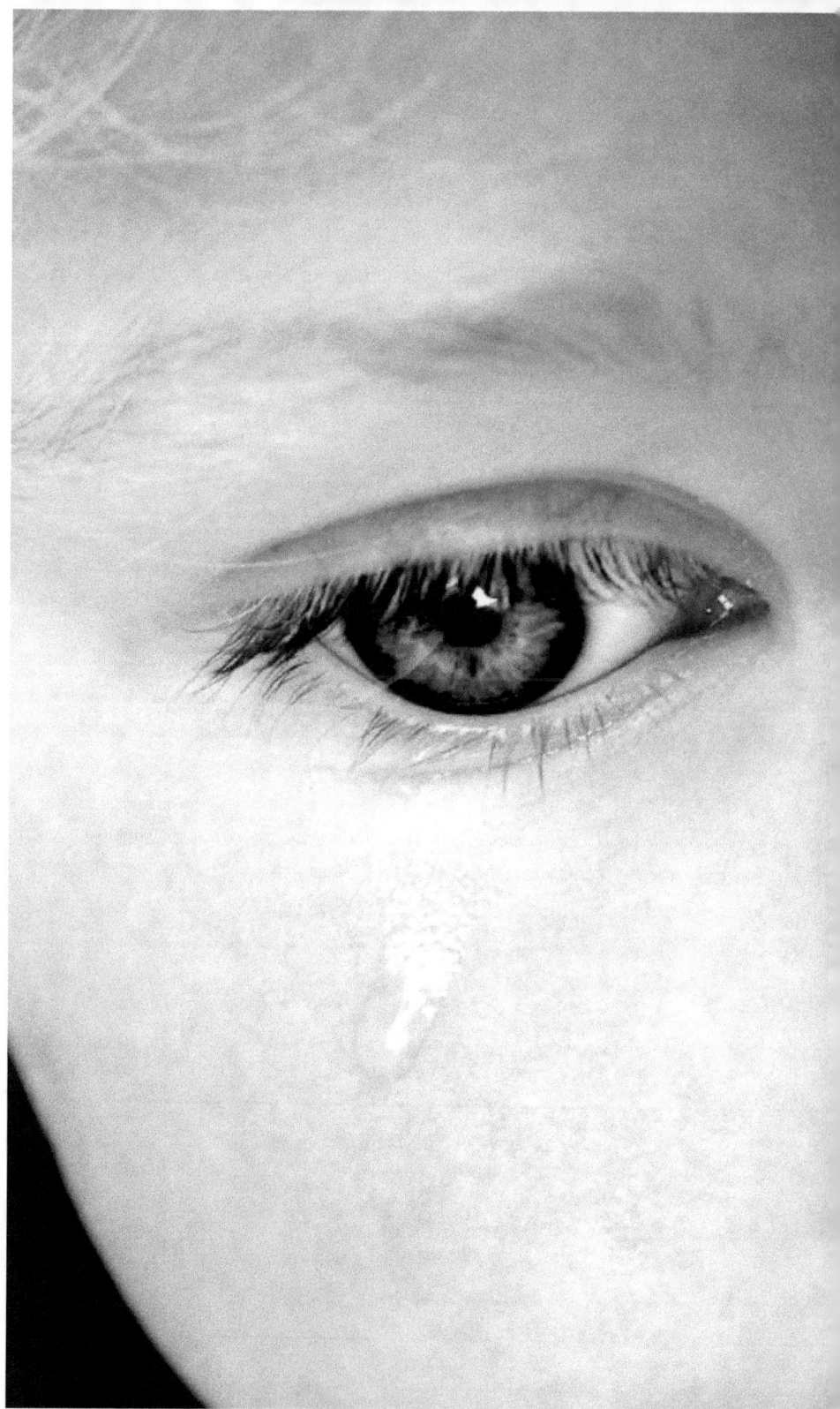

PART I

WHAT CAME BEFORE

"...understand, what is unfolding on this Earth is indeed a monstrous conspiracy so great, so grave, so meticulously planned and so near its completion .... and the vast majority of people are wholly ignorant of it ... And...on such weighty matters concerning the loss of liberty and freedom, of life and death, both physical and spiritual, ignorance is not bliss.

Ian Welsh[1]

ECHOS FROM THE PAST

In February 1945, Joseph Stalin, Winston Churchill and Franklin D. Roosevelt met at Yalta and agreed to the plans proposing the establishment of the United Nations by declaring their resolve to establish "a general international organization to maintain peace and security."

The essential idea of the United Nations was that it would deliver humanity from itself, from its innate warlike nature, by obviating the need to resolve differences between nation, peoples and races by violent means...In this wise, each member nation would send a permanent delegation to represent it in the debates over national and international issues. And, in the event of the failure of diplomacy, the Security Council, made up of the allied victors of WWII USA, UK, Soviet Russia, France and China, would be able to marshal the necessary economic and even military forces to contain a regional conflict, revolution or war.[2]

The United Nations is the creature of the New World Order, planned in secret by men who seek to bring "peace" to the world by establishing a World Empire in which no competing ideologies or spiritual systems are allowed to exist....raising its revenue by "world taxes" and kept in power by a huge sophisticated World Army and World Police that will control the masses with new surveillance and behavior modification technology or, if this fails, with sheer brute force. [3]

Congressional Record of June 7, 1949...a joint resolution...was introduced in the House of Representatives...Concerning this Resolution, the chairman of the National Executive Committee of the United World Federalists, Cord Meyer, declared at a hearing before the Senate Subcommittee on the United Nations Charter that:

> "We in the United States would be declaring our willingness to join with other nations in transferring to the UN constitutional authority to administer and enforce law that was binding on national governments and their individual citizens."[4]

The existences of such documents prove that the government of the United States and the political leaders of the US together with the ruling elite of other countries are working behind the scenes to forge a World Empire under the rule of the UN. These traitors and intriguers have worked ceaselessly to strengthen the United Nations and to move the people of the world towards:

One World Government .... a World Empire[5]

"Whereas it has been proposed that the United States of America become a part of a world federal government; and... This program... would entail the surrender of our national sovereignty and... Bring into being a form of government whose authority would supersede that of the constitution of the United States government; and ... institute a system of laws where-by American citizens could be tried by aliens in controversial of the provisions of the constitution of the United States; and... The veterans of foreign wars is composed solely of men who have worn the uniform of the united states on foreign shores and in hostile waters in time of war and from their personal experiences are familiar with the traditions and operations of other countries; and ... many of our comrades rest forever in foreign soil and their sacrifices were made to retain the dignity and sovereignty of the United States of America: now therefore, be it resolved by the fiftieth annual convention of the Veterans of Foreign Wars of the United States, that we hereby declare that we are unalterably opposed to any program which would entail the surrender of any part of the sovereignty of the United States of America in favor of a world government."

Veterans of Foreign Wars
Resolution objecting to a world federation, VFW Resolution No. 27 presented to House Committee on Foreign Affairs Hearing, 81st Cong., 1st Sess. 10/12-13/49 - Congressional Record (1949)[6]

"It will take a long time to prepare peoples and governments of most nations for acceptance of and participation in a world government ... we will have to be willing to work patiently until peoples or governments are ready for it."

Ambassador Warren Austin
Chief of the US Mission to the UN, United Nations World
(1949)[7]

"Fifty men have run America, and that's a high figure."

Joseph Kennedy

The New York Times. (1936)[8]

"In the 1930's, we put eleven hundred men into the priesthood in order to destroy the Church from within .... Right now they are in the highest places in the Church ... you will not recognize the Catholic Church."

Dr. Bella Dodd

Ex-Communist who was a leader of the Communist Party of America (CPUSA) in the 1930' s and 1940's who converted to Catholicism at the end of her life, speaking about the Communist infiltration of the Roman Catholic Church with the intention of destroying it from within.[9]

"The high office of the president has been used to foment a plot to destroy America's freedom and before I leave this office, I must inform the citizens of their plight."

President John F. Kennedy

Speech at Columbia University ten days before he was assassinated.[10]

"Two centuries ago our forefathers brought forth a new nation; now we must join with others to bring forth a new world order."

32 US Senators and 92 US Representatives

In Washington, D.C. signed a "Declaration of Interdependence"

(1976)[11]

"Mankind's problems can no longer be solved by national government. What is needed is a World Government. This can best be achieved by strengthening the United Nations system."

James Gustave Speth
Yale School of Forestry and Environmental Studies, Bill Clinton's appointee as administrator for the UN Development Program: Human Development Report section "Global Governance for the 21st Century" (1994[12]

"The new world order that is in the making must focus on the creation of a world of democracy, peace and prosperity for all."

Nelson Mandela
The Philadelphia Inquirer (1994)[13]

"What Congress will have before it is not a conventional trade agreement but the architecture of a new international system ... a first step toward a new world order."

Henry Kissinger
Writing in the Los Angeles Times concerning North Atlantic Free Trade Association (NAFTA) (1993)[14]

"It is the sacred principles enshrined in the United Nations charter to which the American people will henceforth pledge their allegiance."

President George Herbert Walker Bush
Address to the General Assembly of the UN (1992)[15]

"The existing order is breaking down at a very rapid rate, and the main uncertainty is whether mankind can exert a positive role in shaping a new world order or is doomed to await collapse in a passive posture. We believe a new order will be born no later than early in the next century and that the death throes of the old and the birth pangs of the new..."

Richard A. Falk

In an article entitled "Toward a New World Order: Modest Methods and Drastic Visions" (1975)[16]

As He was sitting on the Mount of Olives, the disciples came to Him privately, saying, "Tell us, when will these things happen, and what will be the sign of Your coming, and of the end of the age?"

And Jesus answered and said to them, "See to it that no one misleads you."

"For many will come in My name, saying, 'I am the Christ,' and will mislead many."

"You will be hearing of wars and rumors of wars. See that you are not frightened, for those things must take place, but that is not yet the end."

"For nation will rise against nation, and kingdom against kingdom, and in various places there will be famines and earthquakes."

"But all these things are merely the beginning of birth pangs."

Matthew 24:3-8

PART II

THE ISSUES

"We have no government armed with power capable of contending with human passions unbridled by morality and religion. Avarice, ambition, revenge, or gallantry, would break the strongest cords of our Constitution as a whale goes through a net. Our Constitution was made only for a moral and religious people. It is wholly inadequate to the government of any other."

John Adams, October 11, 1798

ALL ABOUT THE ISSUES

The questions about the man's background were varied and numerous. He hated these questions and repeated the mantra over and over that the American people were tired of these questions and wanted nothing more than to be clear on where he stood on the issues and what he could do for their ailing pocketbook.

He was right, each of us had our own particular issues that were near and dear to out hearts. Too many brushed aside the nagging little uneasiness about character and cared more for the balance in the 401k.

However, to anyone who professed Christianity, there are some that should have weighed heavier on the scales and with no room for compromise, since the most heinous of these issues involves murder.

Yes, if the issues were all there were to consider, Barack Obama's record should have been enough to convince us that the years ahead with him at the helm would not bode well.

"Capital must protect itself in every way.... Debts must be collected and loans and mortgages foreclosed as soon as possible. When through a process of law the common people have lost their homes, they will be more tractable and more easily governed by the strong arm of the law applied by the central power of leading financiers. People without homes will not quarrel with their leaders. This is well known among our principal men now engaged in forming an imperialism of capitalism to govern the world. By dividing the people we can get them to expend their energies in fighting over questions of no importance to us except as teachers of the common herd."

Civil Servant's Year Book, The Organizer (1934)

THE ECONOMY

It was all about the economy. Nothing else seemed to matter.

There was enough blame to go around. We were given our script by the media and the politicians on TV. According to them, it was the fault of the evil CEOs of big corporations who were to blame. The politicians would remind us that it was the other political party's fault whose policies, deregulation and reckless spending got us here.

The quick fix was what we were after. There were some who were angry and wanted to hold out for a better solution. But most wanted to just go with whatever plan would allow us to move on and get back to the important things in life...like "Monday Night Football" and "Dancing With The Stars."

Under no circumstances, were we to really sit down and figure out how this all began and what role we played.

Well, guess what? The infamous Bailout of 2008, didn't help. Not us anyway. It started us down the slippery slope that led to our present situation. Actually, let me back up on that, this had really begun decades ago and this merely put a blip on the consciousness of the American people.

I say blip, because even at this point, we were inconvenienced and alittle worried about the balances of our 401k, but still not at the point where we would be shaken to our core. Not yet, but it was coming.

Maybe we would have altered the course of events if we had taken the time to examine our own perceptions and ideologies.

My take on this, is that for me, it started with that first car. Your parents would tell you, credit was good as long as you made your payments. So, you grew up with the notion that it was okay to go out and finance that car, you had every intention of making the payment and...oh, how nice it was to smell that new leather.

This would be the same judgement you would use throughout your lifetime. It was an accepted principle to purchase what you wanted with credit, as long as it was determined that you had a good job to pay for it. Was this the correct way to go about your life? No. As a Christian, everything that you need to know can be found in the Bible. Here's what the Bible has to say:

> Owe no man any thing, but to love one another: for he that loveth
> another hath fulfilled the law.
> ### Romans 13:8

A very simple instruction. Yet, we choose to find a way around those verses that don't quite fit our desires.

Here's another appropriate verse:

> Wealth gained hastily will dwindle, but whoever gathers little by
> little will increase it.
> ### Proverbs 13:11

When we took it upon ourselves to get what we wanted with credit, because we had to have it NOW, it became a matter of disobedience. The American dream of owning a home, became the American nightmare. Our country's own policy of borrowing from the world, put our children's future in the hands of foreign leaders.

So, we found ourselves in a place of desperation. The overwhelming cry was for something or someone who could take our worries and fears and promise to make to make a difference. We cared less about the little nagging questions that we were told by the knowledgeable icons in the media were a distraction from the real issues. So, the issue of character and principles became a minor consideration in the scheme of things.

And that's where we completely unraveled.

According to Investor's Business Daily:
A plan by Barack Obama to redistribute American wealth on a global level is moving forward in the Senate. It follows Marxist theology — from each according to his ability, to each according to his need.

Speaking in Berlin, Obama said: "While the 20th century taught us that we share a common destiny, the 21st has revealed a world more intertwined than at any time in human history."

What the 20th century really showed was a series of totalitarian threats — from fascism to Nazism to communism — defeated by the U.S. military. Hitler's Germany, Mussolini's Italy, Tojo's Japan and the Soviet Union offered destinies we did not share.

Our destiny of peace and freedom through strength was not achieved by a transnationalist fantasy of buying the world a Coke and singing "Kumbaya."

A statement from Obama's office says: "With billions of people living on just dollars a day around the world, global poverty remains one of the greatest challenges and tragedies the international community faces. It must be a priority of American foreign policy to commit to eliminating extreme poverty and ensuring every child has food, shelter and clean drinking water."

These are worthy goals, but note there's no mention of spreading democracy, expanding free trade, promoting entrepreneurial capitalism or ridding the world of despots who rule and ravage countries such as Zimbabwe and Sudan.

Obama would give them all a fish without teaching them how to fish. Pledging to cut global poverty in half on the backs of U.S. taxpayers is a ridiculous and impossible goal.

His legislation refers to the "millennium development goal," a phrase from a declaration adopted by the United Nations Millennium Assembly in 2000 and supported by President Clinton.

It calls for the "eradication of poverty" in part through the "redistribution (of) wealth of land" and "a fair distribution of the earth's resources." In other words: American resources.

It's a mantra of liberals that the U.S. is only a small portion of the world's population yet consumes an unseemly portion of the planet's supposedly finite resources. Never mentioned is the fact that America's population, just 5% of the world's total, also produces a stunning 27% of the world's GDP — to the enormous benefit of other countries. Nonetheless, their solution is to siphon off the product of our free democracy and distribute it.

We already transfer too much national wealth to the United Nations and its busybody agencies. Obama's bill would force U.S. taxpayers to fork over 0.7% of our gross domestic product every year to fund a global war on poverty, spending well above the $16.3 billion in global poverty aid the U.S. already spends.

Over a 13-year period, from 2002, when the U.N.'s Financing for Development Conference was held, to the target year of 2015, when the U.S is expected to meet its part of the U.N. Millennium goals, we would be spending an additional $65 billion annually for a total of $845 billion.

During a time of economic uncertainty, the plan would cost every American taxpayer around $2,500. The Global Poverty Act is the first toe in the water of global socialism.[2]

"The truth is most Americans don't want much. Folks don't want the whole pie. Most Americans feel blessed to thrive a little bit, but that's out of reach for them. The truth is, in order to get things like universal health care and a revamped education system, someone is going to have to give up a piece of their pie so that someone else can have more."

- **Michelle Obama**[3]

Investor's Business Daily also reports that during a speech to the NAACP:

> Before friendly audiences, Barack Obama speaks passionately about something called "economic justice." He uses the term obliquely, though, speaking in code — socialist code....Sen. Obama repeated the term at least four times. "I've been working my entire adult life to help build an America where economic justice is being served," he said at the group's 99th annual convention in Cincinnati.
>
> "Economic justice" simply means punishing the successful and redistributing their wealth by government fiat. It's a euphemism for socialism.
>
> In the past, such rhetoric was just that — rhetoric. But Obama's positioning himself with alarming stealth to put that rhetoric into action on a scale not seen since the birth of the welfare state.
>
> Obama also talks about "restoring fairness to the economy," code for soaking the "rich" — a segment of society he fails to understand that includes mom-and-pop businesses filing individual tax returns.
>
> It's clear from a close reading of his two books that he's a firm believer in class envy. He assumes the economy is a fixed pie, whereby the successful only get rich at the expense of the poor.
>
> Following this discredited Marxist model, he believes government must step in and redistribute pieces of the pie. That requires massive transfers of wealth through government taxing and spending, a return to the entitlement days of old.[4]

The article further stated:

> The seeds of his far-left ideology were planted in his formative years as a teenager in Hawaii — and they were far more radical than any biography or profile in the media has portrayed.
>
> As a Nairobi bureaucrat, Barack Hussein Obama Sr., a Harvard-educated economist, grew to challenge the ruling pro-Western government for not being socialist enough. In an eight-page scholarly paper published in 1965, he argued for eliminating private farming and nationalizing businesses "owned by Asians and Europeans."
>
> His ideas for communist-style expropriation didn't stop there. He also proposed massive taxes on the rich to "redistribute our economic gains to the benefit of all."
>
> "Theoretically, there is nothing that can stop the government from taxing 100% of income so long as the people get benefits from the government commensurate with their income which is taxed," Obama Sr. wrote. "I do not see why the government cannot tax those who have more and syphon some of these revenues into savings which can be utilized in investment for future development."
>
> Taxes and "investment" . . . the fruit truly does not fall far from the vine.
>
> (Voters might also be interested to know that Obama, the supposed straight shooter, does not once mention his father's communist leanings in an entire book dedicated to his memory.) [5]

"Obama learned that revealing his real beliefs can jeopardize his quest for the power needed to put his "redistribution" plans into action." [6]

> "Wealth is within the reach of the masses simply through the process of appropriation."
> - **Che Guevara, Argentine Marxist Revolutionary** [7]

On October 13, 2008 according to FoxNews.com:

> Barack Obama told a tax-burdened plumber over the weekend that his economic philosophy is to "spread the wealth around" -- a comment that may only draw fire from riled-up John McCain supporters who have taken to calling Obama a "socialist" at the Republican's rallies.
>
> "Your new tax plan is going to tax me more, isn't it?" the plumber asked, complaining that he was being taxed "more and more for fulfilling the American dream."
>
> "It's not that I want to punish your success. I just want to make sure that everybody who is behind you, that they've got a chance for success too," Obama responded. "My attitude is that if the economy's good for folks from the bottom up, it's gonna be good for everybody. I think when you spread the wealth around, it's good for everybody." [8]

In addition to Barack Obama's socialistic tax plan, the additional damage he could inflict when combining his philosophies with the current state of the economy, is beyond anything we've witnessed in our country's history.

"We cannot expect the Americans to jump from capitalism to Communism, but we can assist their elected leaders in giving Americans small doses of socialism, until they suddenly awake to find they have Communism."
- Nikita Sergeyevich Khrushchev, Soviet Dictator

The precarious position we find ourselves in when contemplating our financial future is no mistake. There are many who knew this time was coming and warned our government to no avail. There are also lessons that should have been learned with reflection of the Great Depression, but alas, we find ourselves not only repeating history, but actually staring down the prospect of this crisis causing enough panic to change the very fabric of the American way of life.

"When the Federal Reserve Act was passed, the people of these United States did not perceive that a world banking system was being set up here. A super-state controlled by international bankers and international industrialists acting together to enslave the world for their own pleasure. Every effort has been made by the Fed to conceal its powers but the truth is - the FED has usurped the government ... It was not accidental [the 1929 stock-market "crash"]. It was a carefully contrived occurrence ... The international bankers sought to bring about a condition of despair here so that they might emerge as rulers of us all."

- Louis McFadden

Chairman of the House Banking Committee, whose passionate denunciation of International Bankers, their agenda for World Empire and their corrupt creature, central banks, cost him his life, Congressional Record (1934) [9]

"I am a most unhappy man. I have unwittingly ruined my country. A great industrial nation is controlled by its system of credit. Our system of credit is concentrated. The growth of the nation, therefore, and all our activities are in the hands of a few men. We have come to be one of the worst ruled, one of the most completely controlled and dominated governments in the civilized world. No longer a government by free opinion, no longer a government by conviction and the vote of the majority, but a government by the opinion and duress of a small group of dominant men."

- President Woodrow Wilson

Led the United States in World War I and secured the formation of the League of Nations, three years after signing the Federal Reserve Act into law (1916) [9]

"The truly unique power of a central bank is the power to create money, and ultimately the power to create is the power to destroy."

- Paul A Volcker (1979)

Newly installed as Chairman of the Board of Governors of the US Federal Reserve System, gives public expression of a great secret of central banks: their power to create apparent wealth out of thin air and the capacity to destroy economies by the sudden contraction of credit. [10]

"I have spoken about using oil as a weapon. Apart from that, the Arabs keep a lot of money in the US. If we pull out the money, the US can immediately become bankrupt. If we use this strategy, I believe it will be more effective than tying a bomb to your body and blowing up people."

- Dr. Mahathir Mohamad

Former Malaysian Prime Minister, quoted Utusan Malaysia (10/2004) encouraging oil drenched Arab countries and other Muslim nations to pull their money out of the United States of America thereby precipitating an economic meltdown of its economy. [11]

"The invisible money power is working to control and enslave mankind. It financed communism, fascism, Marxism, Zionism and socialism. All of these are directed to making the United States a member of World Government."

- American Mercury Magazine (1957) [12]

"This campaign against the American people -against traditional American culture and values - is systematic psychological warfare. It is orchestrated by a vast array of interests comprising not only the Eastern establishment but also the radical left. Among this group we find the Department of State, the Department of Commerce, the money center banks and multinational corporations, the media, the educational establishment, the entertainment industry, and the large tax-exempt foundations. Mr. President, a careful examination of what is happening behind the scenes reveals that all of these interests are working in concert with the masters of the Kremlin in order to create what some refer to as a New World Order. Private organizations such as the Council on Foreign Relations, the Royal Institute of International Affairs, the Trilateral Commission, the Dartmouth Conference, the Aspen Institute for Humanistic Studies, the Atlantic Institute, and the Bilderberger Group serve to disseminate and to coordinate the plans for this so-called New World Order in powerful business, financial, academic, and official circles ... The psychological campaign that I am describing, as I have said, is the work of groups within the Eastern establishment, that amorphous amalgam of wealth and social connections whose power resides in its control over our financial system and over a large portion of our industrial sector. The principal instrument of this control over the American economy and money is the Federal Reserve System. The policies of the Industrial sectors, primarily the multinational corporations, are influenced by the money center banks through debt financing and through the large blocks of stock controlled by the trust departments of the money center banks. Anyone familiar with American history, and particularly American economic history, cannot fail to notice the control over the Department of State and the Central Intelligence Agency which Wall Street seems to exercise ... The influence of establishment insiders over our foreign policy has become a fact of life in our time. This pervasive influence runs contrary to the real long-term national security of our Nation. It is an influence which, if unchecked, could ultimately subvert our constitutional order. The viewpoint of the establishment today is called globalism. Not so long ago, this viewpoint was called the "one-world" view by its critics. The phrase is no longer fashionable among sophisticates; yet, the phrase "one-world" is still apt because nothing has changed in the minds and actions of those promoting policies consistent with its fundamental tenets. Mr. President, in the globalist point of view, nation-states and national boundaries do not count for anything. Political philosophies and political principles seem to become simply relative. Indeed, even constitutions are irrelevant to the exercise of power. Liberty and tyranny are viewed as neither necessarily good nor evil, and certainly not a component of policy. In this point of view, the activities of international financial and industrial forces should be oriented to bringing this one-world design - with a convergence of the Soviet and American systems as its centerpiece - into being. . . . All that matters to this club is the maximization of profits resulting from the practice of what can be described as finance capitalism, a system which rests upon the twin pillars of debt and monopoly. This isn't real capitalism. It is the road to economic concentration and to political slavery."

- Senator Jesse Helms
Speech before the Senate 15 December (1987)[13]

They shall cast their silver in the streets, and their gold shall be removed: their silver and their gold shall not be able to deliver them in the day of the wrath of the LORD: they shall not satisfy their souls...

Ezekiel 7:19

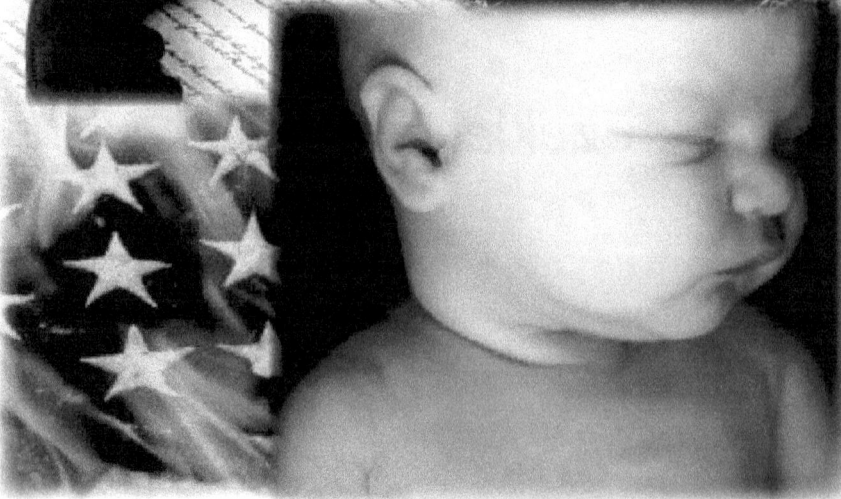

It is necessary ... to be a great feigner and dissembler; and men are so simple and so ready to obey present necessities, that one who deceives will always find those who allow themselves to be deceived ... the conqueror must arrange to commit all his cruelties at once ... in the actions of men ... from which there is no appeal, the end justifies the means."

Niccolo Machiavelli (1469-1527)
Statesman of Florence, Political Theorist and Historian

IN BLACK AND WHITE

MOST LIBERAL SENATOR

Barack Obama

"WAS VOTED THE MOST LIBERAL SENATOR IN 2007, according to National Journal's 27th annual vote ratings." [1]

MISSING IN ACTION AND VOTING "PRESENT"

As David Ignatius of the Washington Post has written, after being elected to the Illinois Senate in 1996, Obama "gained a reputation for skipping tough votes." Interestingly, these included a key gun-control vote in December 1999 because he was vacationing in his home state of Hawaii. [2]

Ignatius quotes a Chicago politician as saying that "the myth developed that when there was a tough vote, he was gone." Obama is the Illinois state senator who voted "present" some 135 times lest he be forced to take a position he would have to intellectually explain and defend.

Obama would appoint justices who would rewrite the liberals' "living Constitution" while legislating from the bench on issues from gun control to national security. It's Obama who lacks the judgment and experience for the position he seeks.[3]

According to GoTrack.us, Barack Obama missed 314 (24%) of 1299 votes since Jan 6, 2005.[4]

PolitiFact says:

In the Illinois state senate, lawmakers sometimes vote "present" instead of "no" to block bills without officially opposing them and Barack Obama was no stranger to the practice. He calls it party tactics, his opponent calls it ducking tough issues.

...the practice has gained national attention after Sen. Hillary Clinton questioned whether Sen. Barack Obama used present votes 129 times over eight years as an Illinois state senator to duck tough votes.

"On issue after issue that really were hard to explain or understand, you voted present . . . And anytime anyone raises that, there's always some kind of explanation," Clinton said.[5]

DEATH PENALTY

"...thinks the death penalty "does little to deter crime." He supports capital punishment in cases in which "the community is justified in expressing the full measure of its outrage." While a state senator, Obama pushed for reform of the Illinois capital punishment system and authored a bill to mandate the videotaping of interrogations and confessions. Obama disagreed with the June 25, 2008 U.S. Supreme Court decision outlawing the execution of child rapists.[6]

HEALTH CARE

According to the Chicago Sun-Times, Barack Obama "vowed to make health insurance available to all Americans by the end of his first term in the White House..."We can have universal health care by the end of the next president's first term, by the end of my first term"... he said he would support rolling back tax cuts for the wealthiest Americans.[7]

In other words, a socialistic model. Here is what one individual from Canada, currently in this type of system had to say about her experience:

"...Canada's bureaucratic health care system transformed me from a human into a number, put me on a waiting list and essentially told me to hope for the best.

Free health care was indeed about money. It refused to pay for treatment outside its borders, even though life-saving surgery was quickly available a short plane-ride away in the U.S.

Movies such as "Sicko" and "John Q," a wave of admiringly reviewed books, newspaper pundits and cable news commentators batter Americans with a daily message that the U.S. needs to embrace a universal, government-run system similar to Canada's or Britain's.

What they don't tell you is that both Canada's and Great Britain's routinely block or delay access to needed treatments and often treat elderly patients with cavalier contempt.

The national health care system in my country is racked by agonizingly long waits and rationing of many vital medical services, starting with a severe shortage of the family physicians who are gatekeepers of our care.

More than 800,000 Canadians currently are in long holding patterns for operations that would be done in the U.S. in a few weeks after the initial diagnosis. Sadly, many will die before they make it to the head of the line. Those who can find a way flee to the U.S. for the quality medical service so often lacking at home.

The benchmark question for any nation's health care system is whether their citizens are forced to go abroad for quality accessible health care treatment. The answer in America is obvious.[8]

FLAG DESECRATION

Barack Obama voted NO on recommending Constitutional ban on flag desecration.

In Obama's statement regarding the issue he said, "Today, there are hundreds of thousands of U.S. troops risking their lives for their country, looking to us to come up with a plan to win the peace so they can come home. Across America, there are millions who are looking for us to do something about health care, about education, about energy. The Senate will likely be in session for about 50 more days for the rest of this year. To spend the precious time we have left battling an epidemic of flag burning that does not exist is a disservice to our country.[9]

I wonder, if the men and women who fight for that flag might have something to say about the "precious time" of Senator Obama that he can't waste on an insignificant issue such as this one.

As a matter of fact, Major General Patrick Brady, who was awarded the Medal of Honor for his service in the Vietnam War during which time he rescued over 5,000 casualties of war,[10] had plenty to say about it:

> Despite what the media would have you believe John McCain and Barack Obama have laid out in some detail where they stand on the issues. As we know they have both changed over the course of the campaign and will continue to do so as they feel the pulse of the people and encounter changing challenges. They are after all politicians one extremely liberal, in fact, socialistic in his life view; and the other semi-conservative. And whoever is elected will continue to change for the same reasons. And that is good. But what they cannot change is their character and their view of our sacred Constitution; both of which define their values.

> Abraham Lincoln said "Don't interfere with anything in the Constitution. That must be maintained for it is the only safeguard of our liberties." He was right. No terrorist, no army, no country in the world can take away our freedom. We will lose our freedom when we lose our Constitution, when the people, our military, and our Founders cease to be the guardians and

guarantors of that sacred document and politicians and judges mutilate it. Some examples of Constitutional and judicial mutilation: Pornography is protected speech but prayer is not; The 10 Commandments are a threat to the public square and displaying them "establishes a religion;" "Under God" should be outlawed from the pledge; the Boy Scouts are bigots; marriage has nothing to do with gender (or, soon to come, numbers); English should not be the language of America and terrorists have constitutional rights on the battlefield. Barack Obama has said he would appoint judges like those who have made these decisions. This is a clear indication of his view of the Constitution and his values.

Of all the litmus tests we have for politicians, I think their vote on a Constitutional amendment to return to the people the right to protect Old Glory is most instructive of their view of the Constitution and their values. That one vote will tell us most of what we need to know about a candidate. Barack Obama voted against the flag amendment and one vote defeated the efforts of the vast majority of the people to recapture their flag from the courts. John McCain voted with the people. Sadly, this issue will not come up in debates and the media, who champion judicial activism and flag burning, will avoid it since it could hurt their candidate who has refused to wear a flag pin, and help John McCain who believes the right to protect our flag is a birth right of all people.

Does Senator Obama, or any candidate, actually believe that flag burning is speech, that he knows more than Webster, is wiser than the founding fathers, (who condemned flag burning) more astute than 80 percent of the people, 50 states and 70 percent of the Congress (who support the people's right to flag protection)? Can Obama tell you what is said when the flag is burned?

Would Obama or any candidate tell our young warriors, to their face, they are fighting for the right to burn Old Glory? (It is easy to wonder if Obama wants to face our troops since he refused to visit our wounded on a recent trip; that should have been the highlight of the trip.) Would he tell that to America's nobility, our Veterans? Would he compare the American flag, protected according to the will of a free people - to flags protected according to the will of tyrants as some politicians have?

Candidates of character who support the right of the people to protect their flag will teach the truth. It is not flag burners that are the problem, the problem is those who call flag burning "speech." Every American should be alarmed, not because flag burning is wrong, but because calling it speech defiles our sacred Constitution.

Candidates who share our values will teach that it is a not true to say the flag amendment criminalizes flag burning, amends the bill of rights and changes the Constitution. It does none of those things, the truth is it restores the Constitution. Such men and women will flush the cultural aliens out of the murky dictatorial darkness of the courts and into the bright democratic light of the public square. They will realize that when they raise their hand and swear to protect and defend the Constitution, that oath carries with it an obligation to correct the errors of the Supreme Court.

Candidates with character will understand that this is a values issue, and the entire debate over values is centered on what we teach our children. Flag burning is wrong, but what it teaches, is worse. It teaches our children disrespect. It teaches that the hateful conduct of a minority is more important than the will of the majority. It teaches that our laws need not reflect our values; and that the courts, not the people, own the Constitution. Every veteran, every American, should be alarmed at what politicians without character, who do not share our values, are doing to our Constitution. If Old Glory is precious enough to cover the coffins of our fallen warriors, it is precious enough to protect.[11]

MILITARY

According to Investor's Business Daily, "In the middle of a war on two fronts, Barack Obama plans to gut the military. He also wants to dismantle our nuclear arsenal. And he wants to keep you in the dark about it."[12]

The article also states:

The Obamatons of the mainstream media have failed to report one of the most chilling campaign promises thus far uttered by the presumptive Democrat nominee for president.

He made it before the Iowa caucus to a left-wing pacifist group that seeks to reallocate defense dollars to welfare programs. The lobbying group, Caucus for Priorities, was so impressed by Obama's anti-military offering that it steered its 10,000 devotees his way.

In a 132-word videotaped pledge (still viewable on YouTube), Obama agreed to hollow out the U.S. military by slashing both conventional and nuclear weapons.

The scope of his planned defense cuts, combined with his angry tone, is breathtaking. He sounds as if the military is the enemy, not the bad guys it's fighting. Here is a transcript:

"I'm the only major candidate who opposed this war from the beginning; and as president, I will end it.

"Second, I will cut tens of billions of dollars in wasteful spending. I will cut investments in unproven missile defense systems. I will not weaponize space. I will slow our development of future combat systems.

"I will institute an independent defense priorities board to ensure that the Quadrennial Review is not used to justify unnecessary defense spending.

"Third, I will set a goal for a world without nuclear weapons. To seek that goal, I will not develop nuclear weapons; I will seek a global ban on the production of missile material; and I will negotiate with Russia to take our ICBMs off hair-trigger alert, and to achieve deep cuts in our nuclear arsenal."

Proposing "deep cuts in our nuclear arsenal" amounts to unilateral disarmament, and it's suicidal given China's and now Russia's aggressive military buildup.

Meanwhile, Iran and North Korea threaten nuclear madness, and Osama bin Laden dreams of unleashing a nuclear 9/11 on America.

In contrast, John McCain has vowed: "We must continue to deploy a safe and reliable nuclear deterrent, robust missile defenses and superior conventional forces that are capable of defending the United States and our allies."[13]

GUN RIGHTS

"Obama would be the most anti-gun President in American history."[14]

Clarification on this issue comes from an article at Newsmax.com:

Although Obama says one thing in public and another in private, the NRA aims to define him by the kinds of legislation for which he has spoken and voted.

When he was a candidate for the Illinois Senate in 1996, a political questionnaire in his name answered "Yes" to a question of whether supported state legislation to "ban the manufacture, sale and possession of handguns?" When this was reported, Obama's campaign claimed that a staffer had filled out the questionnaire and given answers the candidate never approved.

"No, my writing wasn't on that particular questionnaire," Obama told ABC News anchor Charlie Gibson. "As I said, I have never favored an all-out ban on handguns."

But Factcheck.org said, "Actually, Obama's writing was on the 1996 document." Factcheck.org, of the University of Pennsylvania's Annenberg Public Policy Center, described his statement as misleading. A margin note on the questionnaire in Obama's handwriting indicated his approval. The journal Politico also confirmed that Obama had verbally verified his views with members of the liberal group that gave this questionnaire to state candidates.

During Obama's time on the board of the liberal Joyce Foundation, he "oversaw the distribution of $18 million to gun-ban groups, including major funding for the Violence Policy Center," according to the NRA's Wayne LaPierre. This is more than the NRA plans to spend in 2008 to advertise its critique of Obama. "Before he ran for public office, Obama was considered the prime candidate to lead that deep-pocketed anti-gun money machine," LaPierre wrote.

As a member of the Illinois Senate, Obama voted for a bill to ban and confiscate assault weapons that the NRA said was so poorly drafted that "it would have also banned most semiauto and single and double barrel shotguns commonly used by sportsmen."

Obama favors strict controls on both the keeping and bearing of arms, according to the NRA's documentation.

"I am not in favor of concealed weapons," he told the Pittsburgh Tribune. "I think that creates a potential atmosphere where more innocent people could [get shot during] altercations."

Despite his statement that "Chicago is different from Cheyenne," the Feb. 20, 2004, Chicago Tribune quoted Obama saying: "National legislation will prevent other states' flawed concealed-weapons laws from threatening the safety of Illinois residents." In other words, he backed federal legislation to abolish local and state laws that now permit the concealed carrying of handguns.

Obama voted to allow what the NRA calls "reckless lawsuits designed to bankrupt the firearms industry." Obama also voted to make homeowners guilty of a felony if their gun is stolen from their home and then used to harm anyone, thereby making it dangerous for any law-abiding citizen merely to own a gun.

Obama, as NRA documents depict him, is far more extreme than ordinary liberals who favor only gun registration and background checks that could deny firearm purchases to those accused, but not convicted, of crimes such as spousal abuse.

Obama has advocated limiting gun purchases to one a month; restricting how many bullets a gun may carry; requiring technologies that permit a gun to be fired only by its legal owner (and that, if based on a computer chip, would allow the gun to be "turned off" at a distance); and micro-stamping that, in effect, could make it illegal for gun owners to reload their own ammunition.

Obama has supported outlawing assault weapons, defined in a way that could be interpreted to include virtually every semiautomatic weapon, even double-action revolvers. He has voted to outlaw ammunition designed to penetrate a law enforcement officer's bulletproof vest, which could arbitrarily be interpreted to include nearly every cartridge used to hunt game such as deer.

Unless "you're seeing a lot of deer out there wearing bullet-proof vests," Obama said jokingly during a 2004 debate, "then there is no purpose for many of the guns" citizens have been allowed to buy.

Obama has proposed banning inexpensive handguns, so-called Saturday night specials, that poor women and men could afford for self-defense, according to NRA documentation. He also has proposed a 500 percent increase in the federal excise tax on firearms and ammunition. To the extent that he favors any right to keep and bear arms, it appears to be only for the rich, not the poor.

On Sept. 5, at a factory in Duryea, Pa., a woman asked Obama about "a rumor" that, if elected president, he planned some kind of gun ban. His reaction, which only the Wall Street Journal's Christopher Cooper has reported, has been described as Obama's "Gun Meltdown."

Obama tried his usual response, that he respects the "traditions of gun ownership" but favored control measures in big cities to keep guns out of criminal hands.

"If you've got a gun in your house, I'm not taking it," Obama said to the skeptical audience. "This can't be the reason not to vote for me. Can everyone hear me in the back? I see a couple of sportsmen back there. I'm not going to take away your guns."

But during his emotional meltdown, Obama offered a moment of disarming honesty: "Even if I want to take [your guns] away," he said, "I don't have the votes in Congress."   But that, too, could change in the election in November.[15]

"This year will go down in history. For the first time, a civilized nation had full gun registration! Our streets will be safer, our police more efficient, and the world will follow our lead into the future!"

Adolf Hitler

Like other dictators and mass murderers, such as Lenin and Mao Zedong, worked to remove the last vestige of protection the people had against their future tyranny planned for them: their guns (1935)[16]

GAY RIGHTS

According to the Pew Forum:

> Obama says that he personally believes that "marriage is between a man and a woman" but also says that "equality is a moral imperative" for gay and lesbian Americans.

> He advocates the complete repeal of the Defense of Marriage Act (DOMA) because "federal law should not discriminate in any way against gay and lesbian couples, which is precisely what DOMA does."

> He supports granting civil unions for gay couples, and in 2006 he opposed a constitutional amendment to ban gay marriage.

> In March 2007, Obama initially avoided answering questions about a controversial statement by a U.S. general that "homosexual acts" are "immoral," but Obama later told CNN's Larry King, "I don't think that homosexuals are immoral any more than I think heterosexuals are immoral."[17]

Michelle Obama, appearing at a meeting of the Gay & Lesbian Leadership Council of the Democratic National Committee received a standing ovation. Excerpts from her speech include:

> ...cited her husband's efforts to fight discrimination and promote equal rights for lesbians, gays, bisexuals and transgendered people.

> ...said he supported a complete repeal of the federal Defense of Marriage Act, or DOMA, which only recognizes marriages between men and women and upholds states' rights not to honor same-sex marriages performed elsewhere. He also opposes a "don't ask, don't tell" policy toward gays in the U.S. military and was against a constitutional amendment to ban gay marriage, she added.

> ...he supports full family and adoption rights for gay and lesbian couples and believes the federal government should not stand in the way of states that opt for domestic partnerships, civil unions or civil marriage.[18]

In the 2007 Democratic primary debate at Dartmouth College, Obama responded to the following questions.

Q: Last year some parents of second graders in Lexington, Massachusetts, were outraged to learn their children's teacher had read a story about same-sex marriage, about a prince who marries another prince. Would you be comfortable having this story read to your children as part of their school curriculum?

A: My 9-year-old and my 6-year-old are already aware that there are same-sex couples. And my wife and I have talked about it. And one of the things I want to communicate to my children is not to be afraid of people who are different, and because there have been times in our history where I was considered different. And one of the things I think the next president has to do is to stop fanning people's fears.

Q: Have you sat down with your daughters to talk about same-sex marriage?
A: My wife has.[19]

In a the Vice Presidential Debate, between Governor Sarah Palin and Democratic Senator Joe Biden, Senator Biden said:

"Barack Obama nor I support redefining from a civil side what constitutes marriage. We do not support that. That is basically the decision to be able to be left to faiths and people who practice their faiths, the determination, what you call it."[20]

However, in a letter Barack Obama sent to the Lesbian Gay Bisexual Transgender Democratic Club, in June 2008, "he congratulated those in California who recently got married." His letter read:

As the Democratic nominee for President, I am proud to join with and support the LGBT community in an effort to set our nation on a course that recognizes LGBT Americans with full equality under the law. That is why I support extending fully equal rights and benefits to same sex couples under both state and federal law. That is why I support repealing the Defense of

Marriage Act and the "Don't Ask Don't Tell" policy, and the passage of laws to protect LGBT Americans from hate crimes and employment discrimination. And that is why I oppose the divisive and discriminatory efforts to amend the California Constitution, and similar efforts to amend the U.S. Constitution or those of other states.

For too long. issues of LGBT rights have been exploited by those seeking to divide us. It's time to move beyond polarization and live up to our founding promise of equality by treating all our citizens with dignity and respect. This is no less than a core issue about who we are as Democrats and as Americans.

Finally, I want to congratulate all of you who have shown your love for each other by getting married these last few weeks.[21]

EDUCATION

In the 2008 Democratic Compassion Forum at Messiah College, a question was asked regarding Obama's beliefs regarding creationism vs. evolution, his response was:

"What I believe is that God created the universe, and that the 6 days in the Bible may not be 6 days as we understand it. My belief is that the story that the Bible tells about God creating this magnificent Earth, that is fundamentally true. Now whether it happened exactly as we might understand it reading the text of the Bible, that I don't presume to know. But one last point--I do believe in evolution."[22]

In the 2004 Illinois Senate race, controversy erupted when Obama's opponent accused him of supporting a bill for sex education for children as young as kindergarten. The media accepted Obama's explanation who said he wanted to guard against the "possibility of somebody touching them inappropriately, and what that might mean."[23]

But of course, Senate Bill 99 includes language quite different from issues of abuse, "...the bill's intention was to mandate that issues like contraception and the prevention of sexually-transmitted diseases be included in sex-education classes for children before the sixth grade, and as early as kindergarten."[24]

In a February 2008 interview Obama said he supports charter schools "as a way to foster competition in the public school system," and later he said he would double federal funding for charter schools if elected president. Obama is against school vouchers"[25]

The education our children receive has undergone many changes throughout the last few decades. The potential consequences of allowing the these young minds to molded by any group or organization without scrutiny could lead to the greatest moral failure of our time.

In a report from WorldNet Daily, in October 2008:

> A public school in San Francisco bused 18 first-graders to City Hall yesterday, so the youngsters could scatter rose petals in celebration of their lesbian teacher's wedding.
>
> The students, from Creative Arts Charter School, waited on the steps for their teacher with bags of pink rose petals, bottles of bubbles and, at least for some, with political buttons asking Californians to vote down Proposition 8, a ballot measure that seeks to define marriage in the state as a union between one man and one woman.
>
> Chip White, press secretary for the Yes on 8 campaign said, "It's just utterly unreasonable that a public school field trip would be to a same-sex wedding," ..."This is overt indoctrination of children who are too young to have an understanding of its purpose."[26]

It also appears that despite Barack Obama's relatively short time in the public eye, his legacy is already of such proportions that he merits a prominent place in our school's textbooks.

> The mother of an 8th-grader in Wisconsin is blasting school officials over their use of a textbook lauding Democratic presidential candidate Barack Obama's "change" theme and highlighting his 2004 Democratic National Convention as an example of good literature.

"I just found out that my son's new (copyright 2008) Wisconsin – McDougal Littell Literature book has 15 pages covering Barack Obama," she writes. "I was shocked – No John McCain, no Hillary Clinton, no George Bush – Just Barack Obama."

The mother says it "would be one thing, if it was just the tidbit about his boyhood days, but 15 pages, and they talk about his 'Life of Service.'"

"Honestly," she writes, "what has Obama really done to be included in this book? Not only that, but on page 847 there is a photo of Obama at the 2004 Democratic Convention with at least 8 Obama signs in the background!"

The mother says she did some research on McDougal Littell and found chairman and CEO Alfred L. McDougal of Chicago has made contributions to Obama's campaign.[27]

"When an opponent declares, "I will not come over to your side," I calmly say, "Your child belongs to us already... What are you? You will pass on. Your descendants, however, now stand in the new camp. In a short time they will know nothing else but this new community."

Adolph Hitler

"If we want to talk about equality of opportunity for children, then the fact that children are raised in families means there's no equality... In order to raise children with equality, we must take them away from families and communally raise them."

Dr. Mary Jo Bane

Assistant Secretary of Administration for Children and Families in the Department of Health and Human Services in the Clinton Administration (1997)[28]

"Education is thus a most powerful ally of humanism, and every American public school is a school of humanism. What can the theistic Sunday schools, meeting for an hour once a week, teaching only a fraction of the children, do to stem the tide of a five-day program of humanistic teaching?"

C.F. Potter

American educator and humanist who, with John Dewey, profoundly influenced education theory and greatly helped to define child-centred approaches to humanist instruction that destroyed proper education of children in public schools and elsewhere. Potter was a signer of the Humanist Manifesto in 1933, and the betrayer of generations of children and their loving, trusting parents.[29]

"Every child in America entering school at the age of five is insane because he comes to school with certain allegiances toward our Founding Fathers, toward his parents, toward a belief in a supernatural being, toward the sovereignty of this nation as a separate entity... It's up to you teachers to make all of these sick children well by creating the international children of the future."

Dr. Chester M. Pierce

Professor of Education and Psychiatry, Medicine and Graduate School of Education, Harvard University, address to the Association for Childhood Education International in Denver (1972)[30]

"Breaking down inhibitions is the first order of business. That is why so-called "sex education" courses go on for years in some schools. It doesn't take that long to convey the facts of life. But it does take that long to relentlessly undermine what children have been taught at home."

Dr. Thomas Sowell

Cited in USA Today September 10 (1992)[31]

"I am convinced that the battle for humankind's future must be waged and won in the public school classroom by teachers who correctly perceive their roles as the proselytizers of a new faith: a religion of humanity that recognizes and respects the spark of what theologians call divinity in every human being. These teachers must embody the same selfless dedication as the most rabid fundamentalist preachers, for they will be ministers of another sort, utilizing a classroom instead of a pulpit to convey humanist values in whatever they teach, regardless of the educational level - preschool, day care, or large state university. The classroom must and will become an arena of conflict between the old and the new - the rotting corpse of Christianity, together with all its adjacent evils and misery, and the new faith of Humanism, resplendent in its promise of a world in which the never-realized Christian ideal of love thy neighbor will finally be achieved."

John Dunphy, Humanist Magazine (1983)[32]

Lo, children are an heritage of the LORD: and the fruit of the womb is his reward.

Psalms 127:3

Thus saith the LORD, Learn not the way of the heathen, and be not dismayed at the signs of heaven; for the heathen are dismayed at them.

Jeremiah 10:2

He that walketh with wise men shall be wise: but a companion of fools shall be destroyed.

Proverbs 13:20

The Family Research Council gives a synopsis of the typical Christian position on this topic:

> Disabling diseases and injuries, including those for which there is a terminal diagnosis, are tragic. However, there is no such thing as a life not worth living. Every life holds promise, even if disadvantaged by developmental disability, injury, disease, or advanced aging. FRC believes that every human life has inherent dignity, and that it is unethical to deliberately end the life of a suffering person (euthanasia), or assist or enable another person to end their life (assisted suicide). While extraordinary means of life support, such as assistance with respiration and heart function, may be withdrawn from a terminally ill person if that is the person's expressed wish, nutrition and hydration are normal and not extraordinary means of maintaining life, and severe disability is not the same as terminal illness. True compassion means finding ways to ease suffering and provide care for each person, while maintaining the individual's life and dignity.[33]

On October 27, 1997 Oregon enacted the Death with Dignity Act which allows terminally-ill Oregonians to end their lives through the voluntary self-administration of lethal medications, expressly prescribed by a physician for that purpose.[34]

In a March 2008 interview with the Mail Tribune, Obama responded to the following question:

> Q: A couple of other issues of interest to Oregonians involve initiatives passed by the voters that have come into conflict with the federal government: physician-assisted suicide and medical marijuana. Do you support those two concepts?

> A: I am in favor of palliative medicine in circumstances where someone is terminally ill...I'm mindful of the legitimate interests of states to prevent a slide from palliative treatments into euthanasia.

...On the other hand, I think that the people of Oregon did a service for the country in recognizing that as the population gets older we've got to think about issues of end-of-life care....[35]

In February 2008, during a debate with Hillary Clinton, Obama said "his biggest mistake was voting with a unanimous Senate to help save Terri Schiavo."[36]

FreeRepublic.com offers additional information on the case involving Terri Schiavo:

Terri is the disabled Florida woman whose husband won the legal right to starve her to death.

Terri was not on any artificial breathing apparatus and only required a feeding tube to eat and drink. Her family had filed a lawsuit against her former husband to allow them to care for her and give her proper medical and rehabilitative care.

The Senate unanimously approved a compromise bill, which the House eventually supported on a lopsided bipartisan vote and President Bush signed, to help the disabled woman. During the Tuesday debate, Obama said he should have stood up against the life-saving legislation. "It wasn't something I was comfortable with, but it was not something that I stood on the floor and stopped," Obama said.

"And I think that was a mistake, and I think the American people understood that that was a mistake. And as a constitutional law professor, I knew better," he added.

This isn't the first time Obama has said the biggest mistake he made as senator was voting to help try to stop Terri from being euthanized.

During an April 2007 debate, Obama said, "I think professionally the biggest mistake that I made was when I first arrived in the Senate. There was a debate about Terri Schiavo, and a lot of us, including me, left the Senate with a bill that allowed Congress to intrude where it shouldn't have."

"And I think I should have stayed in the Senate and fought more for making sure [Terri's parents couldn't take their case to federal court to save her life]," he explained.[37]

If thou forbear to deliver them that are drawn unto death, and those that are ready to be slain;

If thou sayest, Behold, we knew it not; doth not he that pondereth the heart consider it? and he that keepeth thy soul, doth not he know it? and shall not he render to every man according to his works?

Proverbs 24:11-12

...do justice to the afflicted and needy
...rid them out of the hand of the wicked.

Psalms 82:3-4

ABORTION

Obama's position according to The Pew Forum:

Obama supports abortion rights. In the Illinois State Senate, he voted against a bill to ban late-term abortions because, he said, it did not contain a clause to protect the life of the mother.

During an April 2007 Democratic debate, Obama said, "I trust women to make these decisions in conjunction with their doctors and their families and their clergy."

At an April 2008 candidates' forum on faith and compassion, Obama said that "there is a moral dimension to abortion, which I think that all too often those of us who are pro-choice have not talked about or tried to tamp down." To reduce abortions, Obama advocates a comprehensive sex-education program in which both abstinence and contraception are priorities. He also says, "we should make sure that adoption is an option."[38]

Obama was also asked:

Q: Do you personally believe that life begins at conception?

A: This is something that I have not come to a firm resolution on. I think it's very hard to know what that means, when life begins. Is it when a cell separates? Is it when the soul stirs? So I don't presume to know the answer to that question.[39]

According to LifeSiteNews.com:

Barack Obama...has plans to reward the allies that helped him topple Hillary Clinton from her throne by making total unrestricted abortion in the United States his number one priority as president.

"The first thing I'd do as president is sign the Freedom of Choice Act," Obama said in his July speech to abortion advocates worried about the increase of pro-life legislation at the state level.

The Freedom of Choice Act (FOCA) is legislation Obama has co-sponsored along with 18 other senators that would annihilate every single state law limiting or regulating abortion, including the federal ban on partial birth abortion.

Obama made his remarks in a question-and-answer session after delivering a speech crystallizing for abortion advocates his deep-seated abortion philosophy and his belief that federal legislation will break pro-life resistance on the national debate on abortion.

Besides making abortion on demand a "fundamental right" throughout the United States, FOCA would effectively nullify informed consent laws, waiting periods, health safety regulations for abortion clinics, etc.[40]

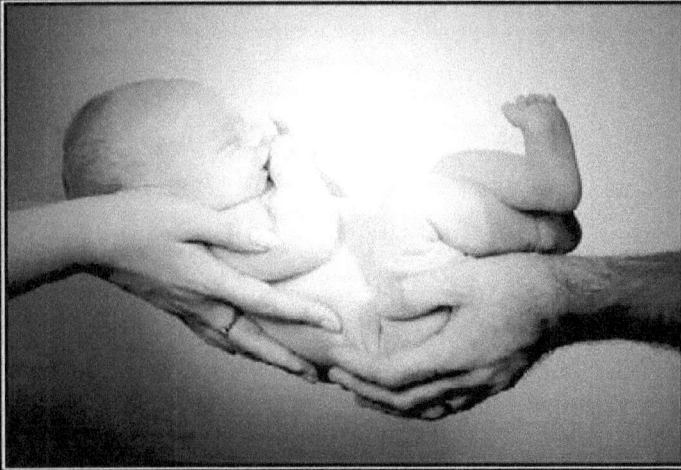

PUNISHMENT

"If [my daughters] make a mistake, I don't want them punished with a baby."
Senator Barack Obama

PHOTO FROM SOUTHERN APPEAL

An article on the WashingtonPost.com site said:

Obama's record on abortion is extreme. He opposed the ban on partial-birth abortion -- a practice a fellow Democrat, the late Daniel Patrick Moynihan, once called "too close to infanticide." Obama strongly criticized the Supreme Court decision upholding the partial-birth ban. In the Illinois state Senate, he opposed a bill similar to the Born-Alive Infants Protection Act, which prevents the killing of infants mistakenly left alive by abortion. And now Obama has oddly claimed that he would not want his daughters to be "punished with a baby" because of a crisis pregnancy -- hardly a welcoming attitude toward new life.[41]

The Partial-Birth Abortion Ban Act defines "partial-birth abortion" as follows:

An abortion in which the person performing the abortion, deliberately and intentionally vaginally delivers a living fetus until, in the case of a head-first presentation, the entire fetal head is outside the body of the mother, or, in the case of breech presentation, any part of the fetal trunk past the navel is outside the body of the mother, for the purpose of performing an overt act that the person knows will kill the partially delivered living fetus; and performs the overt act, other than completion of delivery, that kills the partially delivered living fetus. (18 U.S. Code 1531)[42]

Jill Stanek, a well-known pro-life advocate wrote in an article on her website:

In February 2004, U.S. Senate candidate Barack Obama's wife, Michelle, sent a fund-raising letter with the "alarming news" that "right-wing politicians" had passed a law stopping doctors from stabbing half-born babies in the neck with scissors, suctioning out their brains and crushing their skulls.

Michelle called partial-birth abortion "a legitimate medical procedure," and wouldn't supporters please pay $150 to attend a luncheon for her husband, who would fight against "cynical ploy[s]" to stop it?

Obama insinuated opposition to abortion is based only on religion, lecturing pro-lifers like me to "explain why abortion violates some principle that is accessible to people of all faiths, including those with no faith at all."

I don't recall mentioning religion when I testified against live-birth abortion. I only recall describing a live aborted baby I held in a hospital soiled utility room until he died, and a live aborted baby who was accidentally thrown into the trash.

Neither do I recall religion being brought into the partial-birth abortion ban debate. I recall comparisons made to U.S. laws ensuring animals being killed are treated humanely. I recall testimony that late-term babies feel excruciating pain while being aborted.

Obama stated pro-life proposals must be "amenable to reason."

Then, since you brought it up, explain how, despite all that, you think Jesus should vote for you, either now or in the hereafter, particularly given His statement, "It would be better to be thrown into the sea with a large millstone tied around the neck than to face the punishment in store for harming one of these little ones."[43]

According to the Chicago Sun-Times, March 31, 2001: "A spokesman for Christ Hospital's parent, Advocate Health Care… estimated that between 10 percent and 20 percent of fetuses with genetic defects that are aborted survive for short periods outside the womb.[44]

Obama was the sole senator to ever speak against the Born-Alive Infants Protection Act on the Senate floor.[45]

He stated:

> **"…whenever we define a previable fetus as a person that is protected by the equal protection clause or the other elements in the Constitution, what we're really saying is, in fact, that they are persons that are entitled to the kinds of protections that would be provided to a – child…"**
>
> **Before voting "no" for a second time in the Senate Judiciary Committee on March 5, 2002, Obama stated:**
>
> **"What we are doing here is to create one more burden on women, and I can't support that."[46]**

Since January 1973, there have been over **52 MILLION** babies killed by abortion.

According to AbortionFacts.com:

> There is a direct parallel between the Nazi holocaust and America's abortion holocaust, neither of which could have happened without doctors.[47]

AbortionFacts.com also provides the following revealing similarities:

THEN	NOW
OBEDIENCE TO AUTHORITY	**OBEDIENCE TO AUTHORITY**
"The accused did not act wrongly because they were covered by law [and] were carrying out the laws of the land."(Hadamar Euthanasia Hospital Trial, 1945	"I did nothing which was illegal, immoral or bad medicine. Everything I did was in accordance with law." (Dr. Kenneth C. Edelin, 1975)
SUBHUMANITY OF THE VICTIMS	**SUBHUMANITY OF THE VICTIMS**
"It had nothing to do with humanity — it was a mass. I rarely saw them as individuals. It was always a huge mass." (Franz Stangl, former commandant of Treblinka, 1971)	"What is aborted is a protoplasmic mass and not a real, live grown-up individual." (Drs. Walter Char & John McDermott, 1972)
"If it is now pointed out that the Jew is human, I then reject that totally." (Antisemitic speech, Reichstag, 1895)	"It is a wild contention that new-born babies are persons." (Dr. Michael Tooley, 1972)
THE LANGUAGE OF KILLING	**THE LANGUAGE OF KILLING**
"The treatment was administered to the children of the Haar-Eglfing Institution." (Dr. Pfannmuller, 1945)	"Abortion as treatment for the sexually transmitted disease of unwanted pregnancy."(Dr. Willard Cates & Colleagues, 1976)
THE LANGUAGE OF KILLING	**THE LANGUAGE OF KILLING**
"If you are going to kill all these people, at least take the brains out so that the material could be utilized." (Testimony of Dr. Julius Hallervordan, 1947)	"In the case of abortion the fetus cannot be 'helped' by being experimented upon since it is doomed to death anyhow, but perhaps its death can be ennobled ... when the research has as its objective the saving of lives (or the reduction of defects) of other wanted fetuses." (Drs. Willard Gaylin & Mark Lappe, 1975)

Since his election to the United States Senate Obama has maintained a 100 percent rating....(voted and supported the interests of) Planned Parenthood (as of 2007).[48]

Quotes from Margaret Sanger, Founder of Planned Parenthood:

"Birth control itself, often denounced as a violation of natural law, is nothing more or less than the facilitation of the process of weeding out the unfit, of preventing the birth of defectives or of those who will become defectives."

"The procreation of [the diseased, the feeble-minded and paupers] should be stopped."

"Good and evil are meaningless to things that have no souls."
Plato (428-347 BC)

Before I formed thee in the belly I knew thee; and before thou camest forth out of the womb I sanctified thee, and I ordained thee a prophet unto the nations.

Jeremiah 1:5

Thou shalt not kill.

Exodus 20:13

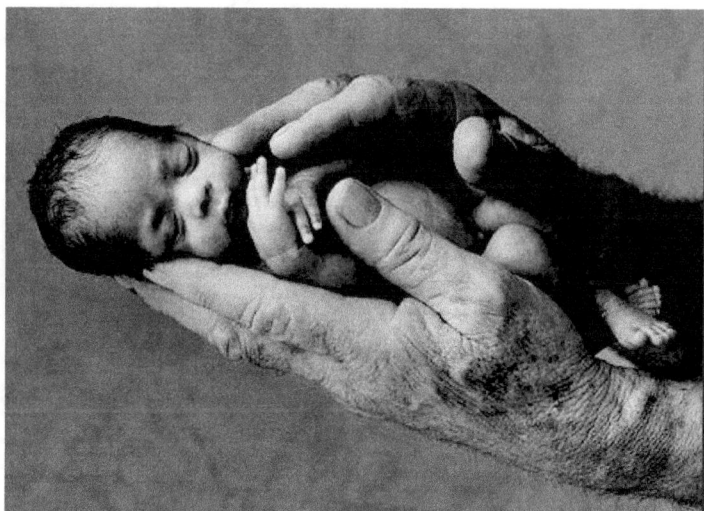

For thou hast possessed my reins: thou hast covered me in my mother's womb.

I will praise thee; for I am fearfully and wonderfully made: marvellous are thy works; and that my soul knoweth right well.

My substance was not hid from thee, when I was made in secret, and curiously wrought in the lowest parts of the earth.

Thine eyes did see my substance, yet being unperfect; and in thy book all my members were written, which in continuance were fashioned, when as yet there was none of them.　　Psalms 139:13-16

"My friends, we live in the greatest nation in the history of the world. I hope you'll join me as we try to change it."
Barack Obama[1]

OBAMA'S VISION

What kind of world will it be with Barack Obama at the helm? With a sickening feeling, we can ascertain from his voting record where our nation will head, how quickly we are headed for the freefall, is another question.

There are a couple of new ideas Obama has though, that are interesting to contemplate and didn't get much media coverage (imagine that!).

LIVING CONSTITUTION

In his book, The Audacity of Hope, Barack elaborates on his opinion of the right to change the Constitution of the United States:

> When we get in a tussle, we appeal to the Founding Fathers and the Constitution's ratifiers to give direction. Some, like Justice Scalia, conclude that the original understanding must be followed and if we obey this rule, democracy is respected.

Others, like Justice Breyers, insist that sometimes the original understanding can take you only so far--that on the truly big arguments, we have to take context, history, and the practical outcomes of a decision into account.

I have to side with Justice Breyer's view of the Constitution--that it is not a static but rather a living document and must be read in the context of an ever-changing world.

I see democracy as a conversation to be had. According to this conception, the genius of Madison's design is not that it provides a fixed blueprint for action. It provides us with a framework and rules, but all its machinery are designed to force us into a conversation.[2]

An article on CBN News clarifies:

...the key issue is how a Supreme Court nominee views the Constitution. Is it a "living document" that judges can interpret as they please? Or should judges stick to what the founding fathers intended?

The U.S. Constitution is the supreme law of the land, created by our founding fathers more than 200 years ago.

But the days of George Washington and Thomas Jefferson are gone. And one lasting document has now turned into two competing philosophies. Because in today's society, some see it as black and white, while others see it a little more blurry.

For social conservatives, the nightmare scenario is a Supreme Court filled with judges who see the Constitution as a living, breathing document. That could lead to gay marriage, to religious expression being removed from the public square, and a host of other liberal causes.

Conservatives say it is a slippery slope that has already begun. "The question is whether we can stop and whether we can trudge back up the hill towards constitutionalism," declared Gaziano.

CBN News asked Gaziano how you accomplish this, and Gaziano replied, "You appoint the right justices to the Supreme Court."[3]

> Barack Obama says, **"We need somebody who's got the heart, the empathy, to recognize what it's like to be a young teenage mom, the empathy to understand what it's like to be poor or African-American or gay or disabled or old - and that's the criterion by which I'll be selecting my judges."**[4]

CIVILIAN NATIONAL SECURITY FORCE

According to Investor's Business Daily:

> In talking about his national service, Obama, the man who seems to be running for "community organizer in chief," also made this startling statement:

> > **"We cannot continue to rely on our military in order to achieve the national security objectives we've set. We've got to have a civilian national security force that's just as powerful, just as strong, just as well-funded."**[5]

This is an idea worthy of Hugo Chavez.

Northwestern University law professor James Lindgren has estimated that this civilian national security force alone would cost somewhere between $100 billion and $500 billion, or between 10% and 50% of all federal tax receipts. And that doesn't include the cost of the brown shirts.

Adults are not exempt from all this, even adults who've already served in the U.S. military. **"People of all ages, stations and skills will be asked to serve,"** Obama says. Will they be asked, or drafted?

"The future of our nation depends on the soldier at Fort Carson," he concedes. **"But it (also) depends on the teacher in East L.A., the nurse in Appalachia, the after-school worker in New Orleans . . ."** So drop down and give Sgt. Obama 50 hours.

Require. Demand. Never allow. Obama's version of "voluntary" service is more appropriate for Havana than middle America. He wants to turn America's students, and even adults, into clones of Elian Gonzalez, compelled to serve the state in ways Obama **"will direct."**[6]

WorldNet Daily's Joseph Farah also addressed this issue, portions of his article are included below:

Are we talking about creating a police state here?

The U.S. Army alone has nearly 500,000 troops. That doesn't count reserves or National Guard. In 2007, the U.S. Defense budget was $439 billion.

Is Obama serious about creating some kind of domestic

security force bigger and more expensive than that?

If not, why did he say it? What did he mean?

So far, despite our attempts to find out, the Obama campaign is not talking.

Who will Obama appoint to administer this new "civilian national security force"? Where will the money come from? Where in the Constitution does he see justification for the federal government creating such a domestic army?

The questions are endless.

But before we can hope to get to the specifics, we need much more in the way of generalizations from Obama.

Certainly there have been initiatives like this elsewhere – Cuba, the Soviet Union, China, Venezuela, North Korea. But has anything like this ever been proposed in a free country?

I have a feeling there would be more questions from the press if I myself had proposed the creation of something as preposterous as a "civilian national security force" than there has been about this proposal by the presidential candidate currently leading in most of the polls. I'm quite sure I would be hung out to dry as some kind of Nazi thug. Meanwhile, Obama makes this wild suggestion and it is met with a collective yawn from the watchdogs.

Help me out here. What am I missing?[7]

An intuitive blogger writes:

The irony of all this is that it looks as though Obama was honest about one thing - he will bring change. If history is any guide, we can expect his sort of change to contain the mores of Marx, the political ambition of Hitler, the foreign policy of Neville Chamberlin, and the economics of Hoover. It's a change that looks remarkably the same. It's a change that, if implemented, could alter this country into something so destitute, so diminished, so destroyed, so devoid of any signs of its origin, that none of us may even recognize it.

If you want change in 2008, and lots of it, vote for Obama. It may be the last vote you ever cast.[8]

INTERNATIONAL CRISIS

In an eerie prediction coming from Senator Joe Biden, the Obama camp's vision includes an international crisis...and very soon after taking office, you just might have to **"gird up your loins,"** and swallow whatever bitter pill that they might give you.

ABC News Online reports:

> Sen. Barack Obama., D-Ill., will be tested by an international crisis within his first six months in power and he will need supporters to stand by him as he makes tough, and possibly unpopular, decisions.

> **"Mark my words,"** the Democratic vice presidential nominee warned at the second of his two Seattle fundraisers Sunday. **"It will not be six months before the world tests Barack Obama like they did John Kennedy. The world is looking. We're about to elect a brilliant 47-year-old senator president of the United States of America. Remember I said it standing here if you don't remember anything else I said. Watch, we're gonna have an international crisis, a generated crisis, to test the mettle of this guy." "I can give you at least four or five scenarios from where it might originate,"** Biden said to Emerald City supporters, mentioning the Middle East and Russia as possibilities. **"And he's**

gonna need help. And the kind of help he's gonna need is, he's gonna need you - not financially to help him - we're gonna need you to use your influence, your influence within the community, to stand with him. Because it's not gonna be apparent initially, it's not gonna be apparent that we're right."

"Gird your loins," Biden told the crowd. "We're gonna win with your help, God willing, we're gonna win, but this is not gonna be an easy ride. This president, the next president, is gonna be left with the most significant task. It's like cleaning the Augean stables, man. This is more than just, this is more than – think about it, literally, think about it – this is more than just a capital crisis, this is more than just markets. This is a systemic problem we have with this economy."

"...This guy has it. But he's gonna need your help. Because I promise you, you all are gonna be sitting here a year from now going, 'Oh my God, why are they there in the polls? Why is the polling so down? Why is this thing so tough?' We're gonna have to make some incredibly tough decisions in the first two years. So I'm asking you now, I'm asking you now, be prepared to stick with us. Remember the faith you had at this point because you're going to have to reinforce us."

"There are gonna be a lot of you who want to go, 'Whoa, wait a minute, yo, whoa, whoa, I don't know about that decision'," Biden continued. "Because if you think the decision is sound when they're made, which I believe you will when they're made, they're not likely to be as popular as they are sound. Because if they're popular, they're probably not sound."[9]

PART III
THE MAN

It is possible that Obama conspired his way to the precipice of the world's biggest job, involving a vast network of people and government agencies over decades of lies. Anything's possible.[1]

Amy Hollifield, St. Petersburg Times

UNIQUE HERITAGE

"He's always wanted to be president"
A close friend of Obama's, would confide after his 2004 Boston Convention speech.[2]

Twice, in kindergarten and also in third grade, Barack Obama, known as Barry Soetoro at the time, wrote an essay titled, 'I Want To Be a President.'

Even at an early age, the Presidency of the United States was uppermost in his mind.

Why? Who or what made young Barry yearn for this position so much that he would write about it over and over again.

Was it just a child's dream, that was a foretelling of things to come? Or had this ambitious idea been placed in his head deliberately? And if so, by whom?

A simple scan of Barack Obama's biography won't yield many clues. However, if you linger over the details a bit longer, there are some revelations that give you cause to consider their place in this mystery.

BIOGRAPHY

Barack Hussein Obama was born on August 4, 1961, in Honolulu, Hawaii.

Born to a black Kenyan father and a white American mother, Obama had a very diverse cultural upbringing. His parents separated when he was two years old and later divorced. His father died in a car accident in Kenya when Obama was 21. He spent his entire childhood in the U.S. state of Hawaii except for four years between ages 6-10 which he spent living in Jakarta Indonesia with his mother and his step-father Lolo Soetoro. After his short time in Indonesia he returned to Honolulu to live with his maternal grandparents until his graduation in 1979.[3]

DIGGING A LITTLE DEEPER

GRANDPARENTS
- PATERNAL

The Obama family is an extended family of Kenyan (Luo), African American, English, Irish, and Indonesian heritage.

Hussein Onyango Obama (1895–1979) is Barack Obama's paternal grandfather who worked as a mission cook. He joined the British Army during World War I. [4]

"His father, Hussein Onyango Obama was a "prominent farmer, and elder of the tribe (Luo), a medicine man with healing powers."[5]

He visited Europe and India, and afterward lived for a time in Zanzibar, where he converted from Christianity to Islam.[6]

- MATERNAL

Madelyn Lee Payne Dunham (born October 26, 1922) and Stanley Armour Dunham (1918 –1992) are the maternal grandparents of Barack Obama.[7]

Obama's maternal grandmother was English, Scottish and Cherokee.[8]

His maternal grandfather's heritage included English, Scottish and French ancestry.[9]

Stanley's mother, Ruth Armour Dunham, committed suicide on November 26, 1926. Her 8 year-old son found her body.

Madelyn and Stanley married in May 1940. She gave birth to Ann Dunham in Fort Leavenworth on November 29, 1942. With Madelyn and Stanley both working full-time and struggling, the family moved to California, Kansas, Texas, and Seattle, Washington (on Mercer Island), where Ann graduated from high school. They then moved to Hawaii, where he worked in a furniture store and she started working at the Bank of Hawaii.[10]

At age 10, Barack Obama went to live with his grandparents. He speaks often of the midwestern values that he was taught by his grandparents, but the portrait that he paints of them in his book, *Dreams of My Father* isn't what most average Americans would consider a moral upbringing.

> "...my grandfather had come to consider himself as something of a freethinker - bohemian, even."

> "...he would enroll the family in the local Unitarian Universalist congregation; he liked the idea that Unitarians drew on the scriptures of all the great religions ("It's like you get five religions in one," he would say).[11]

Obama's grandfather had quite a few black friends and would often take him to see a poet in his eighty's named Frank Davis. Frank Davis was a known Communist.

During these visits, Frank and Stanley would smoke pot,[12] drank whiskey and they had him help them compose "dirty limericks." [13]

His grandfather would take him to bars in the red-light district and Obama mentions looking at the "pornographic" art on the walls.[14]

FATHER

Barack Hussein Obama (1936–1982) was a Kenyan senior governmental economist. He is the main subject of his son's memoir, *Dreams From My Father*.... Obama Sr. was brought up as Muslim. [15]

He married at 18 to a fellow Kenyan, Kezia. Due to a program offering Western educational opportunities to outstanding Kenyan students, Obama Sr. was awarded a scholarship in economics, and at the age of 23, he enrolled at the University of Hawaii. He left behind a pregnant Kezia and their infant son.[16]

On February 21, 1961, Obama Sr. married a fellow student, Ann Dunham in Maui, Hawaii.[17]

Obama's father was not legally divorced from his first wife in Kenya, before he married Obama's mother.[18]

There is no documentation of the marriage of Obama's parents. Obama's father abandoned him and his mother to accept a scholarship at Harvard that would not pay his family expenses when he had an offer from the New School in New York City that would have paid for Obama Sr. to bring his wife and son with him.[19]

Barack Obama's father is interviewed for article published in the Honolulu Star Bulletin upon his graduation. He never once mentions the wife and son at home. Barack says, "No mention is made of my mother or me, and I'm left to wonder whether the omission was intentional on my fathers part..."[20]

He and Dunham divorced in 1963. The divorce was filed in Honolulu, Hawaii in January 1964, and he only saw his son again once, at age 10. He received a Masters degree (AM) from Harvard in 1965.

At Harvard, he met an American-born teacher named Ruth Nidesand who would follow him to Kenya when he returned after completing his Masters degree. She eventually became his third wife and had two children with him before they divorced.[21]

On his return to Kenya, Obama Sr. was hired by an oil company and then served as an economist. As Senator Barack Obama describes in his memoir, his father's conflict with President Kenyatta destroyed his career.

Obama Sr.'s life then took a tailspin into drinking and poverty, from which he never recovered...Obama Sr. lost both legs in an automobile accident, and subsequently lost his job. He died not long afterward at the age of 46 in a car crash in Nairobi.[22]

"Obama's father was a polygamist who failed as a bureaucrat in Kenya and killed himself in the last of a series of drunk-driving incidents in Nairobi."[23]

MOTHER

"In most elections, the deceased mother of a candidate in the primaries is not the subject of a magazine profile. But Ann Soetoro was not like most mothers."[5]

Obama's mother, Stanley Ann Soetoro is somewhat of a mystery. It seems odd that he chose to write more about his absent father than the mother who by all accounts had great aspirations for him...."the person who mattered most in Obama's life is the one we know the least about."[25]

Obama's mother, "was a teen mother who later got a Ph.D. in anthropology; a white woman from the Midwest who was more comfortable in Indonesia; a natural-born mother obsessed with her work"[26]

Stanley Ann Dunham Soetoro (1942–1995), known as Ann Dunham, and later as Ann Soetoro was an anthropologist who specialized in rural development. Born in Kansas, Dunham attended high school near Seattle, Washington, and spent most of her adult life in Hawaii. [27]

Obama writes, "...she was a lonely witness for secular humanism, a soldier for New Deal, Peace Corps, position-paper liberalism."[28]

One high school friend said: "If you were concerned about something going wrong in the world, Stanley [Ann] would know about it first ... We were liberals before we knew what liberals were." Another called her "the original feminist."[29]

In her high school years, she was influenced by two radical teachers at Mercer High School – Val Foubert who taught English…his texts were "cutting edge": "Atlas Shrugged," "The Organization Man," "The Hidden Persuaders," "1984;" and Jim Wichterman, who taught from "The Communist Manifesto."[30]

Ann enrolled at the University of Hawaii, where she studied anthropology. She met Barack Obama Sr., a student from Kenya and the school's first African student, in a Russian language class at the University. When they became engaged, both sets of parents opposed the marriage, with Obama's father in particular objecting. Nevertheless, the couple married on February 2, 1961 in Maui, Hawaii, after discovering she was pregnant.[31]

After her divorce from Obama, Sr…. a few years later, Dunham met an Indonesian student, Lolo Soetoro (1936-1987)…They married in 1967 and moved to Jakarta, Indonesia…where he worked as a government relations consultant with Mobil Corporation, the U.S.-based international petroleum company.[32]

Although a daughter was born in 1970, her second marriage failed.

"She always felt that marriage as an institution was not particularly essential or important," said Nina Nayar, who later became a close friend.[33]

In his memoir, Barack remembers some of the tension in the household:

"Sometimes I would overhear him and my mother arguing in their bedroom, usually about her refusal to attend his company dinner parties, where and boast American businessmen from Texas and Louisiana would slap Lolo's back about the palms they had greased to obtain the new offshore drilling rights, while their wives complained to my mother about the quality of Indonesian help. He would ask her how it would look for him to go alone, and remind her that these were her own people, and my mother's voice would rise to almost a shout."

"'They are not my people.'"[34]

This is an interesting tidbit regarding Ann's true feelings about her heritage and her country. She could identify more with her foreign acquaintances and refused to be aligned with the "American" people.

She returned to Honolulu in 1974 to continue her education, but three years later she was back in Indonesia, leaving Barack with his grandparents.

Ann worked with Indonesia's oldest bank, the United States Agency for International Development, the Ford Foundation, Women's World Banking, and as a consultant in Pakistan. She mingled with leaders from organizations supporting Indonesian human rights, women's rights, and grass-roots development.[35]

"Every so often, Ann would leave Indonesia to live in Hawaii—or New York or even, in the mid-1980s, Pakistan, for a microfinance job. She and her daughter sometimes lived in garage apartments and spare rooms of friends.[36]

Her home became a gathering spot for the powerful and the marginalized: politicians, filmmakers, musicians and labor organizers. "She had, compared with other foundation colleagues, a much more eclectic circle," ..."She brought unlikely conversation partners together."[37]

"Visitors flowed constantly through her Ford Foundation office in downtown Jakarta and through her house...Her guests were leaders in the Indonesian human rights movement, people from women's organizations, representatives of community groups doing grass-roots development."[38]

"I didn't know a lot of them and would often ask after, 'Who was that?' " said David S. McCauley, now an environmental economist at the Asian Development Bank in Manila, who had the office next door. "You'd find out it was the head of some big organization in with thousands of members from central Java or someplace, somebody that she had met some time ago, and they would make a point of coming to see her when they came to Jakarta."[39]

Stanley Ann taught English to Indonesian businessmen at the American Embassy. Obama says, "The Indonesian businessmen weren't much interested in the niceties of the English language, and several made passes at her....The Americans were mostly older men...These men knew the country though...the closets where skeletons were buried... Over lunch or casual conversation they would share with her things she couldn't learn in the published news reports."[40]

What begins to emerge from these facts about Obama's mother, is that she was a woman with many facets, high level connections, keeper of the secrets those connections would entrust her with and was driven to pursue life on her own terms, without any regard for conventionality.

She seemed to have ambitions for her children far beyond the typical mother. Just what these ambitions were, is not clear.

According to Obama: "Five days a week, she came into my room at four in the morning, force-fed me breakfast, and proceeded to teach me my English lessons for three hours before I left for school and she left for work."[41]

Her travels took her to many countries allowing her to expand her knowledge on the world's many cultures and religions. Ann was a professed atheist; however she considered spirituality a different matter. She encouraged her children to be open to all religions, she took great pains to be sure that they were aware of the spirit realm.

Obama discusses his mother's preoccupation in his book *Dreams of My Father*:

"...a book my mother once bought for me, a book called *Origins*, a collection of creation tales from around the world, stories of Genesis and the tree where man was born, Prometheus and the gift of fire, the tortoise of Hindu legend that floated in space, supporting the weight of the world on its back...By the age of five or six I was satisfied to leave these distant mysteries intact, each story self-contained and as true as the next..."[42]

He also recounts how when he and his mother were traveling to Indonesia, during a stopover in Japan, his mother made him walk, "...through bone-chilling rains to see the great bronze Buddha at Kamakura..."[43]

A story in Time magazine recounts:
> She collected treasures from her travels—exquisite things with stories she understood. Antique daggers with an odd number of curves, as required by Javanese tradition."[44] The daggers referenced in the story:

> ...are weapons from South East Asia. It was believed to have originated as a good luck amulet in Java in the 14th century, at the time of the Hindu Majapahit Empire.

> The keris signified manhood and offered a magical potency that could assist its owner. The blade of the keris represents a serpent. This is probably the naga of Hindu mythology, guardian of the earth's treasures. Each keris has its own spirit, reflected by the blade shape and its individual pamor. It was considered important for a prospective owner to acquire a keris whose spiritual persona was compatible with his own. Only then could the weapon's mystical powers be used to his advantage. A keris could help keep disease away...ensure victory in battle...Due to this extraordinary power, many keris were kept as family heirlooms. However, a keris placed in the wrong hands could create havoc and misfortune.[45]

Obama was given his mother's collection. Obama says, "My mother...was one of the most spiritual souls I ever knew. But she had a healthy skepticism of religion......yet for all her professed secularism, my mother was in many ways the most spiritually awakened person that I've ever known...."[46]

> In 1994, Ann Dunham was diagnosed with ovarian cancer and uterine cancer; she moved back to Hawaii to live near her widowed mother. She died there in 1995 at the age of 52.[47]

QUESTIONS

There are unanswered questions flying around in cyberspace on blogs, emails, websites and now the questions are even being voiced at the rallies.

Barack Obama's books regarding his own life are convenient in what they choose to reveal and what parts of his life are conspicuously absent.

"Barack Obama does not say much about his years in New York City. The time he spent as an undergraduate at Columbia College and then working in Manhattan in the early 1980s surfaces only fleetingly in his memoir. In the book, he casts himself as a solitary wanderer in the metropolis, the outsider searching for a way to 'make myself of some use.'"

"He barely mentions Columbia, training ground for the elite, where he transferred in his junior year, majoring in political science and international relations and writing his thesis on Soviet nuclear disarmament."

"...he declined repeated requests to talk about his New York years, release his Columbia transcript or identify even a single fellow student, co-worker, roommate or friend from those years."

"He doesn't remember the names of a lot of people in his life," said Ben LaBolt, a campaign spokesman.

"Mr. Obama has, of course, done plenty of remembering. His 1995 memoir, "Dreams from My Father," weighs in at more than 450 pages. But he also exercised his writer's prerogative to decide what to include or leave out. Now, as he presents himself to voters, a look at his years in New York - other people's accounts and his own - suggest not only what he was like back then but how he chooses to be seen now."

"In a long profile of Mr. Obama in a Columbia alumni magazine in 2005, in which his Columbia years occupied just two paragraphs, he called that time 'an intense period of study.'"

"I spent a lot of time in the library. I didn't socialize that much. I was like a monk."...What is Obama hiding about his years at Columbia? Why the obsessive secrecy? It is likely that this is the decisive moment of his life, when he comes under the guidance of his protector and patron, Zbigniew. "Soviet Nuclear Disarmament" is a thesis title that has Zbigniew Brzezinski written all over it. Zbig was at this time the head of the Institute on Communist Affairs, where he was located from 1960 to 1989, apart from his time in the Carter White House. There is therefore a strong prima facie circumstantial case that Obama entered Brzezinski's orbit between 1982 and 1983 at Columbia.[48]

The Columbia years are a hole in the sprawling Obama hagiography. In his two published memoirs, the 47-year-old Democratic nominee barely mentions his experience there. He refuses to answer questions about Columbia and New York -- which, in this media age, serves only to raise more of them. Why not release his Columbia transcript? Why has his senior essay gone missing? What can be said with some certainty is that Mr. Obama lived off campus while at Columbia in 1981-83 and made few friends. Fox News contacted some 400 of his classmates and found no one who remembered him. [49]

This past April, Obama revealed for the first time at a fundraising event, that he had traveled to Pakistan in 1981 as a college student.

"I traveled to Pakistan when I was in college – I knew what Sunni and Shia was before I joined the Senate Foreign Relations Committee." "The senator had not previously discussed any trip to Pakistan, either in his books or in scores of policy talks regarding Pakistan....Obama visited his mother and sister Maya in Indonesia. Obama then went on to Pakistan with a friend from college whose family was from that country..."[50]

"Obama was in Pakistan for about three weeks...staying with his friend's family in Karachi and also visiting Hyderabad. Pakistan in 1981 was under military rule. It was difficult for U.S. citizens to travel to the country without assistance. It would have been easier for someone to enter Pakistan on an Indonesian passport."

One blogger puts the trip into context:

> NOW, It all sounds very innocent, "a college trip to Pakistan".
>
> Pakistan was in turmoil in 1981 and ruled of martial law. Millions of Afghan refugees were living in Pakistan, while the Afghan Mujahedeen operated from bases inside Pakistan in their war with the Soviets. One of the leaders that based his operation in Quetta, Pakistan was Osama Bin Laden.
>
> Pakistan was on the banned travel list for US Citizens at the time and all non-Muslim visitors were not welcome unless sponsored by their embassy for official business.
>
> Pakistan was not a tourist stop nor the place to hang out with someone's family in 1981.[51]

These are just a few of the areas of Barack Obama's life that leave some unanswered questions. There are also plenty of rumors, some challenge his right to even be running for the office of President, based on his citizenship. Others have less consequences, but still need to be verified to show if this is an additional area that Obama chosen distort and twist to his benefit.

Some of these rumors include:

• No documentation of the marriage of Obama's parents.

• Writer and Radio Host, Kenneth Lamb wrote an in-depth article regarding Barack Obama's heritage. It asserts the claim that Obama should technically be referred to as "Arab-American." Mr. Lamb's article says, "True Negro tribal members of western Kenya where his father was born have Christian names, not Arabic. His father's decision to name him with an Arabic name is a matter of his father establishing his ethnic identity in Africa - it is done deliberately to separate him from the African tribes. He may live among them, but he is not one of them. His father's message is that he is Arabic, not Negro.

- "Many will find these truths unsettling. I'm often asked, "But I thought his father was Kenyan. How could Mr. Obama not be African-American, how could his ethnic composition be so Arabic?"

  "The definitive clue to that answer is to look at his name, his father's name, and the names of all his ancestors on his father's side. They are all Arabic."[52]

- "In Indonesia, which was under tight rule in 1967, Obama clearly took on the last name of his stepfather in school registration documents.

- "Obama's registration in Indonesia under the name "Barry Soetoro" also raises questions as to whether he adopted that name in the U.S. at any time. According to Illinois state filings, when Obama registered as an attorney in 1991, under the name Barack Obama, he stated he did not have any former names."[53]

- Philip Berg, a Philadelphia attorney filed suit in the U.S. District Court for the Eastern District of Pennsylvania against Barack Obama on August 21, 2008, citing more than a few unanswered questions regarding the Senator's background. The suit maintains that Sen. Obama is not a natural born U.S. citizen or that, if he ever was, he lost his citizenship when he was adopted in Indonesia. Berg also cited what he called "dual loyalties" due to his citizenship and ties with Kenya and Indonesia.

Michelle Obama said that Barack talks about "The world as it is" and "The world as it should be..."

It seems that he used this inspiration in writing the story of his life as well. Instead of writing truth "as it is," he wanted you to see how "it should be."

He would prefer you read and believe the fairytale transformation of the disillusioned wanderer to the passionate crusader we see today.

The real story behind the man is a quite a different tale.

The smear campaign
aka
Inconvenient truths

Truth fears no questions.
Unknown

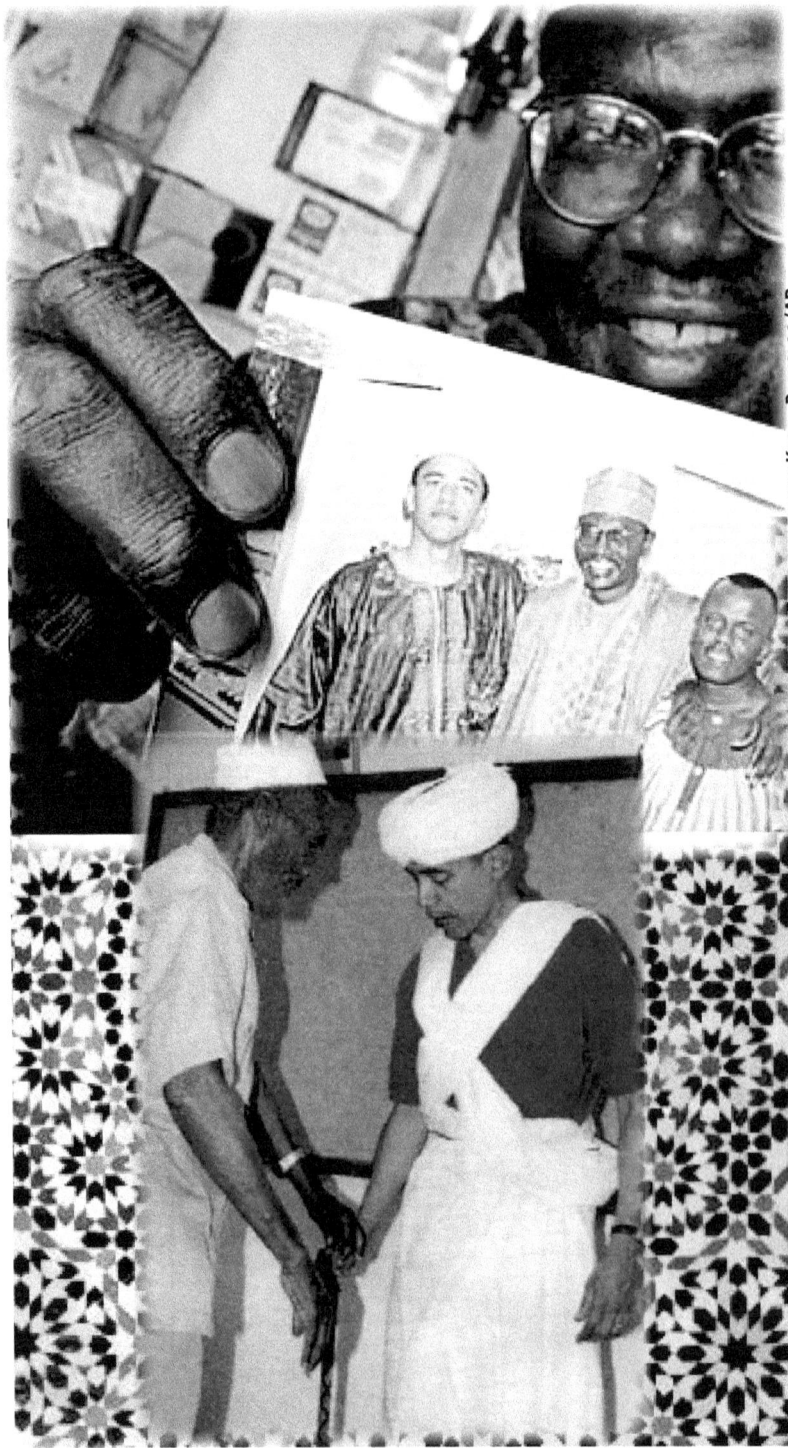

"WAKE UP, WAKE UP! WE ARE AT WAR. WAR HAS BEEN DECLARED ON THE WEST AND WE MUST FIGHT! One or the other must perish."[1]

Oriana Fallaci

MUSLIM?
DOES IT MATTER?

"I will stand with the Muslims should the political winds shift in an ugly direction."[2]

Barack Obama

Is he or isn't he? As Former Secretary of State General Colin Powell put it in an interview..."what if he is?"[3]

Well, if he is, for one thing that makes him a deceiver of the American people. He has categorically and adamantly denied the accusation, stating that he is a Christian.

And if he is a Muslim, like it or not, politically correct or not, that particular piece of information would most definitely make a difference.

Should this issue be put to rest, because he has given us his word on this matter? As we have already seen in the telling of his life story, he has no problem in manipulating the truth to fit the outcome desired.

On October 22, 2002, Oriana Fallaci addressed an audience at the American Enterprise Institute. Following are short excerpts from her talk. Ms. Fallaci, a native of Florence, Italy and a life-long journalist, caused turmoil across Europe with the publication of her book, *The Rage and the Pride*, calling the West to stand up to the Islamic world.

Why am I here, then? Because, since September 11, we are at war. Because the front line of that war is here, in America. Because when I was a war correspondent, I liked to be on the front line. And this time, in this war, I do not feel as a war correspondent. I feel as a soldier. The duty of a soldier is to fight.

From Afghanistan to Sudan, from Palestine to Pakistan, from Malaysia to Iran, from Egypt to Iraq, from Algeria to Senegal, from Syria to Kenya, from Libya to Chad, from Lebanon to Morocco, from Indonesia to Yemen, from Saudi Arabia to Somalia, the hate for the West swells like a fire fed by the wind. And the followers of Islamic fundamentalism multiply like a protozoa of a cell which splits to become two cells then four then eight then sixteen then thirty-two to infinity... The ferocious faces, the threatening fists. The fires that burn the American flag and the photos of Bush.

The clash between us and them is not a military clash. Oh, no. It is a cultural one, a religious one. And our military victories do not solve the offensive of Islamic terrorism. On the contrary, they encourage it. They exacerbate it, they multiply it. The worst is still to come.

President Bush has said, "We refuse to live in fear."

Beautiful sentence, very beautiful. I loved it! But inexact, Mr. President, because the West does live in fear. People are afraid to speak against the Islamic world. Afraid to offend, and to be punished for offending, the sons of Allah. You can insult the Christians, the Buddhists, the Hindus, the Jews. You can slander the Catholics, you can spit on the Madonna and Jesus Christ. But, woe betide the citizen who pronounces a word against the Islamic religion.

My book is also...to accuse us of cowardice, hypocrisy, demagogy, laziness, moral misery, and of all that comes with that. The stupidity of the unbearable fad of political correctness, for instance. The paucity of our schools, our universities, our young people, people who often don't even know the story of their country, the names Jefferson, Franklin, Robespierre, Napoleon, Garibaldi. And no understanding that freedom cannot exist without discipline, self-discipline.

I accuse ourselves also of another crime: the loss of passion. Haven't you understood what drives our enemies? What permits them to fight this war against us? The passion! They have passion! They have so much passion that they can die for it!

Their leaders, too, of course. I met Khomeini. I discussed with him for more than six hours in calm, and I tell you that that man was a man of passion. I never met bin Laden. But I have well observed his eyes. I have well listened to his voice. And I tell you that that man is a man of passion. We have lost passion.

Well, I have not. I boil with passion. I, too, am ready to die for passion. But around me, I see no passion. Even those who hate me and attack me and insult me do this without passion. They are mollusks, not men and women. And a civilization, a culture, cannot survive without passion, cannot be saved without passion. If the West does not wake up, if we do not refind passion, we are lost.

"If we continue to stay inert, they will become always more and more. They will demand always more and more, they will vex and boss us always more and more. 'Til the point of subduing us. Therefore, dealing with them is impossible. Attempting a dialogue, unthinkable. Showing indulgence, suicidal. And he or she who believes the contrary is a fool."[4]

Oriana Fallaci faces jail. In her mid-70s, stricken with a cancer that, for the moment, permits only the consumption of liquids - one of the most renowned journalists of the modern era has been indicted by a judge in her native Italy under provisions of the Italian Penal Code which proscribe the "vilipendio," or "vilification," of "any religion admitted by the state."

In her case, the religion deemed vilified is Islam, and the vilification was perpetrated, apparently, in a book she wrote last year -- and which has sold many more than a million copies all over Europe -- called "The Force of Reason."[5]

Fallaci accused the judge of having disregarded the fact that in 2005, Adel Smith, president of the Union of Italian Muslims called for her murder and defamed Christianity.[6]

Oriana Fallaci, died of cancer on September 15, 2008 at age 77.

Kurdish Media says, "Today the West is being the victim of their own values, such as freedom of speech and _expression, so that Muslims are using 'Democracy' as a tool and taking advantage of democracy to disseminate Islam to all the corners of the world."

After 9/11 many Muslims complained that Islam had been hijacked by Fundamentalism, and many Muslim leaders and political leaders publicly disassociated themselves from radical Islam, but behind closed doors they still continue to preach against the Westerns' values.

Many Muslims are thinking that the war is against Islam, but actually 9/11 accomplished one of their objectives, the application of universal Islamic values, particularly the jihad. After 9/11, thousands of books have been published, and many non-government organizations and Islamic centers have been established to teach Islam to infidels using American tax money.

According to U.S. news online, there are approximately 6 million Muslims in the United States and an estimated 1,450 mosques in the United States.

What does Islamization mean?

It means that from social, political, and cultural institutions to banking and economic operations -- all aspects of the way of life -- will bring the Islamic constitution, the Islamic code of law, to challenge the U.S. Constitution. It is a process by which the spiritual and political leaders disseminate Islam through missionary activities such as holding seminars on university campuses, opening cultural centers and charter schools, sending graduate students to study at ivy league institutions, building mosques, starting newspapers, infiltrating the most sensitive U.S. institutions such as the FBI, the State Department, and offices on Capital Hill...

NASA invited the Counsel on American Islamic Relation to teach sensitivity and diversity training workshops entitled '*Understanding Islam and Muslims at NASA.*' Why has Islam become so delicate a topic and superior to all other religion that non-Muslim Americans should be trained and Islam be taught in American institutions? What about the beliefs of Jews, Christians and other faiths. Are representatives from those groups of faith been invited to discuss their faith as part of cultural sensitivity?

In the Muslim world especially in the Arab countries world, anyone who is not Muslim, such as Christians and other faiths, sometimes even different Islamic sects, as seen currently in Iraq, live in constantl fear of terrorism if they choose to stay among Muslims. Muslims have one agenda, no matter what American or western countries do as humanitarian acts for their people because it is not enough as long as they are infidels.

Bat Ye'or, an Egyptian author, explains in detail the systematic and calculated rise of Islam in Europe in her carefully documented record Eurabia: The Euro-Arab Axis. Once Muslims got their representatives in high public offices, then this will happen. President Bush, European heads of state, and Muslim leaders have already announced that this is a religion of tolerance. Yet, if anyone wants to understand Islam, the student of world affairs must read the history of Islam noting how Mohammed spread Islam beginning with a few people all over the world.

Pope Benedict clearly defines the goal of Islam. The Qu'ran is a total religious law, which regulates the whole of political and social life and insists that the whole order of life be Islamic.

Islam has the universalism agenda to dominate the whole world.[7]

OBAMA CHILDHOOD RECORDS

In an article for the *Israel Insider*, Reuven Koret gives us his take on the issue:

Obama's official campaign site has a page titled "Obama has never been a Muslim, and is a committed Christian." The page states, "Obama never prayed in a mosque. He has never been a Muslim, was not raised a Muslim, and is a committed Christian who attends the United Church of Christ."

Yet the accumulated research from primary sources who knew Obama from his childhood indicate that he was a devout Muslim, the son of a devout Muslim, the step-son of a devout Muslim and the grandson and namesake ("Hussein") of a devout Muslim. He was registered in school as a Muslim and demonstrated his ability to chant praise to Allah in impressive Arab-accented tones even as an adult...

Although as an adult he would register as a Christian, and occasionally attend a Christian Church (but apparently not often enough to listen to the preaching of his pastor, or so he would claim) this was a necessary step for a man who from earliest boyhood has nurtured the precocious ambition to be President of the United States.

He was entered into the Roman Catholic, Franciscus Assisi Primary School, in Jakarta, Indonesia, on January 1, 1968, registered under the name Barry Soetoro, an Indonesian citizen whose religion was listed as Islam.[8]

PHOTO COURTESY ASSOCIATED PRESS

All Indonesian students are required to study religion at school and a young Barry Soetoro, being a Muslim, would have been required to study Islam daily in school. He would have been taught to read and write Arabic, to recite his prayers properly, to read and recite from the Quran and to study the laws of Islam.

In his autobiography, "Dreams From My Father," Obama mentions studying the Koran and describes the public school as "a Muslim school."

"In the Muslim school, the teacher wrote to tell mother I made faces during Koranic studies."

According to Tine Hahiyary, one of Obama's teachers and the principal from 1971 through 1989, Barry actively took part in the Islamic religious lessons during his time at the school:

"I remembered that he had studied "mengaji" (recitation of the Quran)"

The author of the Laotze blog writes from Jakarta: "The actual usage of the word 'mengaji' in Indonesian and Malaysian societies means the study of learning to recite the Quran in the Arabic language rather than the native tongue. "Mengagi" is a word and a term that is accorded the highest value and status in the mindset of fundamentalist societies here in Southeast Asia. To put it quite simply, 'mengaji classes' are not something that a non practicing or so-called moderate Muslim family would ever send their child to. To put this in a Christian context, this is something above and beyond simply enrolling your child in Sunday school classes."

"The fact that Obama had attended mengaji classes is well known in Indonesia and has left many there wondering just when Obama is going to come out of the closet."

Classmate Rony Amiris, now the manager of Bank Mandiri, Jakarta, describes young Barry as enjoying playing football and marbles and of being a very devout Muslim. Amir said:

> "Barry was previously quite religious in Islam. We...often asked him to the prayer room close to the house. If he was wearing a sarong, he looked funny,"...His birth father, Barack Hussein Obama was a Muslim economist from Kenya. Before marrying Ann Dunham, Hussein Obama was married to a woman from Kenya who had seven children. All the relatives of Barry's father were very devout Muslims"

Emirsyah Satar, CEO of Garuda Indonesia, was quoted as saying,

> "He (Obama) was often in the prayer room wearing a 'sarong', at that time."..."He was quite religious in Islam but only after marrying Michelle, he changed his religion."

So Obama, according to his classmates and friends was a Muslim until the confluence of love and ambition caused him to adopt the cloak of Christianity: to marry Michelle and to run for President of the United States.[9]

The majority of his family members were also Muslim. The Israel Insider also points out that:

Obama Senior also had three sons by another woman who are all Muslim. Although Obama claims Senior was an atheist, Senior was buried as a Muslim.

In an interview with the New York Times, published on April 30th, Maya Soetoro-Ng, Obama's younger half sister, told the Times,

"My whole family was Muslim, and most of the people I knew were Muslim."[10]

From his book, Dreams of My Father, Obama advises:

"...his brother Roy opted for Islam over Christianity, as Obama recounted when describing his 1992 wedding."

"The person who made me proudest of all," Obama wrote, "was Roy. Actually, now we call him Abongo, his Luo name, for two years ago he decided to reassert his African heritage. He converted to Islam, and has sworn off pork and tobacco and alcohol."[11]

WHAT'S IN A NAME

According to an article from the *American Thinker*:

Many people seem to think the names "Barack" and "Obama" are African names. They are not.

Baraq [Barack] was the name of the winged horse-like creature that took Mohammed to Paradise in the Night Journey.

Now here is the last little twist to Obama's name.

He called himself Barry, an Irish name, for many years in America. He changed what he wanted to be called after he went to Pakistan for a three-week stay.

He left America as Barry and returned as Barack.[12]

IN HIS OWN WORDS

A blogger recently opined:

Barack Hussein Obama said the Muslim call to prayer is "one of the prettiest sounds on Earth."

"In an interview with Nicholas Kristof, published in The New York Times, Obama recited the Muslim call to prayer, the Adhan, "with a first-class [Arabic] accent.""

The opening lines of the Adhan (Azaan) is the Shahada:

> **"Allah is Supreme! Allah is Supreme!**
> **Allah is Supreme! Allah is Supreme!**
> **I witness that there is no god but Allah**
> **I witness that there is no god but Allah**
> **I witness that Muhammad is his prophet... "**

According to Islamic scholars, reciting the Shahada, the Muslim declaration of faith, makes one a Muslim. This simple yet profound statement expresses a Muslim's complete acceptance of, and total commitment to, the message of Islam.

Obama knows this from his Quranic studies -- and he knows the New York Times will publish this fact and it will be seen throughout the Islamic world.

Regardless of Obama's religion, what message is he sending the world's 1.2 billion Muslims?[13]

The Chicago Sun-Times reported:

A verbal slip by Barack Obama, in which he made a reference to "my Muslim faith," unleashed a barrage of Internet attacks Sunday.

The Democratic presidential candidate appeared on ABC's "This Week" with George Stephanopoulos, which aired Sunday morning.

Obama was -- ironically -- addressing the false rumors that he is Muslim. He suggested that Republican rival John McCain was behind them...

Obama was reminded that McCain denied spreading the rumors.

"You're absolutely right that John McCain has not talked about my Muslim faith," [14]

PART OF HIS CAMPAIGN

In portions of an article by Debbie Schlussel, conservative political commentator, the reader is given an idea of what an Obama White House might look like:

> ...a former Obama insider says that Obama's sudden aversion to NOI and Farrakhan is belied by the fact that Obama employed and continues to employ several Farrakhan acolytes in high positions on his Illinois and U.S. Senate campaign and office staffs.
>
> The insider says he frequently objected to Mr. Obama's placement of Cynthia K. Miller, a member of the Nation of Islam, as the Treasurer of his U.S. Senate campaign. When I contacted Miller, now a Chicago real estate agent, to verify whether she was a member of the Nation of Islam and whether she shared Louis Farrakhan's bigoted views about Jews, she responded, "None of your business! Where are you going with this?" She said her resignation as Obama's treasurer had nothing to do with her Nation of Islam ties. Then, she hung up.
>
> The Obama insider says he also objected to Obama's involvement with Jennifer Mason, whom he says is also a member of the Nation of Islam. Mason is Obama's Director of Constituent Services in his U.S. Senate office and is also in charge of selecting Obama's Senate interns.
>
> But it's not just that he employed these individuals in positions of power in his office, it's that when the former associate raised objections, he says Mr. Obama's position was that he saw nothing wrong with the Nation of Islam and didn't think it was a problem. If true--and the fact that Ms. Mason still holds her prominent Obama Senate staff position bears that out--Obama's condemnation of Farrakhan, this month, is phony.
>
> But the insider says there is more to it than that. Obama's Illinois

State Senate district consisted of prime Nation of Islam territory, including Hyde Park, home to Farrakhan's mansion. It is not possible, Illinois politicos say, to win that district without the blessing of the NOI leader. NOI members, including consultant Shakir Muhammad, held important roles in the Obama state senate campaign.

How many Nation of Islam members will work in an Obama White House?

Barack Obama can denounce Louis Farrakhan ad infinitum. But with supporters like Ms. Saltzman, high-level staffers who are Nation of Islam members, and constantly morphing views on Israel merely for donor appeal, a Barack Obama White House bodes poorly both for Israel and--far more important--for America.[15]

There have been additional campaign staffers who have made news:

- Barack Obama's Muslim Outreach Coordinator, Mazen Asbahi, resigned under pressure in August after it was revealed that he was "a frequent speaker before several groups in the U.S. that scholars have associated with the Muslim Brotherhood."

The Muslim Brotherhood, of course, is engaged **"in America [in] a kind of grand Jihad in eliminating and destroying the Western civilization from within and 'sabotaging' its miserable house by their hands and the hands of the believers so that it is eliminated and Allah's religion is made victorious over all other religions."**

Asbahi has not stopped working on behalf of Obama, though. He appeared at the luncheon to say that despite his official exit he was still "110%" behind Obama and that he was participating in campaign conference calls on Muslim outreach. Stepping down was a "strategic decision," he told the audience.[16]

• According to Dr. Jay and Nathan Lerman of Campus Watch:

> Perhaps most worrisome is Obama's selection for chief
> military advisor and national campaign co-chairman
> General Merrill "Tony" McPeak. In 1976, McPeak
> wrote in an article in Foreign Policy saying that the main
> impediment to peace in the Mideast was Israel's refusal
> to return to its 1967 borders. In a 2003 interview in
> The Oregonian, McPeak accused Jewish and evangelical
> voters of placing their interests in Israel over those of
> the United States. When asked about the single most
> important factor holding back Middle East peace, McPeak
> responded, "New York City. Miami. We have a large
> vote here in favor of Israel. No politician wants to run
> against it." McPeak is a leading candidate for Secretary of
> Defense in an Obama administration and has emerged
> as one of Obama's closest advisors in the campaign.[17]

Barack Obama told a French magazine that he would
organize a summit of the Muslim world if he is elected.
AFP reports:

> Muslim and Western leaders would be invited to the summit
> for **"a discussion about how we can prevent the widening
> misunderstandings and gaps between the Muslim world and
> the West,"** Obama said in the interview to Paris Match.

> **"I will ask them to join us in battling terrorism but we should
> also be willing to listen in terms of some of their concerns,"**
> **he said in the interview to be released Thursday.**

Listen to the concerns the Muslim world has? I wonder what those
concerns might be? How about letting the Muslim world

know about our concerns? Terrorism, denial of human rights, teaching of hatred, the death penalty (which Obama opposes), the impoverishing of the world because of sky high extortionate oil prices which has made a few rich and many desperately poor?[18]

WHAT DO MUSLIMS SAY ABOUT HIM?

"Menashe Amir, the Iranian-born head of Radio Israel's Persian language service, has said: One of the Iranian religious leaders said if Obama will enter the White House, then Islam will conquer the heart of the American nation. The Iranian leadership likes Obama "mainly because he is a Muslim," according to Amir. His first name, Barack, comes from "al-baraq," which is the name of the horse that Muslims believe Muhammad rode on his way to paradise."[19]

His middle name Hussein is also a Muslim name, and he was "born in a Muslim family," said Amir.[20]

What his name means to those abroad....
"The symbolism of a major American presidential candidate with the middle name of Hussein, who went to elementary school in Indonesia," reports Tamara Cofman Wittes of the Brookings Institution from a U.S.-Muslim conference in Qatar, "that certainly speaks to Muslims abroad." Thomas L. Friedman of the New York Times found that Egyptians "don't really understand Obama's family tree, but what they do know is that if America — despite being attacked by Muslim militants on 9/11 — were to elect as its president some guy with the middle name 'Hussein,' it would mark a sea change in America-Muslim world relations."[21]

Malik Zulu Shabazz, New Black Panther Party National Chairman referred to Obama:

"...as a man with a "Muslim background, a man of color."[22]

In a speech that can be seen on AOL Video, Libyan Leader Mu'ammar Al-Qadhafi says:

There are elections in America now, Along came a black citizen of
Kenyan-African origins, a Muslim, Who had studied in an Islamic
school in Indonesia, His name is Obama,
All the people in the Arab and Islamic world
and in Africa should applaud this man,
They welcomed him and prayed for
him and his success and they
may have even been involved in
legitimate contribution campaigns
To enable him to win the American presidency
But we were taken by surprise
When our African-Kenyan brother,
who is an American national
Made statements that shocked
all his supporters in the Arab world,
in Africa and the Islamic world
We hope that this is merely an
elections "clearance sale," as
they say in Egypt
In other words, merely an election lie
As you know this is the farce of elections
A person lies and lies to people,
just so that they will vote for him
And afterwards, when they say to him,
"You promised this and that,"
He says: "This was propaganda, and
you thought I as being serious"
"I was fooling you to get your votes"
Allah willing, it will turn out that
this was merely election propoganda.[23]

The Jihad Candidate
by Rich Carroll

Conspiracy theories make for interesting novels when the storyline is not so absurd that it can grasp our attention. 'The Manchurian Candidate' and 'Seven Days in May' are examples of plausible chains of events that captures the reader's imagination at best-seller level. 'What if' has always been the solid grist of fiction.

Get yourself something cool to drink, find a relaxing position, but before you continue, visualize the television photos of two jet airliners smashing into the Twin Towers in lower Manhattan and remind yourself this cowardly act of Muslim terror was planned for eight years.

How long did it take Islam and their oil money to find a candidate for President of the United States? As long as it took them to place a Senator from Illinois and Minnesota? The same amount of time to create a large Muslim enclave in Detroit? The time it took them to build over 2,000 mosques in America? The same amount of time required to place radical wahabbist clerics in our military and prisons as 'chaplains'?

Find a candidate who can get away with lying about their father being a 'freedom fighter' when he was actually part of the most corrupt and violent government in Kenya's history. Find a candidate with close ties to The Nation of Islam and the violent Muslim overthrow in Africa, a candidate who is educated among white infidel Americans but hides his bitterness and anger behind a superficial toothy smile. Find a candidate who changes his American name of Barry to the Muslim name of Barack Hussein Obama, and dares anyone to question his true ties under the banner of 'racism'. Nurture this candidate in an atmosphere of anti-white American teaching and surround him with Islamic teachers. Provide him with a bitter, racist, anti-white, anti-American wife, and supply him with Muslim middle east connections and Islamic monies. Allow him to be clever enough to get away with his anti-white rhetoric and proclaim he will give $834 billion taxpayer dollars to the Muslim controlled United Nations for use in Africa.

Install your candidate in an atmosphere of deception, because questioning him on any issue involving Africa or Islam would be seen as 'bigoted racism'; two words too powerful to allow the citizenry to be informed of facts. Allow your candidate to employ several black racist Nation of Islam Louis Farrakhan followers as members of his Illinois Senatorial and campaign staffs.

Where is the bloodhound American 'free press' who doggedly overturned every stone in the Watergate case? Where are our nation's reporters that have placed every Presidential candidate under the microscope of detailed scrutiny; the same press who pursue Bush's 'Skull and Bones' club or ran other candidates off with persistent detective and research work? Why haven't 'newsmen' pursued the 65 blatant lies told by this candidate during the Presidential primaries? Where are the stories about this candidate's cousin and the Muslim butchery in Africa? Since when did our national press corps become weak, timid, and silent? Why haven't they regaled us with the long list of socialists and communists who have surrounded this 'out of nowhere' Democrat candidate or the fact that his church re-printed the Hamas Manifesto in their bulletin, and that his 'close pastor friend and mentor' met with Middle East terrorist Muammar Qaddafi, (Guide of the First of September Great Revolution of the Socialist People's Libyan Arab Jamahiriya)? Why isn't the American press telling us this candidate is supported by every Muslim organization in the world?

As an ultimate slap in the face, be blatant in the fact your candidate has ZERO interest in traditional American values and has the most liberal voting record in U.S. Senate history. Why has the American mainstream media clammed up on any negative reporting on Barack Hussein Obama? Why will they print Hillary Rodham Clinton's name but never write his middle name? Is it not his name? Why, suddenly, is ANY information about this candidate not coming from mainstream media, but from the blogosphere by citizens seeking facts and the truth? Why isn't our media connecting the dots with Islam? Why do they focus on 'those bad American soldiers' while Islam slaughters non-Muslims daily in 44 countries around the globe? Why does our media refer to Darfur as 'ethnic cleansing' instead of what it really is: Muslims killing non-Muslims! There is enough strange, anti-American activity surrounding Barack Hussein Obama to pique the curiosity of any reporter. WHERE IS OUR INVESTIGATIVE MEDIA!?

A formal plan for targeting America was devised three years after the Iranian revolution in 1982. The plan was summarized in a 1991 memorandum by Mohammed Akram, an operative of the global Muslim Brotherhood. 'The process of settlement' of Muslims in America, Akram explained, 'is a civilization jihad process.' This means that members of the Brotherhood must understand that their work in 'America is a kind of grand jihad in eliminating and destroying the Western civilization from within and sabotaging its miserable house by their hands and the hands of the believers so that it is eliminated and Allah's religion is made victorious over all other religions.'

There is terrorism we can see, smell and fear, but there is a new kind of terror invading The United States in the form of Sharia law and finance. Condoning it is civilization suicide. Middle East Muslims are coming to America in record numbers and building hate infidel mosques, buying our corporations, suing us for our traditions, but they and the whole subject of Islam is white noise leaving uninformed Americans about who and what is really peaceful. Where is our investigative press? Any criticism of Islam or their intentions, even though Islamic leaders state their intentions daily around the globe, brings forth a volley of 'racist' from the left-wing Democrat crowd.

Lies and deception behind a master plan - the ingredients for 'The Manchurian Candidate' or the placement of an anti-American President in our nation's White House? Is it mere coincidence that an anti-capitalist run for President at the same time Islamic Sharia finance and law is trying to make advancing strides into the United States? Is it mere coincidence this same candidate wants to disarm our nuclear capability at a time when terrorist Muslim nations are expanding their nuclear weapons capability? Is it mere coincidence this candidate wants to reduce our military at a time of global jihad from Muslim nations?

Change for America? What change? To become another 'nation of Islam'?

"MAKE WAR ON THEM UNTIL IDOLATRY IS NO MORE AND ALLAH'S RELIGION REIGNS SUPREME."   KORAN 8:37

"...KILL THE DISBELIEVERS WHEREVER WE FIND THEM"
KORAN 2:191

"FIGHT AND SLAY THE PAGANS, SEIZE THEM, BELEAGUER THEM, AND LIE IN WAIT FOR THEM IN EVERY STRATAGEM"
KORAN 9:5

"MURDER THEM AND TREAT THEM HARSHLY" KORAN 9:123

"STRIKE OFF THE HEADS OF THE DISBELIEVERS"; AND AFTER MAKING A "WIDE SLAUGHTER AMONG THEM, CAREFULLY TIE UP THE REMAINING CAPTIVES"
KORAN 47:4

IT IS ACCEPTABLE TO BREAK TREATIES AND OBLIGATIONS WITH PAGANS AND MAKE WAR ON THEM WHENEVER STRONG ENOUGH TO DO SO   KORAN 9:3

I marvel that ye are so soon removed from him that called you into the grace of Christ unto another gospel:

Which is not another; but there be some that trouble you, and would pervert the gospel of Christ.

But though we, or an angel from heaven, preach any other gospel unto you than that which we have preached unto you, let him be accursed.

As we said before, so say I now again, if any man preach any other gospel unto you than that ye have received, let him be accursed.

For do I now persuade men, or God? or do I seek to please men? for if I yet pleased men, I should not be the servant of Christ.

But I certify you, brethren, that the gospel which was preached of me is not after man.

For I neither received it of man, neither was I taught it, but by the revelation of Jesus Christ.

Galatians 1:6-12

"Our task of creating a socialist America can only succeed when those who would resist us have been totally disarmed."

Sara Brady, Chairman of Handgun Control, (1994)[1]

LET SOCIALISM REIGN

"The American people will never knowingly adopt socialism," said Norman Thomas, a U.S. Socialist Party presidential candidate in the 1940s. "But under the name of 'liberalism,' they will adopt every fragment of the socialist program, until one day, America will be a socialist nation, without knowing how it happened."

Terry Sater, of Investor's Business Dailys says, "If it is to be, let's do it with our eyes open, aware of every ponderous step."[2]

An article by Diane Alden of TYSK News, gives background on the man and the movement that were instrumental in the molding of the "community organizer" aka "agitator" we call Barack Obama:

Saul Alinsky died in 1972. He was a Marxist grassroots organizer who spent much of his life organizing rent strikes and protesting conditions of the poor in Chicago in the 1930s.

However, unlike Christian socialist and activist for the poor, Dorothy Day, Alinsky's real claim to fame was as strategist for anti-establishment '60s radicals and revolutionaries.

Alinsky had a true genius for formulating tactical battle plans for the radical left. He wrote two books outlining his organizational principles and strategies: "Reveille for Radicals" (1946) and "Rules for Radicals" (1971).

"Rules for Radicals" begins with an unusual tribute:

"From all our legends, mythology, and history (and who is to know where mythology leaves off and history begins – or which is which), the first radical known to man who rebelled against the establishment and did it so effectively that he at least won his own kingdom – *Lucifer*."

The devil challenged authority and got his own kingdom, and that goes to the heart of what left is really about. That of course is to get power any way you can, including lying, cheating and stealing. The ultimate rule is that the ends justify the means.

Alinsky asserted that he was more concerned with the acquisition of power than anything else: "My aim here is to suggest how to organize for power: how to get it and how to use it." This is not to be done with assistance to the poor, nor even by organizing the poor to demand assistance: "Even if all the low-income parts of our population were organized ... it would not be powerful enough to get significant, basic, needed changes."

Alinsky advises his followers that the poor have no power and that the real target is the middle class: "Organization for action will now and in the decade ahead center upon America's white middle class. That is where the power is...Our rebels have contemptuously rejected the values and the way of life of the middle class. They have stigmatized it as materialistic, decadent, bourgeois, degenerate, imperialistic, war-mongering, brutalized and corrupt. They are right; but we must begin from where we are if we are to build power for change, and the power and the people are in the middle class majority."

But that didn't stop Alinsky and his followers from using the middle class for their own purposes. They counted on the guilt and shame of the white middle class to get what they wanted. In order to take over institutions and get power, the middle class had to be convinced that they were somehow lucky winners in "life's lottery."

Alinsky's radicals found a perfect vehicle for their destruction of the American system and more particularly for taking and maintaining power. That instrument was the Democratic Party.

Alinsky's influence on the modern Democratic Party indicates that the ends do indeed justify the means. As Alinsky states in "Rules for Radicals" it was foolish to believe that means are just as important as the ends. He states that **"to believe in the immaculate conception of ends and principles ... the practical revolutionary will understand ... [that] in action, one does not always enjoy the luxury of a decision that is consistent both with one's individual conscience and the good of mankind."**[3]

From an article on Investor's Business Daily:

Most Americans revile socialism, yet Barack Obama's poll numbers remain competitive. One explanation: He's a longtime disciple of a man whose mission was to teach radicals to disguise their ideology.

The presumptive Democratic presidential nominee's choice of the word "change" as his campaign's central slogan is not the product of focus-group studies, or the brainstorming sessions of his political consultants.

One of Obama's main inspirations was a man dedicated to revolutionary change that he was convinced "must be preceded by a passive, affirmative, nonchallenging attitude toward change among the mass of our people. They must feel so frustrated, so defeated, so lost, so futureless in the prevailing system that they are willing to let go of the past and change the future."

Senator Obama was trained by Chicago's Industrial Areas Foundation, founded in 1940 by the radical organizer Saul Alinsky. In the 1980s, Obama spent years as director of the Developing Communities Project, which operated using Alinsky's strategies, and was involved with two other Alinsky-oriented entities, Acorn and Project Vote.

On the Obama campaign Web site can be found a photo of him teaching in a University of Chicago classroom with "Power Analysis" and "Relationships Built on Self Interest" written on the blackboard — key terms utilized in the Alinsky method.

The far-left Alinsky had no time for liberalism or liberals, declaring that **"a liberal is (someone) who puts his foot down firmly on thin air."** He wanted nothing less than transformational radicalism. **"America was begun by its radicals,"** he wrote. **"America was built by its radicals. The hope and future of America lies with its radicals."** And so, **"This is the job for today's radical — to fan the embers of hopelessness into a flame to fight. To say. . . let us change it together!"**

Capitalism always was considered the enemy. **"America's corporations are a spiritual slum,"** he wrote, **"and their**

arrogance is the major threat to our future as a free society." Is it surprising that an Alinsky disciple such as Obama can promise so blithely to increase taxes on CEOs?

Obama calls his years as an Alinskyesque community organizer in Chicago **"the best education I ever had, and where I learned the true meaning of my Christian faith."** But as radicalism expert Richard Lawrence Poe has noted, "Camouflage is key to Alinsky-style organizing. In organizing coalitions of black churches in Chicago, Obama caught flak for not attending church himself. He became an instant churchgoer."

Indeed, Alinsky believed in sacrificing ethics and morals for the great cause. **"Ethical standards must be elastic to stretch with the times,"** Alinsky wrote in his last book, "Rules for Radicals," adding that **"all values are relative in a world of political relativity."**

Alinsky's writings even explain what often seems like Obama's oversized ego. In New Hampshire in January, for example, the Senator told an audience that **"a beam of light will come down upon you, you will experience an epiphany . . . and you will suddenly realize that you must go to the polls and vote for Obama."**

It was a bizarre spectacle, but consider that Alinsky believed that **"anyone who is working against the haves is always facing odds, and in many cases heavy odds. If he or she does not have that complete self-confidence (or call it ego) that he can win, then the battle is lost before it is even begun."**

According to Alinsky, **"Ego must be so all-pervading that the personality of the organizer is contagious, that it converts the people from despair to defiance, creating a mass ego."**

Barack Obama's "Change We Can Believe In" is simply socialism — imposed by stratagem because Americans have never believed in Marxist economics. Saul Alinsky understood this, and his ghost is alive and well — and threatening to haunt the White House.[4]

Besides the in-depth training Obama received as a community organizer..."In his books, Obama admits attending "socialist conferences" and coming into contact with Marxist literature."[5]

According to Melanie Scarborough of the DC Examiner:

When Barack Obama accepts the Democratic nomination later this week, he will portray himself as a shining example of the Great American Dream. With his impressive rhetorical skill, he will speak of embracing America's common ideals and securing them for future generations and continuing on that glorious path established by our founding fathers, yada, yada. And he won't mean a word of it.

To the contrary, Obama largely rejects the principles of individual liberty on which this nation was founded. His thinking is more closely aligned with Karl Marx's than John Locke's.

"... Obama openly scorns the idea that individual families should take care of themselves... "In Washington, they call this the Ownership Society," he continues. "And it is especially tempting because each of us believes we will always be the winner in life's lottery, that we're the one who will be the next Donald Trump, or at least we won't be the chump who Donald Trump says: "You're fired!"

Got that? Only chumps dare to dream. (This from the candidate peddling hope.)[6]

Even Obama's wife is well educated in the "Alinsky" way:

> Michelle Obama has delivered some rousing statements at the Democratic National Convention...the statements appear to have been drawn from "Rules for Radicals," a book by dedicated socialist Saul Alinsky.
>
> "What to make of Michelle Obama's use of the terms, 'The world as it is' and 'The world as it should be?'"... Try Chapter 2 of Saul Alinksy's book, 'Rules for Radicals.'"
>
> "In last night's speech, Michelle Obama said...'Barack stood up that day,' talking about a visit to Chicago neighborhoods, 'and spoke words that have stayed with me ever since. He talked about 'The world as it is' and 'The world as it should be...'"[7]

According to the American Thinker:

> One of Obama's early mentors in the Alinsky method was Mike Kruglik, who had this to say to an Ryan Lizza of The New Republic, about Obama:

> "He was a natural, the undisputed master of agitation, who could engage a room full of recruiting targets in a rapid-fire Socratic dialogue, nudging them to admit that they were not living up to their own standards. As with the panhandler, he could be aggressive and confrontational. With probing, sometimes personal questions, he would pinpoint the source of pain in their lives, tearing down their egos just enough before dangling a carrot of hope that they could make things better."

> The agitator's job, according to Alinsky, is first to bring folks to the "realization" that they are indeed miserable, that their misery is the fault of unresponsive governments or greedy corporations, then help them to bond together to demand what they deserve, and to

make such an almighty stink that the dastardly governments and corporations will see imminent "self-interest" in granting whatever it is that will cause the harassment to cease.

In these methods, euphemistically labeled "community organizing," Obama had a four-year education, which he often says was the best education he ever got anywhere.[8]

A RINGING ENDORSEMENT

Barack Obama's training in Chicago by the great community organizers is showing its effectiveness. It is an amazingly powerful format, and the method of my late father always works to get the message out and get the supporters on board. When executed meticulously and thoughtfully, it is a powerful strategy for initiating change and making it really happen. Obama learned his lesson well.

I am proud to see that my father's model for organizing is being applied successfully beyond local community organizing to affect the Democratic campaign in 2008. It is a fine tribute to Saul Alinsky as we approach his 100th birthday.

L. DAVID ALINSKY[9]

"Most people who read "The Communist Manifesto" probably have no idea that it was written by a couple of young men who had never worked a day in their lives, and who nevertheless spoke boldly in the name of "the workers."
Thomas Sowell
Writer and Economist

"To take from one, because it is thought that his own industry and that of his fathers has acquired too much, in order to spare others, who, or whose fathers have not exercised equal industry and skill, is to violate arbitrarily the first principle of association, 'the guarantee to every one of a free exercise of his industry, and the fruits acquired by it.'"
Thomas Jefferson

"Socialism is a philosophy of failure, the creed of ignorance, and the gospel of envy, its inherent virtue is the equal sharing of misery."
Winston Churchill

"You cannot bring prosperity by discouraging thrift.
You cannot help small men by tearing down big men.
You cannot strengthen the weak by weakening the strong.
You cannot lift the wage earner by pulling down the wage payer.
You cannot help the poor man by destroying the rich.
You cannot keep out of trouble by spending more than your income.
You cannot further brotherhood of men by inciting class hatred.
You cannot establish security on borrowed money.
You cannot build character and courage by taking away man's initiative and independence.
You cannot help men permanently by doing for them what they could and should do for themselves."
Rev. William J. H. Boetcker

Therefore the LORD God sent him forth from the garden of Eden, to till the ground from whence he was taken.

Genesis 3:23

Say not, I will do so to him as he hath done to me: I will render to the man according to his work.

I went by the field of the slothful, and by the vineyard of the man void of understanding;

And, lo, it was all grown over with thorns, and nettles had covered the face thereof, and the stone wall thereof was broken down.

Then I saw, and considered it well: I looked upon it, and received instruction.

Yet a little sleep, a little slumber, a little folding of the hands to sleep:

So shall thy poverty come as one that travelleth; and thy want as an armed man.

Proverbs 24:29-34

"And, behold, I come quickly; and my reward is with me,
to give every man according as his work shall be."

Revelation 22:12

"I found a solace in nursing a pervasive sense of grievance and
animosity against my mother's race."[1]
Barack Obama

SO THIS IS UNITY?

"Obama wants to run from this radical past, but his first memoir —
written long before he had serious White House aspirations — is a
peek into his soul. "Dreams" has become more of a nightmare, and
he may just come to regret ever writing it."

Investor's Business Daily[2]

Wow, the discrepancies just keep piling up. As they say...the *hits* keep
on coming. In his attempt to gain the coveted prize of the White
House, suddenly "Barack the Agitator's" fondest desire is to usher in
a peaceful coexistence among the races. In a speech given on March
18, 2008, Barack Obama says:

"But I have asserted a firm conviction...that working together
we can move beyond some of our old racial wounds, and that
in fact we have no choice if we are to continue on the path of a
more perfect union."[3]

Yet, in his book, *Dreams of My Father*, he says:

"Nationalism provided that history, an unambiguous morality tale that was easily communicated and easily grasped. A steady attack on the white race, the constant recitation of black people's brutal experience in this country...Yes, the nationalist would say, whites are responsible for your sorry state, not any inherent flaws in you. In fact, whites are so heartless and devious that we can no longer expect anything from them....Rid them from your mind and find your true power liberated. Rise up, ye mighty race!...Rafiq was right when he insisted that, deep down, all blacks were potential nationalists."[4]

Most Americans are understandably caught up in the things that make their own lives run smoothly and believe that if you just treat others as you would like to be treated, you are doing your part in living at peace with other races and cultures.

Families have enough to worry about when they focus on their own backyard, what with...bills, kids, college, health, ailing parents, etc....But what they don't realize is that there is a movement, alive and well, that perpetuates the superiority of a people based on their common history and race. Black Liberation Theology.

The Action Institute gives us further insight into Black Liberation Theology:

"Black theology is a theology of black liberation...."Jesus was a poor black man" because he lived in oppression at the hands of "rich White people." The overall emphasis of Black liberation theology is the Black struggle for liberation from various forms of "White racism" and oppression."[5]

In the controversy spread "round the world," we all heard the Reverend Jeremiah Wright YouTube video and then the denouncement by Obama.

In an interview, author Webster Tarpley discusses this subject:

"He denounced him after sitting at his knee for 20 years, 20 years! Practically half of Obama's life he was sitting at Wright's knee, imbibing hatred and the philosophy of racist provocation and indeed, some would say indeed Satanism. In other words, a religion based on hatred cannot be identified with Christianity but is something else.

He first said he could not denounce him. He said:"I can no more disown him then I can disown my own mother or the black community."

That was until the temperature got too high. And once Wright had paraded his insanity [and his racist provocations] at the National Press Club, then, then and only then did Obama finally turn around and separated himself from him or attempted to, because he can't. You can't sit at the knee of somebody for 20 years and say: "I'm his disciple, he is my mentor, he is my guru, he is my boss," and then say:"Oh, sorry, it's now expedient for me to break contact."[6]

According to Obama's book, he was forewarned by the Reverend Jeremiah Wright himself at their first meeting of the church's reputation for being "radical." Reverend Wright said, "Some of my fellow clergy don't appreciate what we're about. They feel like we're too radical."[7]

At that first visit to Trinity United Church of Christ, Obama picked up a brochure from the reception area titled, a "Black Value System" that the congregation had adopted in 1979. Obama called these values "a heartfelt, sensible list."[8]

According to Let Us Reason Ministries, "James Cone is one of the leading voices of this theology, he wrote that the United States was a white racist nation and the white church was the Antichrist for having supported slavery and segregation."[9]

Information regarding the some of the tenants of this theology:

- "Defines liberation as the "emancipation of black people from white oppression by whatever means black people deem necessary" —selective buying, boycotting, marching, even rebellion."

- "Black theology refuses to accept a God who is not identified totally with the goals of the black community. If God is not for us and against white people, then he is a murderer, and we had better kill him. The task of black theology is to kill Gods who do not belong to the black community. Black theology will accept only the love of God which participates in the destruction of the white enemy."

- "The time has come for white America to be silent and listen to black people. . . . All white men are responsible for white oppression... Theologically, Malcolm X was not far wrong when he called the white man 'the devil.' The white structure of this American society, personified in every racist, must be at least part of what the New Testament meant by the demonic forces."[10]

In an interview, Cone, when he was asked which church most embodied his message, "I would point to that church (Trinity) first." Cone also said he thought that Wright's successor, the Rev. Otis Moss III, would continue the tradition.[11]

In the sermon that so inspired Obama, that he named his next book after it, *The Audacity of Hope*, Reverend Jeremiah Wright says, "In this world...where white folks' greed runs a world in need."[12]

There is no doubt that Barack Obama knew exactly where his

pastor stood. He made that very clear in each and every service, and Obama embraced both the man and the church.

After reading the past literary works of Obama, his truth speaks louder than a candidates empty rhetoric in the heat of the battle. If you go back to his youth, you find:

> Obama started to spend quite a bit of time doing research and reading various authors works in an attempt to reconcile his confusion. His states that Malcolm X's autobiography "spoke to me; the blunt poetry of his words, his unadorned insistence on respect, promised a new and uncompromising order, martial in its discipline, forged through sheer force of will....**one line in the book stayed with me. He spoke of a wish he'd once had, the wish that the white blood that ran through him...might somehow be expunged.**"[13]

Barack Obama lets you know in his own words that he won't let it go.

> **"I had stumbled upon one of the well-kept secrets about black people: that most of us were tired of thinking about race all the time;...easier than spending all your time mad or trying to guess whatever it was that white folks were thinking about you....So why couldn't I let it go?"**[14]

After seeing a movie with his mother he realized their mutual perceptions of race would always be different:

> **"...the same thought occurred to me as I left the movie theater with my mother and sister: The emotions between races could never be pure; even love was tarnished by the desire to find in the other some element that was missing in ourselves. Whether we sought out our demons or salvation, the other race would always remain just that: menacing, alien, and apart."**[15]

Obama says:

> "I had begun to see a new map of the world"..."We were
> always playing on the white man's court"..."by the white man's
> rules.".."The only thing you could choose as your own was
> withdrawal into a smaller and smaller coil of rage, until being
> black meant only the knowledge of your own powerlessness,
> of your own defeat. And the final irony: Should you refuse this
> defeat and lash out at your captors, they would have a name for
> that, too, a name that could cage you just as good. Paranoid.
> Militant. Violent. Nigger."[16]

In another portion of the book he says:

> "...at night, lying in bed, I would let the slogans drift away, to
> be replaced with a series of images, romantic images, of a past
> I had never known. They were of the civil rights movement...
> Such images became of form of prayer for me, bolstering my
> spirits, channeling my emotions in a way that words never
> could."[17]

During Obama's time as a community organizer, he conducted interviews
with individuals in the local neighborhood to find out their concerns and
the issues important to them, one of the observances he made, **"in these
stories, wherever black and white met, the result was sure to be anger
and grief."**[18] In his book he says, **"Once I found an issue enough people
cared alone, I could take them into action. With enough actions, I
could start to build power."**[19]

Obama says that he made the decision to become a community organizer in
1983 and already was using his slogan for "change." He says, **"That's what
I'll do, I'll organize black folks. At the grass roots. For change."**[20]

Obama mentions a book he read called *Heart of Darkness*, in explaining his reasons for reading it, he says:

> "...because the book teaches me things....It's about the man who wrote it. The European. The American. A particular way of looking at the world....So I read the book to help me understand just what it is that makes white people so afraid. Their demons. The way ideas get twisted around. It helps me understand how people learn to hate."[21]

After a fight between Obama's grandmother and grandfather over an incident in which Obama's grandmother had been frightened by a panhandler who was black, Obama went over to talk to family friend, Frank Davis. Frank told Obama,

> "...your grandma's right to be scared....She understands that black people have a reason to hate. That's just how it is."[22]

During his college years, Barack Obama tells of going to hear Kwame Toure, formerly Stokely Carmichael, known for his association with the Black Panthers and is known for the phrase "Black Power."

As James Haskins recorded in his book, *Profiles in Black Power*, Carmichael explained to one crowd, "When you talk of 'Black Power,' you talk of building a movement that will smash everything Western civilization has created." Carmichael and his movement continued to be seen by many in America as a movement that could spark a "Race War." In his famous 1966 speech Black Power at a college campus in California, Stokely Carmichael said:

> "...white America cannot condemn herself for her criminal acts against black America. So black people

have done it–you stand condemned.

We must urge you to fight now to be the leaders of today, not tomorrow. This country is a nation of thieves. It stands on the brink of becoming a nation of murderers. We must stop it. We must stop it.

We are on the move for our liberation. We're tired of trying to prove things to white people. We are tired of trying to explain to white people that we're not going to hurt them. We are concerned with getting the things we want, the things we have to have to be able to function.

The question is, Will white people overcome their racism and allow for that to happen in this country? If not, we have no choice but to say very clearly, "Move on over, or we're going to move over you."[23]

An article in the Weekly Standard says:

"...the question of race plays so large a role in Obama's own thought and action that it is all but impossible to discuss his political trajectory without acknowledging the extent to which it engrosses him. Obama settled in Chicago with the declared intention of "organizing black folks." His first book is subtitled "A Story of Race and Inheritance," and his second book contains an important chapter on race. On his return to Chicago in 1991, Obama practiced civil rights law and for many years taught a seminar on racism and law at the University of Chicago. When he entered the Illinois senate, it was to represent the heavily (although not exclusively) minority 13th district on the South Side of Chicago. Indeed, race functions for Obama as a kind of master-category, pervading and organizing a wide array of issues that many Americans may not think of as racial at all."[24]

In an interview on John Batchelor's radio program, New Black Panther Party leader Malik Zulu Shabazz said:

> **"Sen. Obama, as president, fits in with Nation of Islam theology, or black liberation theology, that says black people ruled in the beginning and scriptures say "we will rule in the end," that Sen. Obama is a "sign" that Africa will rise next, that black people will rise to glory now, that Sen. Obama is the leading sign of that right now."[25]**

Glenn Beck conducted an interview with Malik Shabazz, the following are portions of the transcript:

BECK: A possible future president has spent the last 20 years in a church where radical black nationalism is being preached, and it seems like only half the country cares right now.

First, let me talk about the double standard here, in my opinion. Obama's Reverend Wright has said unforgivable things about white people in America. Remember, racism is a human flaw, not a white one. You wouldn't excuse a racist or anti-American comments from a friend or a co-worker or--dare I say it--Don Imus. Why should we be expected to accept it from a man who is advising a presidential candidate?

If John McCain's priest had said that poor blacks are the problem in America, the media, including me, would be calling for his head. He wouldn't have had time to make an important speech.

Obama has spent decades listening to a true believer in black liberation theology. This is an extremist belief system that wants to kill a god who isn't against white people, calls for God's destruction of the white enemy.

BECK: Barack Obama says that Reverend Wright is responsible for his foundation of faith. Well, if that doesn't fill you with rage, it should, at least fill you with a few questions. And if it doesn't fill you with rage, I don't know what will. No, wait, I do.

Tonight, America, here's what you need to know. Reverend Wright and radical black theology are one thing, but now we've got an endorsement by the New Black Panther Party. That's quite another thing.

And the other part, the New Black Panther Party, just as bad as the KKK. They are identified as an extremist hate group by the Southern Poverty Law Center.

In addition to the widely-held belief that they advocate violence, they demand slavery reparations, the release of all black prisoners, and a separate country for African-Americans.

SHABAZZ: How would you feel -- the reason why -- how would you feel, Glenn, if you had to understand that your ancestors had been in slavery and bondage for 300 years, that your ancestors had been denied the right to become policemen, firemen, attend schools and get mortgages, how would you feel if...

BECK: I'll tell you -- I would feel -- I'll tell you, I would feel -- I would feel so unbelievably proud that that country has made so much progress that the richest woman in America is Oprah Winfrey and possibly the next president is also an African-American. I'd feel pretty darn good that we've made an awful lot of progress.

Obama's message is to come together, yet your message, according to your Web site, is the trials of blacks only, by all black juries, end of all black cooperation with police departments, and a separate country for African-Americans. How is Obama your man?

SHABAZZ: Obama is my man, because I believe he can change America, and I pray to almighty God that America will listen to and follow Barack Obama, black or white or whoever you are.

BECK: So where is the -- where is the line? How come Don Imus gets fired for saying things in a comedy routine, but a guy like Obama`s Reverend Wright only gets away with, you know, saying what he`s said so far and it`s far worse. You know, he`s saying it to a man who could be president.[26]

Larry Johnson at No Quarter concludes:

This is the disaster of Barack. Instead of transcending race, he has embraced and lived in the heart of a radical theology that preaches racial division and black dominance.

Obama says he doesn't agree with Wright about everything. Fine. And maybe he doesn't agree with his wife when she (twice) said that she'd never been proud of her country until its people began to support her husband. But then, what did he mean when he said on March 4 that making a little girl proud to say she is an American is the "change we are calling for"? One suspects that beneath the soothing talk, there is bitterness in the man that we'd best learn more about before voting.[27]

A scoundrel and villain,
who goes about with a corrupt mouth,

who winks with his eye,
signals with his feet
and motions with his fingers,

who plots evil with deceit in his heart—
he always stirs up dissension.

Proverbs 6:12-14

Thou shalt not avenge, nor bear any grudge against the children of thy people, but thou shalt love thy neighbour as thyself: I am the LORD.

Leviticus 19:18

Hatred stirreth up strifes: but love covereth all sins.

Proverbs 10:12

He that walketh with wise men shall be wise: but a
companion of fools shall be destroyed.
Proverbs 13:20

THOSE PESKY CONNECTIONS

They say a man is known by the company he keeps. Barack Obama would
have you believe that he should be known by words he says.

It has become standard procedure that when one of Obama's old associates
or his current affiliations pop up, with the potential to embarrass him for
their radical words and deeds, the campaign uses a systematic approach and
expects their answer to be the end of the issue.

It's not one or two questionable affiliations, but a full cast of characters that
are too colorful to be made into a Hollywood movie. Too unbelievable.

If it were anyone else, the campaign would've already been derailed. But as
we have already seen, Barack Obama has an uncanny ability to deflect and
move on.

The real problem with these connections is that with most of them, Obama
won't admit the depth of their association or the extent of the role that they
played in developing his ideals and philosophies.

FRANK DAVIS

In his biography of Barack Obama, David Mendell writes about Obama's life as a "secret smoker" and how he "went to great lengths to conceal the habit." But what about Obama's secret political life? It turns out that Obama's childhood mentor, Frank Marshall Davis, was a communist.

In Obama's own book, Dreams From My Father... He writes about **"a poet named Frank,"** who visited them in Hawaii, read poetry, and was full of **"hard-earned knowledge"** and advice.[1]

The UK Telegraph Newspaper reports:

Although identified only as Frank in Mr. Obama's memoir *Dreams from My Father*, it has now been established that he was Frank Marshall Davis, a radical activist and journalist who had been suspected of being a member of the Communist Party in the 1950's.

Mr. Davis moved to Honolulu from Chicago in 1948 with his second wife Helen Canfield, a white socialite, at the suggestion of his friend, the actor Paul Robeson, who advised them that there would be more tolerance of a mixed race couple in Hawaii than on the American mainland.

A bohemian libertine who drank heavily and loved jazz, he became friends with Stanley Dunham, Mr. Obama's maternal grandfather in the 1960's. Mr. Davis died in 1987 at the age of 81, five years before Mr. Dunham.

"He knew Stan real well," said Dawna Weatherly-Williams, a close friend of Mr Davis "They'd play Scrabble and drink and crack jokes and argue. Frank always won and he was always very braggadocio about it too. It was all jocular. They didn't get polluted drunk. And Frank never really did drugs, though he and Stan would smoke pot together."

While his mother was in Indonesia during part of his teenage years,

Mr. Obama lived with his white grandparents. Mrs. Weatherly-Williams said that the poet was first introduced to the future Democratic presidential candidate in 1970 at the age of 10.

"Stan had been promising to bring Barry by because we all had that in common - Frank's kids were half-white, Stan's grandson was half-black and my son was half-black. We all had that in common and we all really enjoyed it. We got a real kick out of reality." Maya Soetoro-Ng, Obama's half-sister, told the Associated Press recently that her grandfather had seen Mr. Davis was "a point of connection, a bridge if you will, to the larger African-American experience for my brother."

In his memoir, Mr Obama recounts how he visited Mr Davis on several occasions, apparently at junctures when he was grappling with racial issues, to seek his counsel. At one point in 1979, Mr. Davis described university as "an advanced degree in compromise" that was designed to keep blacks in their place.

Mr. Obama quoted him as saying: "Leaving your race at the door. Leaving your people behind. Understand something, boy. You're not going to college to get educated. You're going there to get trained."

He added that "they'll tank on your chain and let you know that you may be a well-trained, well-paid nigger, but you're a nigger just the same."

It has also been established that Mr. Davis, who divorced in 1970, was the author of a hard-core pornographic autobiography published in San Diego in 1968 by Greenleaf Classics under the pseudonym Bob Greene.

He stated that "under certain circumstances I am bisexual" and that he was " a voyeur and an exhibitionist" who was "occasionally mildly interested in sado-masochism."

The book, which closely tracks Mr. Davis's life in Chicago and Hawaii and the fact that his first wife was black and his second white, describes in lurid detail a series of shockingly sordid sexual encounters, often involving group sex.

One chapter concerns the seduction by Mr. Davis and his first wife of a 13-year-old girl called Anne.[2]

NewsWithViews.com says:

One Davis poem, *"Christ is a Dixie Nigger,"* dismisses Christ as "another New White Hope" and declares:

> "Remember this, you wise guys
> Your tales about Jesus of Nazareth are no-go with me
> I've got a dozen Christs in Dixie all bloody and black..."

The revelations about Davis' poetry will add to the controversy over what kind of role Davis played in shaping Obama's political views. Davis (1905-1987) seems to have had the same kind of anti-American outlook that animated Obama's longtime pastor, Jeremiah Wright. In fact, Davis was pro-Soviet, not just anti-American.

One Davis poem, "Onward Christian Soldiers," mocks the Christian hymn by the same name. It talks of Africans being killed with a "Christian gun" instead of a spear by the missionaries following "the religion of Sweet Jesus." Another Davis poem refers to Christians "who buy righteousness like groceries."

Davis' writings have become an issue because he became a father-figure to Obama...during their time in Hawaii.[3]

EDWARD W. SAID

Edward Said was a Palestinian American literary theorist, cultural critic, political activist, and an outspoken advocate of Palestinian rights. He was University Professor of English and

Comparative Literature at Columbia University.[4]

He is seen here with Barack and Michelle Obama in 1998. Obama was an honored guest at a gala dinner in Burbank, IL. Hosting the event was an anti-Israeli organization, the Arab American Action Network.

PHOTO COURTESY DEBBIESCHLUSSEL.COM

Said has been called "the most prominent spokesperson for the Palestinian cause in the United States."[5]

Barack Obama in 1998 attended a speech by Edward Said...According to a news account of the speech, Said called that day for a nonviolent campaign "against settlements, against Israeli apartheid."[6]

In an interview with The Progressive in 2001, Said commented on September 11th and his views on terrorism.

Regarding September 11th and how it should be handled.

SAID: We need a much more...defined...campaign, as well as one that surveys...the root causes of terrorism...They come out of…U.S. involvement in the affairs of the Islamic world…the U.S. has played a very distinctive role…

…In all of this rather heady mixture of violence… it's not hard for demagogues, especially people who claim to speak in the name of religion, in this case Islam, to raise a crusade against the United States and say that we must somehow bring America down…

…Ironically, many of these people, including Osama bin Laden and the mujahedeen, were, in fact, nourished by the United States in the early eighties in its efforts to drive the Soviets out of Afghanistan…

…The definition of terrorism has to be more precise, so that we are able to discriminate between, for example, what it is that the Palestinians are doing to fight the Israeli military occupation and terrorism of the sort that resulted in the World Trade Center bombing….

BARSAMIAN: What's the distinction you're drawing?

SAID: Take a young man from Gaza living in the most horrendous conditions--most of it imposed by Israel--who straps dynamite around himself and then throws himself into a crowd of Israelis. I've never condoned or agreed with it, but at least it is understandable.

He wants to do something, to strike back. That can be understood as the act of a truly desperate person trying to free himself from unjustly imposed conditions.[7]

TONY REZKO

Antoin "Tony" Rezko, was born in 1955 in Aleppo, Syria to a prominent Catholic family. Rezko is an American political fundraiser, restaurateur, and real estate developer in Chicago, Illinois, convicted on several counts of fraud and bribery in 2008. Rezko has been involved in fundraising for local Illinois Democratic and Republican politicians since the 1980's.[8]

An article in Investor's Business Daily highlights the relationship between Obama and Rezko:

> Barack Obama mocks John McCain for not knowing the number of his residences. Does that include the Hanoi Hilton? At least McCain's real estate broker is not a felon he did favors for.

> Rezko, who Hillary Clinton once labeled a "slumlord," was among Obama's earliest supporters.

> In 1995, when Obama ran for a seat in the Illinois Senate, Rezko, through two of his companies, gave Obama $2,000.

> Obama won election in 1996 in a district that coincidentally contained 11 of Rezko's 30 low-income housing projects. In 2003, when Obama said he'd run for the U.S. Senate, Rezko held a lavish fundraiser at his Wilmette, Ill. mansion.

> In 2005, when Rezko was under federal investigation of influence-peddling in Illinois Gov. Rod Blagojevich's administration, Obama bought a house in Chicago's upscale Hyde Park neighborhood for $1.65 million, $300,000 below the asking price, while Rezko's wife paid full price, $625,000, for an adjacent vacant lot.

> Six months later, Obama overpaid Rezko's wife $104,500 for a 10-foot-wide strip of her land, allegedly so he could have a bigger yard. Obama has admitted that at the time, he knew Rezko "was going to have some significant legal problems" with his land deals. He calls their deal a "boneheaded move."

After Rezko's 2008 conviction on 16 counts of wire fraud, mail fraud, money laundering and soliciting bribes, Obama said, "This isn't the Tony Rezko I knew." Uh-huh. Just as he said the Rev. Jeremiah Wright, after his anti-American rants became public, was "not the person I met 20 years ago."[9]

ALI ABUNIMAH

Ali Abunimah is a Palestinian American who serves as the Board of Directors Member for the Chicago-based Arab American Action Network. He is also a co-founder of the Electronic Intifada website, which was created by activists affiliated with the International Solidarity Movement.

In Abunimah's calculus, Palestinian violence and terrorism is caused entirely by Israel's "land confiscation," its "ongoing orgy of violence," and its "routine human-rights abuses" that have "made life under a seemingly endless occupation so intolerable."[10]

Ali Abunimah claims that "Mr. Obama would unequivocally be the most pro-Palestinian president in history." And he has his own personal history with Obama upon which to base that judgment. Having first met Obama ten years ago, he has observed that Obama has been "close to some prominent Arab-Americans and has received their best advice." And, according to Ali Abunimah, Obama had been strongly influenced by their views, consistently and forthrightly criticizing U.S. policy and calling for an even-handed approach to the Palestinian-Israeli conflict.

And once Obama realized that these anti-Israel positions would hurt his political future, he also showed a willingness to play the crudest of disingenuous old-style politics, openly claiming that his words did not represent his true beliefs. According to Ali Abunimah, Obama said, "Hey, I'm sorry I haven't said more about Palestine right now, but we are in a tough primary race. I'm hoping when things calm down I can be more up-front." [11]

Dr. Khalid al-Mansour

Newsmax.com reports:

> New evidence has emerged that Democratic presidential candidate Barack Obama was closely associated as early as age 25 to a key adviser to a Saudi billionaire who had mentored the founding members of the Black Panthers.
>
> Percy Sutton, the former borough president of Manhattan, offhandedly revealed the unusual circumstances about his first encounter with the young Obama.
>
> "I was introduced to (Obama) by a friend who was raising money for him," Sutton told NY1 city hall reporter Dominic Carter.
>
> "The friend's name is Dr. Khalid al-Mansour, from Texas," Sutton said. "He is the principal adviser to one of the world's richest men. He told me about Obama."
>
> Sutton, the founder of Inner City Broadcasting, said al-Mansour contacted him to ask a favor: Would Sutton write a letter in support of Obama's application to Harvard Law School?
>
> "I wrote a letter of support of him to my friends at Harvard, saying to them I thought there was a genius that was going to be available and I certainly hoped they would treat him kindly,"...
>
> Sutton did not say why al-Mansour was helping Obama, how he discovered him, or from whom he was raising money on Obama's behalf.
>
> The details of Obama's academic performance are well known: At Harvard, Obama rose to academic distinction becoming the editor of the Harvard Law Review and graduating magna cum laude.

Less known are the reasons al-Mansour, an activist African-American Muslim, would be a key backer for a young man from Hawaii seeking to attend the most Ivy of the Ivy League law schools.

In an exclusive interview with Newsmax from his home in San Antonio, Texas, al-Mansour said he would not comment specifically on the statement by Percy Sutton because he was afraid anything he said would get "distorted."
Although many Americans have never heard of Khalid Abdullah Tariq al-Mansour (his full name), he is well known within the black community as a lawyer, an orthodox Muslim, a black nationalist, an author, an international deal-maker, an educator, and an outspoken enemy of Israel.

A graduate of Howard University with a law degree from the University of California, al-Mansour sits on numerous corporate boards, including the Saudi African Bank and Chicago-based LaGray Chemical Co. LaGray, which was formed to do business in Africa, counts former Nigerian President General Abdusalam Abubakar on its advisory board.

But his writings and books are packed with anti-American rhetoric reminiscent of the Rev. Jeremiah Wright, Obama's disgraced former pastor.

In a 1995 book, "The Lost Books of Africa Rediscovered," he alleged that the United States was plotting genocide against black Americans.

The first "genocide against the black man began 300 years ago," he told an audience in Harlem at a book-signing, while a second "genocide" was on the way "to remove 15 million Black people, considered disposable, of no relevance, value or benefit to the American society."

In the 1960's, when he founded the African American Association in the San Francisco Bay area, he was known as Donald Warden.

According to the Social Activism Project at the University of California at Berkley, Warden, a.k.a. Khalid al-Mansour, was the mentor of Black Panther Party founder Huey Newton and his cohort, Bobby Seale.

Al-Mansour's more recent videotaped speeches focus on Muslim themes, and abound with anti-Semitic theories and anti-Israel vitriol.

"Today, the Palestinians are being brutalized like savages," he told an audience in South Africa. "If you protest you will go to jail, and you may be killed. And they say they are the only democratic country in the Middle East. ... They are lying on God."

He accused the Jews of "stealing the land the same way the Christians stole the land from the Indians in America."

But al-Mansour's sponsorship of Obama as a prospective Harvard law student is important for another reason beyond his Islamic and anti-American rhetoric and early Black Panther ties.

At the time Percy Sutton, a former lawyer for Malcolm X and a former business partner of al-Mansour, says he was raising money for Obama's graduate school education, al-Mansour was representing top members of the Saudi Royal family seeking to do business and exert influence in the United States.

At the same time, he was also advising Prince Alwaleed bin Talal in his U.S. investments, and sits on the board of his premier investment vehicle, Kingdom Holdings.

Since then, Prince Alwaleed's Kingdom Foundation has given millions of dollars to Muslim charities in the United States, including several whose leaders have been indicted on terrorism-related charges in federal courts.

He also has given tens of millions of dollars to Harvard and other major U.S. universities, to establish programs in Islamic studies.

The casual statement by Percy Sutton...is the first time anyone has hinted at a relationship between Obama and the Saudi royal family.

He told Newsmax that he has personally introduced Prince Alwaleed to "51 of the 53 leaders of Africa," traveling from country to country on the Saudi prince's private jet.

He knows virtually every black leader in America, from the business community, to community activists, to the worlds of politics and entertainment.

Sutton gives no clues as to why al-Mansour would be raising money to help Obama go to law school. Obama has said during his campaign that he paid his way through Harvard with student loans.

For Jesse Lee Peterson, founder of the Los Angeles-based Brotherhood Organization of a New Destiny (BOND), these latest revelations about Obama's ties to Saudi financiers were an important wake-up call.

"To me, this opened up more questions about Barack Obama and his relationship to the Muslim world," Peterson told Newsmax.

"I think there's more to this story and to Barack Obama than we realize," Peterson said. "As all the truth comes out before the election, I don't think he has a chance. I can't see American's taking that kind of risk." [13]

WILLIAM AYERS

William Ayers is an American elementary education theorist and former 1960's anti-war activist. He is known for the radical nature of his activism in the 1960's and 1970's...In 1969, he cofounded the radical left organization the Weather Underground, which conducted a campaign of bombing public buildings during the 1960's and 1970's.[14]

The National Review says:

> The problem of Barack Obama's relationship with Bill Ayers will not go away. Ayers and his wife, Bernardine Dohrn were terrorists for the notorious Weather Underground during the turbulent 1960's, turning fugitive when a bomb — designed to kill army officers in New Jersey — accidentally exploded in a New York townhouse.
>
> Prior to that, Ayers and his cohorts succeeded in bombing the Pentagon. Ayers and Dohrn remain unrepentant for their terrorist past. Ayers was pictured in a 2001 article for Chicago magazine, stomping on an American flag, and told the New York Times just before 9/11 that the notion of the United States as a just and fair and decent place "makes me want to puke."
>
> Although Obama actually launched his political career at an event at Ayers's and Dohrn's home, Obama has dismissed Ayers as just "a guy who lives in my neighborhood," and "not somebody who I exchange ideas from on a regular basis." [15]

PHOTO COURTESY MINDFULLY.ORG

PHOTO COURTESY FREEREPUBLIC.COM

Investor's Business Daily further clarifies:

> Tuesday's release of papers from a Chicago school reform project known as the Annenberg Challenge shows once again Barack Obama has a problem with the truth.
>
> Obama has tried to distance himself from Ayers, his former campaign contributor and foundation colleague. When asked in the Pennsylvania debate if he could "explain that relationship for the voters and explain to Democrats why it won't be a problem?" Obama's lame response was that "the notion that somehow, as a consequence of me knowing somebody who engaged in detestable acts 40 years ago when I was 8 years old somehow reflects on me and my values doesn't make much sense to me."
>
> It makes sense to us. Ayers, a founder of the Weather Underground organization that bombed the U.S. Capitol and Pentagon four decades ago wasn't just a passing acquaintance to Obama.
>
> When Obama was making his first run for the Illinois Senate, Ayers and terrorist wife Bernadine Dohrn had Obama to his house for a 1995 campaign event. Ayers also served with Obama on the board of the Woods Fund of Chicago for three years and made a donation to the Friends of Barack Obama in 2001.
>
> The only thing needing investigating is why Obama is trying so hard to hide his past. Full disclosure is change we can believe in.[16]

"'I don't regret setting bombs. I feel we didn't do enough."

Spoken during an interview on September 11th.[17]

"Kill all the rich people. Break up their cars and apartments. Bring the revolution home, kill your parents, that's where it's really at."[18]

"Everything was absolutely ideal on the day I bombed the Pentagon."[19]

FATHER MICHAEL PFLEGER

Michael Louis Pfleger is a Roman Catholic priest and social activist in Chicago, Illinois.[20]

Below are portions of an article regarding Father Pfleger from American Thinker:

> ...one of Obama's mentors, one Father Michael Pfleger -- a white race-baiting Marxist. Like Rev. Wright, you have to hear the truly demonic tones in his voice --- simply reading the text isn't enough. Your inner "reading voice" just won't say it like he does.
>
> To give you an idea, Father Pfleger sounds like Jeremiah Wright on a really bad acid trip. He is hateful; he is sadistically gleeful; he preaches a vicious anti-White race hatred; and he has the congregation screaming with joy. This is a sight and sound to behold, something out of the worst parts of the Middle Ages, with priests demagoguing their congregations to go out and kill Jews, or Protestant infidels, Catholics, or Orthodox Christians. But this is right here in America, brough to you by the compassion of Black Liberation Theology.
>
> Father Pfleger brings public scandal to the Church. He clearly and obviously, on videotape, preaches racial hatred.
>
> Today, everybody in the world knows. They can see it on YouTube.
>
> As for Senator Barack Obama, it does bring his history and political backers into sharper and sharper focus, doesn't it?[21]

ZBIGNIEW BRZEZINSKI

Zbigniew Brzezinski is a Polish-American political scientist, geostrategist, and statesman who served as United States National Security Advisor to President Jimmy Carter from 1977 to 1981.[22]

In February 2008, Israel National Radio conducted an interview with Prof. Paul Eidelberg, Founder and President of the Foundation for Constitutional Democracy, a Jerusalem-based think tank for improving Israel's system of governance. Here are a portion of his observations from that interview:

> It was reported in the New York Sun on February 15 that Barack Hussain Obama has chosen Zbigniew Brzezinski to advise him on Middle East policy.
>
> Back in 1985, I wrote an article on Brzezinski for The Intercollegiate Review. Before citing some of the more relevant passages of that article, it should be borne in mind that Brzezinski, a political scientist, served as President Jimmy Carter's national security adviser. One does not have to read Carter's *Palestine: Peace Not Apartheid* to know that Carter is an anti-Semite. Brzezinski has earned the same reputation.
>
> Not only has Brzezinski publicly defended the anti-Semitic canard that the relationship between America and Israel is the result of Jewish pressure, but he also signed a letter demanding dialogue with Hamas, whose charter calls for Israel 's destruction. It behooves us to understand the mentality of Obama's Middle East adviser—and more deeply than our so-called experts.
>
> The influence of political scientists like Brzezinski is wide and deep. His moral relativism or neutrality prompts politicians to negotiate with and appease terrorist regimes. Mr. Obama may not be a moral

relativist, but with Brzezinski as his adviser, he will be more disposed than other presidential candidates to appease Iran.

Brzezinski views history through the lens of Marxism, which, despite its atheism, has much in common with Islam. Both Communism and Islam are universalistic ideologies that reject the idea of the nation-state. Both do not regard adherence to treaties between nations as obligatory. Both Communism and Islam are militaristic and expansionist creeds that do not recognize international borders. Brzezinski's globalism has become evident in Jimmy Carter . Under Brzezinski's influence, Carter lowered the defense budget and pursued a soft line toward the Soviet Union. We can expect an Obama White House to pursue a very soft line toward Islam.

With Zbigniew Brzezinski as his national security adviser, it was Jimmy Carter who facilitated the return of Ayatollah Khomeini to Iran. The Carter-Brzezinski axis is very much responsible for the Islamic revolution—the most dangerous revolution that has occurred in human history, a revolution that threatens the existence of every nation-state.

As a crypto-Marxist, Brzezinski deplores the nation-state .

"That is why Marxism," he contends, **"represents a further vital and creative stage in the maturing and man's universal vision."** Marxism, he says, **"was the most powerful doctrine for generating a universal and secular human consciousness. "**

Brzezinski, a self-professed secularist, is an internationalist whose moral relativism contradicts the moral law or natural rights doctrine of America's Declaration of Independence. His relativism and internationalism contradict the teachings of the America 's Founding Fathers, who endowed the United States with a national identity and character, the same that animated Abraham Lincoln and Theodore Roosevelt. To put it more bluntly: Brzezinski's mode of thought or political mentality — like that of countless other American academics — is anti-American. An Obama-Brzezinski axis has revolutionary significance. It might accelerate the de-Americanization and decline of the United States.

Terminate the nation-state and you are heading for world government. But a world government must also have a monopoly of power. Its agents must be everywhere, to make sure that no opposition group in any country secretly develops weapons of mass destruction. A world government must have the equivalent of the KGB in every country. A world government would be the greatest tyranny in human history.

Israel is the target of all those who oppose the nation-state if only because the Bible of Israel not only prescribes a multiplicity of nations, but a moral code that contradicts the moral relativism of the Brzezinskis and of Israel's ruling elites.

Will Israel be the target of CHANGE — the mantra of the Democratic Party chanted most ominously by Barack Hussein Obama?[23]

BRZEZINSKI'S ROLE IN THE RISE OF AL-QUAEDA

A video can be seen on YouTube of Zbigniew Brzezinski in late 70's, telling Afghan Jihadists: **"Your cause is right. God is on your side."**[24]

In 1979, the US government, under then-president Jimmy Carter and his national security adviser, Zbigniew Brzezinski, began to covertly arm and train the mujahideen through the Pakistani military's Inter Services Intelligence (ISI) service. Between 1979 and 1992, Washington provided at least $6 billion worth of weapons and training to the various militias.[25]

According to an article by the Socialist Alternative:
One of the first non-Afghan volunteers to join the ranks of the mujahideen was Osama bin Laden, hailing from a wealthy construction family in Saudi Arabia. Bin Laden recruited 4,000 volunteers from his own country and developed close relations with the most radical mujahideen leaders.

According to journalist John Cooley, "the CIA gave Osama free reign in Afghanistan, as did Pakistan's intelligence generals.[26]

**BRZEZINSKI CHECKS OUT BIN LADEN'S GUN ON THE
BORDER OF AFGHANISTAN IN 1980.**

PHOTO COURTESY NWOTRUTH.COM

Mr. Brzezinski gave an interview to Foreign Policy International in October
2007. Here is a portion of the transcript:

> **FP:** You've defended your decision under the Carter administration
> to back the mujahedin in Afghanistan on the grounds that backing
> the jihad was crucial to defeating the Soviet Union. But wouldn't
> the Soviet Union have collapsed on its own, for economic reasons?
> Was it worth it to support a movement that led to the rise of the
> Taliban and al Qaeda?

> **ZB:** I think that question is so crazy that it really makes you
> wonder. Afghanistan was destroyed by the Soviets, and that is
> what has bred the Taliban years after. The support for Afghan
> resistance has created support of America for a whole generation
> of Afghans who are still on our side. We would be in a terrible
> mess if we hadn't supported the Afghans.

FP: What are your thoughts on the upcoming Middle East peace conference, especially in light of Israel's recent attack on Syria? Do you think any progress can be made?

ZB: Progress will be made at the forthcoming conference only if the United States forthcomingly leads and starts out by defining explicitly the minimum requirements of an eventual settlement. That is: no right of return, the genuine sharing of Jerusalem, lines with reciprocal accommodations, and a demilitarized Palestinian state.[27]

The New York Sun reported in February 2008:

A foreign policy adviser to Senator Obama is scheduled to arrive in Syria today as the leader of a RAND Corp. delegation.

Mr. Brzezinski's visit to Syria, a country President Bush has accused of arming terrorists and ordering political assassinations in Lebanon, is in many ways in keeping with a theme of the Obama campaign. The Illinois senator in August said during a Democratic debate that he would be willing to meet with foreign adversaries...

Mr. Brzezinski, a one-time national security adviser to President Carter, announced in an interview on Bloomberg's satellite news channel that he was endorsing Mr. Obama, and he has been an adviser to the campaign since.

A spokesman for the senator's presidential campaign, Tommy Vietor, said the campaign did not know Mr. Brzezinski was leading the delegation. "The first we heard of this trip was from you," he said. He added: "Brzezinski is not a day-to-day adviser for the campaign, he is someone whose guidance Senator Obama seeks on Iraq."

...Rep. Eliot Engel, a Democrat from New York, said he found it hard to believe that one of the Illinois senator's main advisers would not know that his visit to Syria would appear to have the tacit consent of the Obama campaign.

"People are going to say if you are advising Obama, you are representing Obama," Mr. Engel said. "At this time when we are in the middle of an election, I can't believe that for him to go to Syria at this moment would not appear he was going with at least some tacit approval of the candidate he is advising. I would think he would realize that...."[28]

According to the American Thinker:
"...on the far reaches of the Web can be found conspiracies about former Carter national security adviser Zbigniew Brzezinski, who became the candidate's "guru and controller" while at Columbia in the early 1980's. Mr. Brzezinski laughs, and tells us he doesn't **"remember meeting him."**[29]

The Washington Post reports on Brzezinski's endorsement:
Obama **"recognizes that the challenge is a new face, a new sense of direction, a new definition of America's role in the world,"** said Brzezinski, who keeps an office at the Center for Strategic and International Studies. **"Obama is clearly more effective and has the upper hand. He has a sense of what is historically relevant and what is needed from the United States in relationship to the world."**[30]

How did Barack feel about Brzezinski? From Investor's Business Daily:

> Barack Obama has also been very forthright in his praise of Brzezinski as **"someone I have learned an immense amount from,"** and **"one of our most outstanding scholars and thinkers."**[31]

In what how now become a familiar scenario, Obama made an about face on this trusted guru. Recently when Brzezinski made statements that riled Jewish voters, Obama "threw him under the bus" (a phrase now made famous by Obama).

According to New York Daily News:

> A high-profile supporter of Barack Obama accused American Jewish groups of engaging in "McCarthyism," a statement that could further complicate the Illinois senator's appeal to Jewish voters.
>
> **"It's not unique to the Jewish community - but there is a McCarthy-ite tendency among some people in the Jewish community,"**…**"They operate not by arguing but by slandering, vilifying, demonizing."**
>
> **"They very promptly wheel out anti-Semitism,"** he said.
>
> **"There is an element of paranoia in this inclination to view any serious attempt at a compromised peace as somehow directed against Israel."**
>
> Reached for comment, Obama spokeswoman Jen Psaki said Brzezinski **"is not an adviser to our campaign, and does**

not speak for the campaign. Sen. Obama profoundly disagrees with the sentiments he expressed."[32]

Another denial reported by the Chicago Sun-Times:

"I do not share his views with respect to Israel. I have said so clearly and unequivocally," Obama said. "He's not one of my key advisers. I've had lunch with him once. I've exchanged e-mails with him maybe three times. He came to Iowa to introduce ... for a speech on Iraq."[33]

"Though Stalinism may have been a needless tragedy for both the Russian people and communism as an ideal, there is the intellectually tantalizing possibility that for the world at large it was, as we shall see, a blessing in disguise."

Zbigniew Brzezinski

"The technetronic era involves the gradual appearance of a more controlled society. Such a society would be dominated by an elite, unrestrained by traditional values. Soon it will be possible to assert almost continuous surveillance over every citizen and maintain up-to-date complete files containing even the most personal information about the citizen. These files will be subject to instantaneous retrieval by the authorities."

Zbigniew Brzezinski

"Today we are again witnessing the emergence of transnational elites ... [Whose] ties cut across national boundaries ...It is likely that before long the social elites of most of the more advanced countries will be highly internationalist or globalist in spirit and outlook ... The nation-state is gradually yielding its sovereignty... Further progress will require greater American sacrifices. More intensive efforts to shape a new world monetary structure will have to be undertaken, with some consequent risk to the present relatively favorable American position."

Zbigniew Brzezinski

"Marxism represents a further vital and creative stage in the maturing of man's universal vision ... Marxism is simultaneously a victory of the external, active man over the inner, passive man and a victory of reason over belief ... Marxism, disseminated on the popular level in the form of communism, represents a major advance in man's ability to conceptualize his relationship to the world."

Zbigniew Brzezinski

These are but a few of the unusual characters that play a part in this cast of the drama entitled, "This is Your Life Barack Obama." You really could go on and on with the digging, from Pakistani college roomates to rumors of homosexual trysts during the Columbia years, to the 300 advisors that are in his circle of acquaintances. But, just these few mentioned here, should give one pause.

The National Review Online put it best:

> There are two disturbing—and now predictable—patterns to Obama's serial distancing from prior intimates. First, the post facto embarrassment is personalized in terms of "I" and "me," as if a Wright or Rezko is somehow doing something out of character aimed at Obama, rather than persisting in entirely predictable behavior that offends society at large. Thus in reaction to the racist Wright, we get "That's a show of disrespect to me," while Pfleger's venom prompts, "I am deeply disappointed in Father's Pfleger." But the issue is racial hatred, not a matter of pleasing or respecting Obama himself.
>
> The second reaction is a sort of amnesia: So suddenly the past benefactor Rezko has radically changed with his indictment: "That isn't the Tony Rezko I knew." And after Rev. Wright himself confirmed that his hatred once labeled as "snippets" and "loops" was, in fact, representative of his world view, Obama pivoted with "Well, I may not know him as well as I thought."
>
> The truth?
>
> Obama has required a vocabulary of needed ostracism, as he insidiously sheds most of his prior life and environment of the last twenty years. Wright, Moss, Pfleger, Ayers, Rezko, etc. are all figures that have to be "disavowed" or, better, Trostkyized in some fashion. The method apparently is to suggest that they, not Obama, have suddenly changed (when, in truth, they, not Obama, have remained

entirely consistent) and are now out to hurt or embarrass Obama (when, again, they are surprised that their longtime predictable behavior is suddenly producing different results).

Like many of his prior positions on the Middle East, Iran, guns, abortion, taxes, the war, etc. Obama must metamorphosize from a hard-core Chicago racial leftwing activist, into a liberal idealist who transcends politics.

Will it work? Two things are in his favor. One, his message is messianic ("this was the moment when the rise of the oceans began to slow and our planet began to heal"), and the devoted not only don't want to know of their prophet's mortal lapses, but like all devotees will turn in anger on those who remind them of such mortality. Second, many of these bombs have been exploded in the primaries, months before the election. Even in Chicago, there are only so many Rezkos and Wrights.[34]

He keeps company with evildoers; he associates with wicked men.
Job 34:8

Not a word from their mouth can be trusted; their heart is filled with destruction. Their throat is an open grave; with their tongue they speak deceit.

Declare them guilty, O God! Let their intrigues be their downfall. Banish them for their many sins, for they have rebelled against you.
Psalms 5:9-10

BEING BARACK OBAMA

What you do speaks so loud that I cannot hear what you say.

Ralph Waldo Emerson

"In all great deceivers a remarkable process is at work to which they owe their power. In the very act of deception with all its preparations, the dreadful voice, expression, and gestures, they are overcome by their belief in themselves; it is this belief which then speaks, so persuasively, so miracle-like, to the audience.

Friedrich Nietzsche, "The Genealogy of Morals"

WILL THE REAL BARACK OBAMA, PLEASE STAND UP

What makes him tick? If you peer behind the curtain, what will it reveal?

The subtle nuances of speech, the actions of a man filled with his own grand notions of his place in history.

If you look closely, with the eyes of one who will not be blinded by the surrounding extravaganza of manufactured euphoria, you will find the truth.

It's there; in fact, he has made it easy...we've just not been able to sew all the little pieces into a cohesive pattern...until now.

An age is called "dark," not because the light fails to shine but because people refuse to see it.

James Michener

MANCHURIAN CANDIDATE

Investor's Business Daily's discusses the phenomenon of a lab created candidate:

> ...the Democrats are compounding the fraud by foisting him off on the voters. The Barack Obama they are peddling is a media-created virtual person endowed by his creators with characteristics that do not represent the real Barack Obama. Millions of people are being duped.
>
> The fictional Barack Obama may win the election in November, but if he does, it will be the real Barack Obama who will occupy the White House and exercise nearly untrammeled power over the lives and livelihoods of 300 million Americans. Therein lies the enormity of the trick the Democrats are playing on the American people.
>
> Padding a resume is one thing — exaggeration is, after all, a part of politics — but it is quite another thing to paper over discomfiting parts of a candidate's resume and condemn those who ask or wonder why. The Democrats are insulting people's intelligence and making a mockery of the electoral process by asking them to vote for a figment of the media's imagination.[1]

TRAINED TO DECEIVE

> Marty Kaufman, looking to hire Obama as a community organizer, said, **"You must be angry about something...anger's a requirement for the job."**[2]

The Alinsky method of training would serve Obama well in his future endeavors. Saul Alinsky believed that "the end justifies the means." This explains the ability of Barack Obama to be able to deceive to achieve the desired outcome:

In his college years, Obama writes, "Later, I would realize that the position of most black students in predominately white colleges was already too tenuous, our identities too scrambled, to admit to ourselves that our black pride remained incomplete. And to admit our doubt and confusion to whites, to open up our psyches to general examination by those who had caused so much of the damage in the first place, seemed ludicrous, itself an expression of self-hatred...**It was in observing this division, I think, between what we talked about privately and what we addressed publicly...**"[3]

In a different chapter of Obama's book, Dreams of My Father, he admits that he had developed a strategy to anesthetize those he came in contact with:

> **"It was usually an effective tactic, another one of those tricks I had learned: People were satisfied so long as you were courteous and smiled and made no sudden moves. They were more than satisfied, they were relieved - such a pleasant surprise to find a well-mannered young black man who didn't seem angry all the time."**[4]

He succumbed to the idea that it was okay to manipulate:

> **"The man was starting to get on my nerves. I asked him if he ever worried about becoming too calculating, if the idea of probing people's psyches and gaining their trust just to build an organization ever felt manipulative.** He sighed. **"I'm not a poet, Barack. I'm an organizer...Later, I had to admit that Marty was right."**[5]

THE MASK SLIPS

We can find those rare incidences when he has shown that he is human and has been caught - saying what he **really** means. And the words of truth coming from his mouth, don't align with the message of "hope."

> **"...that, I suppose, is what I'd been trying to tell my mother that day: that her faith in justice and rationality was misplaced, that we couldn't overcome after all, that all the education and good intentions in the world couldn't help plug up the holes in the universe or give you the power to change its blind, mindless course."**[6]

Obama likened working at a consulting house to multinational corporations as being a **"spy behind enemy lines."**[7]

One of the most offensive statements Obama made was regarding 9/11:

> "Just eight days after 9/11, in an op-ed for the Hyde Park Herald, the senator blamed the attacks on **"a failure of empathy"** that **"grows out of a climate of poverty and ignorance, helplessness, and despair."** ...Obama made no mention of the role radical Islam played in the hijackers' lives."[8]

And in one of the most replayed gaffes, according to the National Review:

> Senator Barack Obama finds himself in the midst of a controversy in the aftermath of comments that he made at a private fundraiser in San Francisco on April 6, during which he explained his difficulty appealing to working-class voters in Pennsylvania. He said, "It's not surprising that they get bitter, they cling to guns or religion or antipathy to people who aren't like them or anti-immigrant sentiment or anti-trade sentiment. . . ."[9]

Senator Obama's words are significant because they were said off-the-record, meaning they provided a more authentic glimpse into the attitudes of Obama than a carefully scripted event. Nonetheless, his words were not merely careless; his comments were based on a carefully constructed, if deeply condescending, explanation.[10]

The New York Times found the remark oddly similar to a statement made by Karl Marx:

This sent me to Marx's famous statement about religion in the introduction to his "Contribution to the Critique of Hegel's Philosophy of Right":

Religious suffering is at the same time an expression of real suffering and a protest against real suffering. Religion is the sigh of the oppressed creature, the sentiment of a heartless world, and the soul of a soulless condition. It is the opium of the people."

But it's one thing for a German thinker to assert that "religion is the sigh of the oppressed creature." It's another thing for an American presidential candidate to claim that we "cling to ... religion" out of economic frustration.[11]

According to FreeRepublic.com, Obama's even resorted to instructing his followers to do more than vote, he says take action:

...at a Nevada rally...Obama said this to about 14,000 people:

"I need you to go out and talk to your friends and talk to your neighbors. I want you to talk to them whether they are independent or whether they are Republican. I want you to argue with them and get in their face..."

Nice. So much for the politics of hope and unity. So much for teaching our youth how to be good citizens and neighbors.[12]

So much for teaching tolerance, respect, and bi-partisanship. If someone doesn't agree with you, especially if they don't choose Obama, just get in their face and pick a fight.

Is this how Obama plans to train his National Citizen Service Corps?

How presidential. Teaching young people how to be Chicago thugs.[13]

Reuven Koret for the Israel Insider says:

Obama wants it both ways, has always wanted it both ways. Black and white, Indonesian and American, Muslim and Christian. He loves playing one off the other, using one to hide the other even as the traces of the truth may be assembled to reveal the whole cloth of deception and self-promotion he has been weaving so skillfully since his childhood. No wonder he is a man of change. He IS a changeling, a veritable chameleon, adapting and amending his life story to fit the circumstances.[14]

On Alinsky's personality...obviously taught to his best student:

"'His charm lies in his ability to commit himself completely to the people in the room with him. In a shrewd though subtle way, he often manipulates them while speaking directly to their experience.'[15]

"The art of propaganda lies in understanding the emotional ideas of the great masses and finding, through a psychologically correct form, the way to the attention and thence to the heart of the broad masses. The receptivity of the great masses is very limited, their intelligence is small, but their power of forgetting is enormous. In consequence of these facts, all effective propaganda must be limited to a very few points and must harp on these slogans until the last member of the public understands what you want him to understand [or believe]...

Adolf Hitler, Mein Kampf

The words of his mouth were
smoother than butter,
but war was in his heart:
his words were softer than oil,
yet were they drawn swords.

Psalms 55:21

> By the skillful and sustained use of propaganda,
> one can make a people see even heaven as hell or
> an extremely wretched life as paradise.
>
> *Adolf Hitler*

SILENCING THE CRITICS

Did you ever think there would come a time when the nation known for freedom, would have an election where you could be investigated for saying a candidate's full name? As the GOPUSA.com website recently reported, that time has come:

> We have seen many changes in this great nation which have been brought about by left wing activists. As kids, we used to say the Pledge of Allegiance. Now, it's being attacked in the courts. We used to say a prayer in the morning before school or at football games. Socialists in America have deemed that "offensive" and the practice has all but disappeared. Christmas displays honoring the birth of Christ trigger convulsions by the Left, who say that we shouldn't make people feel "uncomfortable" with our manger scenes.
>
> Now, we can't even say what we want to say in public because

not only will the thought police be on patrol, but, using a recent event in Florida as an example, saying **"Hussein Obama"** in public might just get you a visit from the FBI. Just ask Florida's Lee County Sheriff Mike Scott who is under fire -- and investigation -- for referring to Obama at a campaign rally by his -- gasp -- full name. What is going on with America?

Oh, the shock of it all! Speaking someone's full legal name in public! When asked about the "incident," Sheriff Scott responded by saying:

> **"I absolutely, unequivocally don't regret saying it,"** Scott told the News-Press on Monday. **"In order to be a speaker at this event, I had to give my full name — Michael Joseph Scott — to the Secret Service, even though I'm the sheriff of Lee County. So why would I apologize? Is there some kind of double standard here where I have to give my full name, but I can't use his?"**

> **"Unless he changed his name, my position hasn't changed,"** said Scott of Obama. **"It seems very clear to me that people have one of three stances on this thing: There are those who dislike it, there are those who like it, and there are those who think it's a whole big deal about nothing, which is where I stand."**

Sheriff Scott's remark has now earned him an investigation by the federal government.

The NBC station reports that officials with the U.S. Office of Special Counsel have started an investigation of the Sheriff under the question of "did he use his position as sheriff to influence an election?

The question is this... If Sheriff Scott had not said **"Barack Hussein Obama,"** do you really think he would now be under investigation? If you answered "no," then that should send a shiver down your spine, because it means that the government is imposing pressure and creating a public example of Scott for simply saying someone's name.

Whether the investigation leads to charges or legal action is not the point. The point is that government intimidation is being brought to bear for someone exercising his first amendment right to free speech.[1]

In response to the creation of an Obama Missouri "Truth Squad," which is comprised of lawmakers, prosecutors and law enforcement, whose mission is to "respond quickly, forcefully, and aggressively when John McCain or his allies launch inaccurate claims or character attacks about Barack Obama,"[2] Missouri Governor Matt Blunt recently issued the following news release regarding Barack Obama's attempts to silence the opposition:

> Gov. Matt Blunt today issued the following statement on news reports that have exposed plans by U.S. Senator Barack Obama to use Missouri law enforcement to threaten and intimidate his critics.

> "St. Louis County Circuit Attorney Bob McCulloch, St. Louis City Circuit Attorney Jennifer Joyce, Jefferson County Sheriff Glenn Boyer, and Obama and the leader of his Missouri campaign Senator Claire McCaskill have attached the stench of police state tactics to the Obama-Biden campaign."

> "What Senator Obama and his helpers are doing is scandalous beyond words, the party that claims to be the party of Thomas Jefferson is abusing the justice system and offices of public trust

trust to silence political criticism with threats of prosecution and criminal punishment."

"Barack Obama needs to grow up. Leftist blogs and others in the press constantly say false things about me and my family.

Usually, we ignore false and scurrilous accusations because the purveyors have no credibility. When necessary, we refute them. Enlisting Missouri law enforcement to intimidate people and kill free debate is reminiscent of the Sedition Acts - not a free society."

"This abuse of the law for intimidation insults the most sacred principles and ideals of Jefferson. I can think of nothing more offensive to Jefferson's thinking than using the power of the state to deprive Americans of their civil rights. The only conceivable purpose of Messrs. McCulloch, Obama and the others is to frighten people away from expressing themselves, to chill-free and open debate, to suppress support and donations to conservative organizations targeted by this anti-civil rights, to strangle criticism of Mr. Obama, to suppress ads about his support of higher taxes, and to choke out criticism on television, radio, the Internet, blogs, e-mail and daily conversation about the election."[3]

According to Real Clear Politics:

If Barack Obama gets his way, the Oxford English Dictionary will have updated its definition of "distraction" by the end of the campaign: "Diversion of the mind, attention, etc., from any object or course that tends to advance the political interests of Barack Obama."

Here are the Obama rules in detail:

- He can't be called a "liberal" ("the same names and labels they pin on everyone," as Obama puts it);

- His toughness on the war on terror can't be questioned ("attempts to play on our fears");

- His extreme positions on social issues can't be exposed ("the same efforts to distract us from the issues that affect our lives" and "turn us against each other");

- His Chicago background too is off-limits ("pouncing on every gaffe and association and fake controversy").

Besides that, it should be a freewheeling and spirited campaign.

We could take Obama's rules in good faith if he never calls John McCain a "conservative" or labels him in any other way. If he never criticizes him for his association with George Bush. If he doesn't jump on his gaffes (like McCain's 100-years-in-Iraq comment that Obama distorted and harped on for weeks). And if he never says anything that would tend to make Americans fearful about the future or divide them (i.e., say things that some people agree with and others don't).

This is, of course, an impossible standard. Obama doesn't expect anyone to live up to it except John McCain.[4]

"The degree by which people's minds are moulded by their leaders is truly staggering yet depressing in equal measure ....
a state of affairs gloated upon by despots and tyrants-in-waiting alike.
Just as Hitler said: "What luck for the rulers that men do not think."
The Rise and Fall of the Third Reich (1959)

TIME

THE WEEKLY NEWSMAGAZINE

MAN OF 1938

From the unholy organist, a hymn of hate.
(Foreign News)

Adolf Hitler
1938
Man of The Year

He graced the cover once...
could he be 2008's
"Man of The Year?"

"Obama is the hope of the entire world." - Louis Farrakhan[1]
"Hitler was a very great man." - Louis Farrakhan[2]

DICTATOR RISING

Three main factors that swayed people to follow Hitler:[3]

1. The state of the German people after World War I, feeling hopeless and divided, looking for a leader.

2. Hitler's promise of change and prominent nationalism.

3. Hitler's rhetoric and charisma.

Author Joel Richardson wrote an article regarding Barack Obama's unusual stage set-up for his acceptance speech at the 2008 Democratic National Convention:

Apparently Barack Obama's big speech on Thursday night will be delivered from an elaborate columned stage resembling a miniature Greek temple.

When I heard this, I couldn't help but be reminded of another famous world leader who also loved to deliver his propaganda to the quivering masses from a podium that was created specifically to resemble a Greek temple. A little bit of history:

In two campaigns, starting in 1879, the Pergamon Altar in Pergamos, Turkey was excavated by a German archaeological team lead by Carl Humann. The altar was shipped out of the Ottoman Empire from the original location and was reconstructed in the Pergamon Museum in Berlin in the 19th century. Today the altar still sits in Berlin where it can be seen alongside other monumental structures such as the Ishtar Gate from Babylon.

THE PERGAMON ALTAR, BERLIN

PHOTO COURTESY JOELSTRUMPET.COM

In 1934 Adolph Hitler became the dictator of Germany. Hitler ordered construction of the Tribune at Zeppelin Field in Nuremberg specifically for the purpose of his Nazi rallies.

Several volumes have been written detailing the deeply occult nature of Hitler and the Nazi regime. Not surprisingly then the Nazi architect of the Zeppelintribüne, Albert Speer, actually used the Pergamon Altar as the model for what essentially became the premier Nazi pulpit. The Führer's podium was located in the middle of the replica Pergamon Altar.

HITLER'S PODIUM AT ZEPPELIN TRIBUNE FIELD

PHOTO COURTESY JOELSTRUMPET.COM

PHOTO COURTESY CHICAGOTRIBUNE.COM

PHOTO COURTESY GUARDIAN.CO.UK

PHOTO COURTESY CLEVELAND.COM

What is also noteworthy is that Biblical Scholars are in near universal agreement that it was this very Altar that was referred to by Jesus in the Book of Revelation as "the throne of Satan":

To the angel of the church in Pergamum write: These are the words of him who has the sharp, double-edged sword. I know where you live—where Satan has his throne.

Revelation 2:12-13

After comparing the design of Obama's podium to the Pergamum Altar, it is clear that the two are nearly identical. While some are claiming that Obama's Temple is modeled after the Russian Kazan Cathedral, it is clear that Obama's Temple bears a much closer resemblance to the Pergamum Altar.[4]

Richardson continues his observation:

So, for those who are accustomed to watching "the signs all around us," in what must be seen as prophetic, Obama's acceptance speech will be delivered from a replica of what Jesus Himself refers to as "Satan's Throne."

Now, please do not get me wrong, I am not comparing Barack Obama to Satan. I'm comparing him to Hitler.

First, the two are/were extraordinary orators who had seemingly magical powers to hypnotize the glassy eyed masses.

Secondly, they are both extreme leftists.

Third, the two think very highly of themselves. Few will argue that Barack Obama has done very little to discourage his Messiah-image. The set design of this speech a perfect example.

And now fourthly, we find that the two share some very unusual tastes:

- They both found it appropriate to model their respective power-podiums after Greek Temples dedicated to the "gods."
- Both have chosen to give perhaps the most important political speeches of their lives in replica Greek Temples, under the lights, in an open field, to the masses of their cheering fans.
- And lastly, but most importantly both Barack Obama and Adolph Hitler share the commonality in that they both proudly place their stamp of approval on the wholesale slaughter of millions upon millions of fellow human beings. In Hitler's case, it was the Jewish people, those who God has referred to as "the apple of my eye." And in Obama's case, his support is for the slaughter of the most innocent little lambs that this world has to offer; those who our Creator no doubt would refer to as "the least of these."

So when you see Barack Obama step up to his pulpit of power, remember the other man who not so long ago made powerful speeches in a strikingly similar fashion to the masses about how he was going to better all of their lives.[5]

Unfortunately, there are more similarities that we should observe between Barack Obama and Adolf Hitler. First, it would be helpful to give you the characteristics of a narcissistic leader. According to a study by Dr. Sam Vaknin:

> Narcissistic leadership is about theatre, not about life. To enjoy the spectacle...the leader demands the suspension of judgment, depersonalization, and de-realization.

> Narcissistic leadership often poses as a rebellion against the "old ways"...the upper classes, the established religions, the superpowers, the corrupt order.

> This is precisely the source of the fascination with Hitler, diagnosed by Erich Fromm - together with Stalin - as a malignant narcissist. He was not the devil. He was one of us. He was what Arendt aptly called the banality of evil...He was the perfect mirror, a channel, a voice, and the very depth of our souls.

> The narcissistic leader prefers the sparkle and glamour of well-orchestrated illusions to the tedium and method of real accomplishments. His reign is all smoke and mirrors, devoid of substances, consisting of mere appearances and mass delusions. In the aftermath of his regime - the narcissistic leader having died, been deposed, or voted out of office - it all unravels.

> Thus, a narcissist who regards himself as the benefactor of the poor, a member of the common folk, the representative of the disenfranchised, the champion of the dispossessed against the corrupt elite - is highly unlikely to use violence at first.

The pacific mask crumbles when the narcissist has become convinced that the very people he purported to speak for, his constituency, his grassroots fans, the prime sources of his narcissistic supply - have turned against him. At first, in a desperate effort to maintain the fiction underlying his chaotic personality, the narcissist strives to explain away the sudden reversal of sentiment. "The people are being duped by (the media, big industry, the military, the elite, etc.)", "they don't really know what they are doing", "following a rude awakening, they will revert to form", etc.

When these flimsy attempts to patch a tattered personal mythology fail - the narcissist is injured. Narcissistic injury inevitably leads to narcissistic rage and to a terrifying display of unbridled aggression...[6]

"The leader of genius must have the ability to make different opponents appear as if they belonged to one category."
Adolph Hitler

From CNNPolitics.com:

Obama accused McCain of supporting a track record from the Bush administration that included the failure to find weapons of mass destruction in Iraq, a longer and more expensive war in Iraq than was initially projected, the continued freedom of September 11th mastermind Osama bin Laden and the strengthening of Iran after the U.S.-led invasion of Iraq.[7]

The Times of India report:

> McCain was on the offensive throughout the 90-minute encounter. He rebuked Obama for his frequent claims that he is too close to the policies of President George W. Bush.

> "Senator Obama, I am not President Bush. If you wanted to run against President Bush you should have run four years ago," [8]

Dr. Joseph Goebbels "was one of German dictator Adolf Hitler's closest associates and most devout followers."[9]

In the German Propaganda Archive, Goebbels shares insight on the characteristics crucial in propelling Adolf Hitler to unimaginable power:

> The important thing is not whether an idea is right; the decisive thing is whether one can present it effectively to the masses so that they become its adherents.

> It is difficult to place the Führer within these categories. His ability to reach the masses is unique and remarkable, fitting no organizational scheme or dogma.

> He speaks his heart, and therefore reaches the hearts of those who hear him. He has the amazing gift of sensing what is in the air. He has the ability to express things so clearly, logically and directly that listeners are convinced that that is what they have always thought themselves. That is the true secret of the effectiveness of Adolf Hitler's speeches. The Führer is neither a speaker from reason nor from the heart. He uses both, depending on the needs of the moment.

The Führer is the first person in Germany to use speech to make history.

He did not speak like everyone else. He could not be compared with them. He understood the cares and worries of the little man and spoke about them, but they were for him only brush strokes on the dreadful painting of Germany's collapse. He did more than simply talk about them, he was not a mere reporter like the others. He took the events of the day and gave them a larger national significance that put them in context. He appealed to the good, not the bad instincts of the masses. His speaking was a magnet that drew to him whatever in the people still had iron in its blood.

Ordinary life is presented in a way that grips the hearers. The problems of the day are not explained only with the difficult tools of a worldview, but with wit and biting irony. His humor triumphs; one cries with one eye and laughs with the other. Every tone of daily life is touched upon.

The Führer is at his best, however, before a small audience. Here he is able to reach each individual member of the audience. His speaking carries away the listener, who never loses interest because he always feels spoken to directly. He may speak about a random theme with an expertise that astonishes the specialists, or in speaking about everyday matters suddenly raise them to universal significance.

On such occasions the Führer can be more intimate and precise than a public speech permits. He can go into the heart of things with irrefutable logic. Only one who has heard him in such a setting can understand his full brilliance as a speaker.

One can say that his speeches to his people and the world have an audience unprecedented in world history. They are words that inspire the heart and have a lasting impact in forming a new international epoch. There is probably no educated person in the world who has not heard the sound of his voice and who, whether he understood the words or not, felt that his heart was spoken to by magical words. Our people are fortunate to know the voice the world hears, a voice that puts words into thoughts and uses those thoughts to move an era.

Millions of people are suffering from bitter sorrow, great troubles, and terrible need. They see hardly a star of hope through the dark clouds that cover Europe's sky. No one is able to dispel the despair they face. But in Germany, God chose one from countless millions to speak our pain![10]

An article at Speigel Online shows that Hitler started to believe that he was the chosen one to lead Germany during this time:

Finally, there was the impact of the expanded Führer cult on Hitler himself. Some of those in his close proximity later claimed to have detected a change in Hitler around 1935-6. He became, so it was said, more dismissive than earlier of the slightest criticism, more convinced of his own infallibility. His speeches started to develop a more pronounced messianic tone. He saw himself ever more -- the tendency had been long implanted in his personality, but was now much exaggerated -- as chosen by Providence. When, following the successful Rhineland coup, he remarked, in one of his "election" speeches: **"I follow the path assigned to me by Providence with the instinctive sureness of a sleepwalker,"** it was more than a piece of campaign rhetoric. Hitler truly believed it. He increasingly felt infallible.[11]

Of our own Barack Obama, Peter Wehner of the National Review Online says:

> Beneath the enormous charm and cool persona of Obama beats the heart of an arrogant man. With increasing frequency, the 46-year-old one-term senator from Illinois orates as though he resides at Olympian Heights. By his presumptuous demeanor, he suggests that he sees what no one else sees, and can do what no other person can do; he is America's healing balm.[12]

WhatReallyHappened.com summarizes the way a people can so easily be led to drop their guard:

> It's easy to look back and realize what a jerk Hitler was. But at the time, Hitler looked pretty good to the German people, with the help of the media. He was TIME Magazine's Man Of The Year in 1938. The German people assumed they were safe from a tyrant. They lived in a Republic, after all, with strict laws regarding what the government could and more importantly could not do. Their leader was a devoutly religious man, and had even sung with the boy's choir of a monastery in his youth.[13]

The article that accompanied the TIME Magazine Man Of The Year designation (written in January 1939) stated:

> ...the German Republic collapsed under the weight of the 1929-34 depression in which German unemployment soared to 7,000,000 above a nationwide wind drift of bankruptcies and failures. Called to power as Chancellor of the Third Reich on January 30, 1933... Chancellor Hitler began to turn the Reich inside out.[14]

NAZI SYMBOL

What Adolf Hitler & Co. did to Germany in less than six years was applauded wildly and ecstatically by most Germans. He lifted the nation from post-War defeatism. Under the swastika Germany was unified.

His was no ordinary dictatorship, but rather one of great energy and magnificent planning. The "socialist" part of National Socialism might be scoffed at by hard-&-fast Marxists, but the Nazi movement nevertheless had a mass basis...

What Adolf Hitler & Co. did to the German people in that time left civilized men and women aghast. Civil rights and liberties have disappeared. Opposition to the Nazi regime has become tantamount to suicide or worse. Free speech and free assembly are anachronisms. The reputations of the once-vaunted German centres of learning have vanished. Education has been reduced to a National Socialist catechism.

BARACK OBAMA SYMBOL

Most cruel joke of all, however, has been played by Hitler & Co. on those German capitalists and small businessmen who once backed National Socialism as a means of saving Germany's bourgeois economic structure from radicalism. The Nazi credo that the individual belongs to the state also applies to business. Some businesses have been confiscated outright, on others what amounts to a capital tax has been levied. Profits have been strictly controlled.

Nor were signs lacking that many Germans disliked the cruelties of their Government, but were afraid to protest them. Having a hard time to provide enough bread to go round, Führer Hitler was being driven to give the German people another diverting circus. The Nazi controlled press, jumping the rope at the count of Propaganda Minister Paul Joseph Goebbels, shrieked insults at real and imagined enemies.

Meanwhile an estimated 1,133 streets and squares...acquired the name of Adolf Hitler. He delivered 96 public speeches...sold 900,000 new copies of Mein Kampf...

To those who watched the closing events of the year it seemed more than probable that the Man of 1938 may make 1939 a year to be remembered.[15]

If TIME Magazine makes Barack Obama their choice for 2008 Man of The Year...what will 2009 hold for America?

ULTIMATE POWER

On May 9 2007, President George W Bush signed a directive granting extraordinary powers to the office of the president in the event of a "declared national emergency." With a stroke of a pen, Bush arrogated for the office of the president executive powers unknown to any of his predecessors.[16]

The directive says:

"In the event of a catastrophic emergency and a declared national emergency such as any incident, regardless of location, that results in extraordinary levels of mass casualties, damage, or disruption severely affecting the US population, infrastructure, environment, economy, or government functions .... The president will assume National Essential Functions to ensure that the US will emerge from the emergency with an enduring constitutional government."[17]

WhatReallyHappened.com continues their observation:

"...when confronted with a situation demanding individual courage, in the form of a government gone wrong, the German people simply pretended that the situation did not exist. And in that simple self-deception lay the ruin of an entire nation and the coming of the second World War."

"...so trapped were the Germans by their belief in their own bravery that they willed themselves to be blind to the evidence before their eyes, so that they could nod in agreement with Der Fuhrer while still imagining themselves to have courage, even as they avoided the one situation which most required real courage; to stand up to Hitler's lies and deceptions."

When Hitler requested temporary extraordinary powers, powers specifically banned under German law, but powers Hitler claimed he needed to have to deal with the "terrorists", the German people, having already sold their souls to their self-delusions, agreed. The temporary powers were conferred, and once conferred lasted until Germany itself was destroyed.[18]

PHOTO COURTESY
FLICKR.COM

"It is not the Germany of the first decade that followed the war- broken, dejected and bowed down with a sense of apprehension and impotence. It is now full of hope and confidence, and of a renewed sense of determination to lead its own life without interference from any influence outside its own frontiers. One man has accomplished this miracle. He is a born leader of men. A magnetic and dynamic personality with a single-minded purpose, a resolute will and a dauntless heart."

David Lloyd George
Prime Minister

He has a supreme intellect. I have known only two other men to whom I could apply such distinction - Lord Northcliffe and Lloyd George. If one puts a question to Hitler, he gives an immediate, brilliant clear answer. There is no human being living whose promise on important matters I would trust more readily. He believes that Germany has a Divine calling and that the German people are destined to save Europe from the revolutionary attacks of Communism. He values family life very highly, whereas Communism is its worst enemy. He has thoroughly cleansed the moral, ethical life of Germany"

Viscount Rothermere

PHOTO COURTESY AMERICANTHINKER.COM

"This is the moment that the world is waiting for.
I have become a symbol of the possibility of
America returning to our best traditions."
Barack Obama[19]

PHOTO COURTESY GUARDIAN.CO.UK

PHOTO COURTESY CITY-DATA.COM

Let them alone: they be blind leaders of the blind.
And if the blind lead the blind, both shall fall into the
ditch.

Matthew 15:14

The wicked are estranged from the womb: they
go astray as soon as they be born, speaking lies.

Psalms 58:3

Ye are of your father the devil,
and the lusts of your father ye will do.
He was a murderer from the beginning,
and abode not in the truth,
because there is no truth in him.
When he speaketh a lie,
he speaketh of his own:
for he is a liar, and the father of it.
John 8:44

"We are no longer just a Christian nation....
We are also a Jewish nation, a Muslim nation, a Buddhist nation, a Hindu
nation, and a nation of nonbelievers."[1]

Barack Obama

A GLIMPSE INTO THE SOUL

Is is clear, that while Barack Obama's spiritual upbringing was not conventional, it was spiritual, none the less.

He reflected in his book, *The Audacity of Hope*:

> I was not raised in a religious household. For my mother, organized religion too often dressed up closed-mindedness in the garb of piety, cruelty and oppression in the cloak of righteousness. However, in her mind, a working knowledge of the world's great religions was a necessary part of any well-rounded education. In our household the Bible, the Koran, and the Bhagavad Gita sat on the shelf alongside books of Greek and Norse and African mythology. On Easter or Christmas Day my mother might drag me to church, just as she dragged me to the Buddhist temple, the Chinese New Year celebration, the Shinto shrine, and ancient Hawaiian burial sites. In sum, my mother viewed religion through the eyes of the anthropologist;

it was a phenomenon to be treated with a suitable respect, but with a suitable detachment as well.

This spirit of hers guided me on the path I would ultimately take.[2]

Obama said in a 2007 speech:

"My mother, whose parents were nonpracticing Baptists and Methodists, was one of the most spiritual souls I ever knew," "But she had a healthy skepticism of religion as an institution. And as a consequence, so did I."[3]

Barack Obama's stepfather Lolo also contributed to the spiritual knowledge that he acquired:

"...Lolo followed a brand of Islam that could make room for the remnants of more ancient animist and Hindu faiths. He explained that a man took on the powers of whatever he ate: One day soon, he promised, he would bring home a piece of tiger meat for us to share."[4]

"...Lolo appeared not to hear me. Instead he touched my arm and motioned ahead of us. "Look," he said, pointing upward. There, standing astride the road, was a towering giant at least ten stories tall, with the body of a man and the face of an ape. "That's Hanuman," Lolo said as we circled the statue, "the monkey god." I turned around in my seat, mesmerized by the solitary figure..."He's a great warrior," Lolo said firmly. "Strong as a hundred men. When he fights the demons, he's never defeated."[5]

Barack Obama's personal spiritual philosophies and accompanying actions are quite different than the glib answer he gives when he says, "I'm a Christian." His broad view of taking bits and pieces of many religions, doesn't ring true for those with a true professing belief in Christianity, since this requires you to believe in one way only, through Jesus Christ.

The New York Post recently reported:

Obama, campaigning in New Mexico, revealed to a group of voters in a cafe the pocket full of charms that he carries with him.

Obama has also carried a small gold statue of the Monkey King, revered in India because Hindus believe monkeys are descendants of the monkey god, Hanuman.

BARACK REVEALING HIS POCKET OF CHARMS

PHOTO COURTESY TRADITIONALVALUES.ORG

WorldNet Daily posted an article regarding a special presentation:

A group of Hindus in India have presented Sen. Barack Obama's campaign with a two-foot Hindu monkey-god idol after hearing the candidate carries a smaller version of the Lord Hanuman good-luck charm with him as he vies for the presidency.

Earlier this week, according to reports in India, Obama representative Carolyn Sauvage-Mar accepted the gold-plated statue, promising to pass it on to the candidate after is it sanctified through ritual Hindu prayers.

"The idol is being presented to Obama as he is reported to be a Lord Hanuman devotee and carries with him a locket of the monkey god along with other good luck charms," reported the Times of India.

An hour-long prayer meeting to sanctify the idol was conducted by Congress party leader Brijmohan Bhama and temple priests.

"Obama has deep faith in Lord Hanuman, and that is why we are presenting an idol of Hanuman to him," said Bhama.[7]

This might explain Oprah's fascination and adoration of Obama; he has no problem with her New Age guru, Eckhart Tolle. An article on HumanEvents. com examined this connection:

Barack Obama's connections to Oprah Winfrey and her New Age guru, Eckhart Tolle, are the least examined, yet most revealing, and by far the most potentially ruinous of the senator's controversial associations. Obama claims to be a "committed Christian," yet appears to support Oprah in the worldwide dissemination of Tolle's and her virulent anti-Christian doctrine.

Oprah sees Barack Obama as having "awakened" and "evolved" as well.

Oprah called Obama "an evolved leader who can bring evolved leadership to our country." This suggests that Oprah, who describes her relationship with Obama as "very, very personal," knows the senator to be one who subscribes to the Oprah/Tolle doctrine.

At a UCLA rally, Oprah said, "I'm just following my own truth, and that truth has led to Barack Obama." Oprah's "own truth" is the anti-Christian Oprah/Tolle doctrine. Is the real Obama the Obama Oprah knows?[8]

There are more than a few of those candid moments where you find Barack tells you exactly what his brand of Christianity is all about in his own words.

He admits in his book, *Dreams of My Father*, that he was prompted to attend church and become part of this religious scene, to further his community organizing initiative, he was told:

> **"With the unions in the shape they're in, the churches are the only game in town."**[9]

> **"It might help your mission if you had a church home, though. It doesn't matter where really."**[10]

Other documented comments by Obama include:

> **"...there were many churches, many faiths....we all clung to our own foolish magic."**[11]

> **"The right wing, the Christian right, has done a good job of building these organizations of accountability, much better than the left or progressive forces have. But it's always easier to organize around intolerance, narrow-mindedness, and false nostalgia. And they also have**

hijacked the higher moral ground with this language of family values and moral responsibility."[12]

In this speech, now made into a TV ad, Obama mocks the Bible:

> "...even if we did have only Christians in our midst, if we expelled every non-Christian from the United States of America, whose Christianity would we teach in the schools? Would we go with James Dobson's, or Al Sharpton's? Which passages of Scripture should guide our public policy? Should we go with Leviticus, which suggests slavery is ok and that eating shellfish is abomination? How about Deuteronomy, which suggests stoning your child if he strays from the faith? Or should we just stick to the Sermon on the Mount - a passage that is so radical that it's doubtful that our own Defense Department would survive its application? So before we get carried away, let's read our Bibles. Folks haven't been reading their Bibles."[13]

On their website, the Christian Anti-Defamation Commission analyzed an interview Obama gave regarding his Christian views. A portion of that interview and analysis is included below:

> Cathleen Falsani, the author of *The God Factor: Inside the Spiritual Lives of Public People*, interviewed Barack Obama about his faith March 27, 2004, a few days after he clinched the Democratic nomination for the U.S. Senate seat that he eventually won.

> What emerges is a man who is not comfortable discussing spiritual matters, and is a spiritually confused theological eclectic. He is clearly not a Christian by any biblical, historic measure. He repeatedly affirms then denies Christ, says he believes but is filled with doubt.

> Obama's faith reflects the Universalistic beliefs of his grandparents. The fact that he felt comfortable in Trinity United

Church of Christ, one of the most radical churches in one
of the most liberal denominations, is entirely understandable.

When Falsani asks, "What do you believe?" Obama effectively calls
himself a Buddhist, agnostic, Muslim, Jewish, Christian. If you read
the whole interview you will see a person who seems to be trying very
hard to not take a stand on the Christian faith, yet at the same time tries
to identify as a Christian.

OBAMA: I believe that there are many paths to the same place,
and that is a belief that there is a higher power, a belief that we are
connected as a people. That there are values that transcend race or
culture, that move us forward, and there's an obligation for all of
us individually as well as collectively to take responsibility to make
those values lived.

OBAMA: So I don't think as a child we were, or I had a structured religious education. But my mother was deeply spiritual person, and would spend a lot of time talking about values and give me books about the world's religions, and talk to me about them. And I think always, her view always was that underlying these religions were a common set of beliefs about how you treat other people and how you aspire to act, not just for yourself but also for the greater good.

GG (Falsani): So you got yourself born again?

OBAMA: Yeah, although I don't, I retain from my childhood and my experiences growing up a suspicion of dogma. And I'm not somebody who is always comfortable with language that implies I've got a monopoly on the truth, or that my faith is automatically transferable to others.

I'm a big believer in tolerance. I think that religion at it's best comes with a big dose of doubt. I'm suspicious of too much certainty in the pursuit of understanding just because I think people are limited in their understanding.

I think that, particularly as somebody who's now in the public realm and is a student of what brings people together and what drives them apart, there's an enormous amount of damage done around the world in the name of religion and certainty.

When I'm talking to a group and I'm saying something truthful, I can feel a power that comes out of those statements that is different than when I'm just being glib or clever.

Not to try to intellectualize it but what I see is there are moments that happen within a sermon where the minister gets out of his ego and is speaking from a deeper source. And it's powerful.

There are also times when you can see the ego getting in the way. Where the minister is performing and clearly straining for applause or an Amen. And those are distinct moments. I think those former moments are sacred.

GG (Falsani): Who's Jesus to you?
(He laughs nervously)

OBAMA: Right. Jesus is an historical figure for me, and he's also a bridge between God and man, in the Christian faith, and one that I think is powerful precisely because he serves as that means of us reaching something higher. And he's also a wonderful teacher. I think it's important for all of us, of whatever faith, to have teachers in the flesh and also teachers in history.

GG (Falsani): Do you have people in your life that you look to for guidance?

OBAMA: Well, my pastor is certainly someone who I have an enormous amount of respect for. I have a number of friends who are ministers. Reverend Meeks is a close friend and colleague of mine in the state Senate. Father Michael Pfleger is a dear friend, and somebody I interact with closely.

There's the belief, certainly in some quarters, that people haven't embraced Jesus Christ as their personal savior that they're going to hell.

GG (Falsani): You don't believe that?

OBAMA: I find it hard to believe that my God would consign four-fifths of the world to hell. I can't imagine that my God would allow some little Hindu kid in India who never interacts with the Christian faith to somehow burn for all eternity. That's just not part of my religious makeup.

The more specific and detailed you are on issues as personal and fundamental as your faith, the more potentially dangerous it is.

GG (Falsani): Do you get questions about your faith?

OBAMA: Obviously as an African American politician rooted in the African American community, I spend a lot of time in the black church. I have no qualms in those settings in participating fully in those services and celebrating my God in that wonderful community that is the black church.

If all it took was someone proclaiming I believe Jesus Christ and that he died for my sins, and that was all there was to it, people wouldn't have to keep coming to church, would they.

GG (Falsani): Do you believe in heaven?

OBAMA: Do I believe in the harps and clouds and wings?

GG (Falsani): A place spiritually you go to after you die?

OBAMA: What I believe in is that if I live my life as well as I can, that I will be rewarded. I don't presume to have knowledge of what happens after I die. But I feel very strongly that whether the reward is in the here and now or in the hereafter, the aligning myself to my faith and my values is a good thing.

GG (Falsani): Do you believe in sin?

OBAMA: Yes.

GG (Falsani): What is sin?

OBAMA: Being out of alignment with my values.

GG (Falsani): What happens if you have sin in your life?

OBAMA: I think it's the same thing as the question about heaven. In the same way that if I'm true to myself and my faith that that is its own reward, when I'm not true to it, it's its own punishment.

GG (Falsani): Is there something that you go back to as a touchstone, a book, a particular piece of music, a place ...

OBAMA: As I said before, in my own sort of mental library, the Civil Rights movement has a powerful hold on me. It's a point in time where I think heaven and earth meet. Because it's a moment in which a collective faith transforms everything. So when I read Gandhi or I read King or I read certain passages of Abraham Lincoln and I think about those times where people's values are tested, I think those inspire me.

GG (Falsani): An example of a role model, who combined everything you said you want to do in your life, and your faith?

OBAMA: I think Gandhi is a great example of a profoundly spiritual man who acted and risked everything on behalf of those values but never slipped into intolerance or dogma. He seemed to always maintain an air of doubt about him. I think Dr. King, and Lincoln. Those three are good examples for me of people who applied their faith to a larger canvas without allowing that faith to metastasize into something that is hurtful.[14]

PHOTO COURTESY TELEGRAPH.CO.UK

For out of the heart proceed evil thoughts…false witness…
These are the things which defile a man..
Matthew 15:19

Barack Obama, in his own words...

"I believe that there are many paths to the same place,
and that is a belief that there is a higher power." [15]

"I think that religion at it's best comes with a big dose of
doubt."[16]

"Jesus is an historical figure for me..."[17]

"I find it hard to believe that my God would consign
four-fifths of the world to hell."[18]

"If all it took was someone proclaiming I believe Jesus
Christ and that he died for my sins, and that was all
there was to it, people wouldn't have to keep coming to
church, would they."[19]

"I don't presume to have knowledge of what happens
after I die."[20]

If we say that we have fellowship with him, and walk in darkness,
we lie, and do not the truth.

John 1:6

He that saith, I know him, and keepeth not his commandments, is
a liar, and the truth is not in him.

1 John 2:4

Behold, ye trust in lying words, that cannot profit. Will ye…
swear falsely…and walk after other gods…?

Jeremiah 7:8-9

And they bend their tongues like their bow for lies: but they are
not valiant for the truth upon the earth; for they proceed from
evil to evil, and they know not me, saith the LORD.

Jeremiah 9:3

"…thou hast tried them which say they are apostles, and are
not, and hast found them liars.."

Revelation 2:2

PART IV
ADORATION OF THE MASSES

For there are many unruly and vain talkers and deceivers...
Whose mouths must be stopped...
teaching things which they ought not,
for filthy lucre's sake.
...but even their mind and conscience is defiled.

Titus 1:10,11,15

CAMPAIGNING WITH THE STARS

The celebrities have really outdone themselves this time.

Every day you can open your newspaper and find a new endorsement.

What would we do without this wisdom? Actually, there are few of their lives that we would want to emulate in any way.

In fact, their endorsement should make us want to run, not walk, in the opposite direction. It does tell you something about the man, when he is so heartily endorsed by scores of famous faces.

The television show "The View" is one of those that tries to pretend that they are fair and balanced, with opposing views, liberal and conservative, but their ratio is 4-1, respectively. They routinely dismiss anything that Elizabeth Hasselbeck has to say with Barbara Walters playing the "smear" card. Anything that is genuinely questionable in Barack Obama's past, Barbara will dismiss it in the following manner:

1. The question has been answered, it's in the past, drop it.
2. Whine about the negativity and nasty turn that the campaign has taken.
3. Admonish Elizabeth to concentrate on the issues, saying that the American people have more to worry about (issues) than the same old rumors and lies.

It is unfortunate that Barbara Walters and the rest of the general media like to tell us that we are not concerned with these questions, but the "issues" are more important. Character no longer counts, according to them.

Barack Obama's most well-known celebrity backer, is of course, Ms. Oprah Winfrey. For the first time, since she has been a celebrity, she has come out in favor of a candidate. But it is actually more like "gushing" over a candidate. She raised over $3 million for his campaign, was quoted as saying she "cried her eyelashes off" at his Democratic acceptance speech and although Barack Obama has been on her show twice, she has denied any airtime to the opposing party.

It was recently reported that she might be in the running for a position in his administration. The Herald Sun says:

> Oprah Winfrey is being talked about as a possible U.S. ambassador to Great Britain in a Barack Obama administration.

> The scenario was suggested yesterday in an item in the London Times that quoted "well-placed sources" as saying her name had been "floated" for the job, considered the top rung of all U.S. ambassadorships.

The appointment would be seen as a reward for Winfrey's endorsement of Senator Obama's run for president. She made that official last December, the first time she had publicly backed a candidate.

Senator Obama is reportedly considering appointing a high-profile policy cabinet to steer America through troubled times.[1]

How comforting. Barack Obama will appoint a **high profile** cabinet. With Ms. Winfrey, it has recently come to light that she has long been dabbling in New Age doctrine and is now bringing it to her audience in full force. A flurry of news articles have reported on her recent ratings decline and drop in magazine sales.

A few other celebrity endorsements:

> **Woody Allen:**...says it will be no laughing matter if Barack Obama fails to win the race for the White House.
>
> "It would be a disgrace and a humiliation if Barack Obama does not win...It would be a very, very terrible thing for the United States in many, many ways."[2]
>
> **George Clooney:** A self-proclaimed "Obama guy" Clooney says the senator has the "aura of a rock star."[3]

Rev. Al Sharpton, Gayle King, Cicely Tyson, Lou Gossett Jr., Alfrie Woodard, Blair Underwood and many more gathered for a unity breakfast organized by Barack Obama's campaign. As reported by ABC.com:

> Firing up a crowd of about 500 black Democratic delegates, celebrities and faith leaders, the Rev. Joseph Lowery, president of the Coalition for the People's Agenda, said Obama doesn't have to be a civil rights leader between now and November.

"He can go ahead and be president and leave the agitating to us," he said to cheers and whoops of "That's right!"

"The most important thing he can do for the nation is get elected," Lowery said.

Bernice King also brought the crowd to its feet, arguing that, despite Obama's historic accomplishment, her father's work is far from done.

"He declared that he may not get there with us," she said, "and we are on our way to the promised land, but we are not there yet and our next step is unity."

"Let us be satisfied when our young men are going to college not going to jail," she said to loud cheers and applause. "The movement is not there, let's continue the movement!"

Not to be outdone, Sharpton brought the crowd again to their feet with a verbal slap against President George W. Bush.

"The media keeps talking about passing the baton," he said of news coverage about former President Bill Clinton's solid endorsement last night of Obama. "The only baton that we're going to pass is from George Bush to Barack Obama."

Sharpton said civil rights leaders will go in November to "states that seem to have difficulty counting votes."

"We're going to make sure that the names of African American voters don't mysteriously disappear," he said, "Not this time! We will not be divided. Not this time!"

"To have it occur on the 45th anniversary of the march on Washington -- that it was destined to be. It could have never been anyone else," Tyson said.

"My old friend Jane Pittman used to say that when a child is born, folks look into its face and ask, 'Are you the one? Are you the one?' Well, he is definitely the one," she said.

According to the Culture and Media Institute:

Just a few weeks ago, the rapper calling himself Ludacris lauded Obama and slashed Bush and McCain in a YouTube video entitled "Obama's Here." In the lyrics, Ludacris called himself Obama's favorite rapper, noting the candidate said (to Rolling Stone magazine) that he listens to Ludacris on his iPod.

First, Ludacris offended all the Hillary-adoring feminists.... Then came the Republican-bashing: "Paint the White House black and I'm sure that's got 'em terrified, McCain don't belong in any chair unless he's paralyzed." McCain deserves a wheelchair, and Bush is a moron: "Yeah I said it cause Bush is mentally handicapped, ball up all of his speeches and just throw 'em like candy wrap."

It says something about our screwed-up culture that the President of the United States, a man with an MBA from Harvard Business School, is mocked as a special-needs student by a guy with no college degree who misspells his album titles ("Word of Mouf") to look hip.

Obama spokesman Bill Burton expressed great shock and outrage: "As Barack Obama has said many, many times in the past, rap lyrics today too often perpetuate misogyny, materialism and degrading images that he doesn't want his daughters or any children exposed to....it is offensive to all of us who are trying to raise our children with the values we hold dear."

Really? When he spoke to Rolling Stone, Obama lauded Ludacris as one of several "great talents and great businessmen" and hailed "the genius of the art form." He said he was "troubled sometimes by the misogyny and materialism" in rap lyrics and added "It would be nice if I could have my daughters listen to their music without me worrying they were getting bad images of themselves." He didn't even claim his little girls didn't listen to it.[5]

"We're here to evolve to a higher plane ...
he is an evolved leader ...
[he] has an ear for eloquence and
a Tongue dipped in the Unvarnished Truth."

Oprah Winfrey[6]

PHOTO COURTESY GOTHAMIST.COM

This I say therefore, and testify in the Lord, that ye henceforth walk not as other Gentiles walk, in the vanity of their mind,

Having the understanding darkened, being alienated from the life of God through the ignorance that is in them, because of the blindness of their heart:

Ephesians 4:17-18

"I speak to you not as a candidate for President, but as a… fellow citizen of the world.......with resolve in our hearts, let us ...answer our destiny, and remake the world once again."
Barack Obama[1]

KING OF THE WORLD

It would appear that Barack Obama has an even more ambitious plan than mere President of the United States.

As reported on Politico:

> Addressing more than 200,000 elated Europeans massed in Berlin at twilight, presumptive Democratic nominee Barack Obama promised Thursday that he would work to unite Christians, Muslims and Jews in a safer, more united world.
>
> His 27-minute speech at the gold-topped Victory Column was interrupted by applause at least 30 times, with occasional audience chants of "O-ba-MA!"
>
> Billed as a speech about Transatlantic relations, it turned out to be a manifesto for the planet, with an appeal to "the burdens of global citizenship."[2]

In an article regarding the Global Poverty Act, NewsWithViews.com says:

"Clearly, Obama's bill has been introduced to assure the United States falls in line with the Millennium Declaration and all that it stands for. After all, the UN needs the money to pay for its new found power. Truth, science and American taxpayer interests be hanged. Barack Obama wants to be a "world" leader."[3]

ENDORSEMENTS FROM AROUND THE GLOBE

Barack Obama has made a series of strategic moves that have been observed in all parts of the world.

The Times of India reports:

Obama, because of his eclectic and unusual upbringing, may be different: He's the only American leader who has been heard to pronounce Gandhi and Pakistan correctly — just like it's pronounced in the subcontinent (Gaan-dhi, not Gain-dee; Paak-isthaan, not Pack-is-tan). In other conversations, Obama has also referred to Indian success in technology fields, and drawn comparisons between his father (who came to the US "without money, but with a student visa and a determination to succeed") and the experiences of Indian immigrants.

Such empathy and "connection" to immigrants from the subcontinent is only one part of Obama's plural multi-ethnic background and wide-ranging eclectic education (American, African, even part-Asian) that makes him arguably the most unusual and exciting presidential candidate in US history — more universalist than American.[4]

OnTheIssues.org says:

> Greeted as hero on visit to ancestral Kenya...Rapturous crowds of Kenyans wearing T-shirts emblazoned with his name and likeness chanted "Come to us, Obama!" as he visited a memorial at the site of the US embassy bombing in Nairobi."

> Obama and his family flew to Kisumu where 1000s lined the route, many climbing trees for a better view of the motorcade carrying the American that the local Luo tribespeople loudly claimed as their own.[5]

> Obama was quoted as saying, "Even though I had grown up on the other side of the world, I felt the spirit among the people who told me that I belonged."[6]

According to the The Guardian Newspaper Online - UK:

> Obama has stirred an excitement around the globe unmatched by any American politician in living memory. Polling in Germany, France, Britain and Russia shows that Obama would win by whopping majorities, with the pattern repeated in Africa, Asia, the Middle East and Latin America. If November 4 were a global ballot, Obama would win it handsomely. If the free world could choose its leader, it would be Barack Obama.[7]

Barack Obama: More Popular
Than Jesus, Angelina Jolie
Gawker.com[1]

THE MEDIA'S PET

According to WorldNet Daily, this is the "Year The Media Died."[2]

The mask is off. The pretense over.

After decades of pretending they're not biased leftward – even though everyone else knew it – America's "mainstream media" have finally, during 2008, dropped the façade of fairness and impartiality.

"It doesn't matter how dangerous the reality of Obama is – a hardcore leftist whose intended tax-and-spend policies would, experts say, plunge American into a full-bore depression," said WND Managing Editor and best-selling author David Kupelian. "It doesn't matter how surreal and creepy his campaign gets – enlisting sheriffs and prosecutors to intimidate voters, exploiting children into singing 'Obama's gonna lead us' songs stunningly reminiscent of Chinese Maoist indoctrination. The mainstream press ignores it all, because, very simply, they just really want Obama to be president."[3]

NewsBusters.org reports:

> "...the media is especially compliant where it concerns the Obama campaign's graphic designs, displays that can be so easily compared to religious iconography or even old style communist propaganda. The overblown, obscenely reverential posters featuring Obama's upturned face in Jesus-like poses have gone uncommented upon by what should be a hard-nosed, doubtful media. These over-the-top graphic images in the form of posters and campaign literature design are amazing for their obvious propagandistic style, yet the media seem not to find any reason to be off put by the absurdity of these graphics. Nor have they noticed the campaign art's similarity to communist imagery. One can't help but wonder why this blatant re-use of the graphic style used by Stalin, Hitler and Mao has raised not the slightest question in the minds of the American media?[4]

In an additional NewsBusters.org article:

> "The American press has traditionally been even harder on our politicians and government than even the average American. Since the first days of our country, the press has savaged, doubted, dug up dirt and attacked our politicians, seeming to never believe a word the polls say. From George Washington to George Bush, the press has been at odds with politicians. Yet, for some unexplainable reason, the pretentiousness and presumption of Barack Obama is being allowed to pass uncommented upon. The media especially is allowing him to make all sorts of claims that they should never allow anyone else to get away with. They are unquestioning with his claim to be the candidate of "change" and the candidate that will "reach across the aisle." Neither claim can be substantiated by the man's career thus

far. He does not reach across the aisle and he is responsible for no great program of change. A properly skeptical press would ask for the proof of Obmam's claims, but they merely smile and allow him to ramble on as if what he is saying is unassailable."

"...the media has also made of Obama a sort of religious icon... Reuters, the Associated Press, and various other news services, news papers and media outlets have joined in to portray Obama in all sorts of images that recall religious iconography. Some images seem to show Obama with a halo. Or preaching from the pulpit... surrounded by worshippers seeking his touch as if he were a faith healer...Juxtaposed with religious symbols...Or in otherwise ethereal poses. One has to wonder why an otherwise hard bitten, cynical media establishment is allowing itself to be so used in this way? The obvious answer, of course, is that the media is not an observer, not a "reporter" or commentator on American politics. The media is an active participant and they have chosen sides. They have joined the Barack Obama team and are more than happy to put their normal cynicism aside to help Barack Obama to achieve elevation from a junior Senator with little experience with nothing to sell to president of the United States of America."[5]

"I myself was to experience how easily one is taken
in by a lying and censored press and radio in a
totalitarian state ...Nazi sources, a steady diet
over the years of falsifications and distortions
made a certain impression on one's
mind and often misled it."
William Shirer
The Rise and Fall of the Third Reich

He ventured forth to bring light to the world

The anointed one's pilgrimage to the

Holy Land is a miracle in action -

and a blessing to all his faithful followers...

suddenly, with the men appeared the archangel

Gabriel and the whole host of the heavenly choir,

ranks of cherubim and seraphim,

all praising God and singing: "Yes, We Can."

The Times Online[1]

THE "ANOINTED' ONE

An article in the San Francisco Chronicle asks... is Obama an enlightened being? They discuss the possibility:

"Barack Obama isn't really one of us. Not in the normal way, anyway.... ...all right, you want to know what it is? The appeal, the pull, the ethereal and magical thing that seems to enthrall millions of people from all over the world, that keeps opening up and firing into new channels of the culture normally completely unaffected by politics?"

"No, it's not merely his youthful vigor, or handsomeness, or even inspiring rhetoric. It is not fresh ideas or cool charisma or the fact that a black president will be historic and revolutionary in about a thousand different ways. It is something more. Even Bill Clinton, with all his effortless, winking charm, didn't have what Obama has, which is a sort of powerful luminosity, a unique high-vibration integrity. "

"Dismiss it all you like, but I've heard from far too many enormously smart, wise, spiritually attuned people who've been intuitively blown away by Obama's presence - not speeches, not policies, but sheer presence..."

"Many spiritually advanced people I know (not coweringly religious, mind you, but deeply spiritual) identify Obama as a Lightworker, that rare kind of attuned being who has the ability to lead us not merely to new foreign policies or health care plans or whatnot, but who can actually help usher in a new way of being on the planet, of relating and connecting and engaging with this bizarre earthly experiment. These kinds of people actually help us evolve. They are philosophers and peacemakers of a very high order, and they speak not just to reason or emotion, but to the soul."[2]

There have been more than a few observations of Obama's unusual presence and the effect it has on mere mortals.

According to WorldNet Daily, Louis Farrakhan certainly waxes poetic about Mr. Obama's possibilities. Addressing a large crowd behind a podium Feb. 24 with a Nation of Islam Saviour's Day 2008 sign, Farrakhan proclaims:

"You are the instruments that God is going to use to bring about universal change, and that is why Barack has captured the youth. And he has involved young people in a political process that they didn't care anything about. That's a sign.

When the Messiah speaks, the youth will hear, and the Messiah is absolutely speaking."

"**Brothers and sisters,**" Farrakhan said, "**Barack Obama to me, is a herald of the Messiah. Barack Obama is like the trumpet that alerts you something new, something better is on the way.**"

Farrakhan points out that the man Nation of Islam followers refer to as "the Savior," Fard Muhammad, had a black father and a white mother, just as Obama did.

"**A black man with a white mother became a savior to us,**" he said. "**A black man with a white mother could turn out to be one who can lift America from her fall.**

"**Would God allow Barack to be president of a country that has been so racist, so evil in its treatment of Hispanics, native Americans, blacks?**" he asked. "**Would God do something like that? Yeah. Of course he would. That's to show you that the stone that the builders rejected has become the headstone of the corner. This is a sign to you. It's the time of our rise. It's the time that we should take our place. The future is all about you.**"

Farrakhan suggested he would keep a low profile in the campaign, despite his enthusiasm for Obama.

"**That's why you have never heard me make any comment,**" he explained. "**I love that brother, and I want to see that brother successful. I don't want to say anything that would hurt that brother, and I don't want them to use me or the Nation of Islam.**"

He went on to point out that when religious scholars talk about Christ or the Islamic Mahdi, they never talk in racial terms – again, pointing to Obama's mixed racial background.[3]

> Is Barack the one we have been waiting for? Or is it the other way around? Are we the people we have been waiting for? Barack Obama is giving voice and space to an awakening beyond his wildest expectations, a social force that may lead him far beyond his modest policy agenda.
>
> *Tom Hayden[4]*

National Review Online says:

Whether it's Billy Ayers or Bernadine Dohrn, Tom Hayden or Jane Fonda, or any of the other lesser-knowns, 60's Marxist radicals are lining up behind Obama.

Obama's young worshippers think they see something altogether new, a unique persona, seemingly magically transported to this moment in history to help them finally be the ones to net the elusive butterfly of socialism's never-realized promise.

Obama's followers make high-tech videos, mindlessly chanting, "Yes, we can" instead of making bombs to blow up government buildings, or holding up armored trucks and killing police officers.

This new generation seems to have the opportunity to do now with mere votes what their predecessors tried and failed to do through violence. We can finally seal the deal on the real revolution — democratically. Obama, the Closer, is at hand.

He is the One they've been waiting for. Biding their time during the dark, dreary days of Reagan, throughout the self-absorbed Boomer years, into the Yuppie sellout decade, and on through the compromising Clinton years, they've waited and planned and hoped.[5]

All right, already: so Barack Obama is not just some far-left putz from Chicago, but something more than human, a being on a higher plane. Not just some dork who thinks there are 57 states in the Union, but a Lightworker.

But which higher being is he? An archangel? A genie? Zeus? Hercules? The Mothman? It's important to know these things.

The evidence is overwhelming: Barack Obama is Maitreya.

"Who is Maitreya? He has been expected for generations by all of the major religions... Although the names are different, many believe that they all refer to the same individual: the World Teacher, whose personal name is Maitreya... Preferring to be known simply as the Teacher, Maitreya has not come as a religious leader, or to found a new religion, but as a teacher and guide for people of every religion and those of no religion. If Obama is not Maitreya, then he and Maitreya have the same speechwriters. But there's no way Obama intuitively flabbergasts all those spiritually attuned people in San Francisco without being the World Teacher.

At this point we ought to be asking ourselves, Why even hold the election? I mean, this guy is Maitreya, man! Aside from the undeniable fact that anyone who votes against him has got to be a racist, and so shouldn't be allowed to vote at all, it's, like, karma that Barack Obama be the president. We need the World Teacher in the White House!

"Under Maitreya's inspiration, humanity itself will make the required changes and create a saner and more just world for all"--it says so on the Internet. For "Maitreya" read "Obama."

And this fallen world deserves him.

Lee Duigon, Christian Freelance Writer[6]

"We just like to say his name.
We are considering taking it as a mantra."
Chicago Sun-Times[7]

"Does it not feel as if some special hand is guiding Obama on his journey, I mean, as he has said, the utter improbability of it all?"
Daily Kos[8]

"He communicates God-like energy..."
Steve Davis (Charleston, SC)[9]

"Not just an ordinary human being
but indeed an Advanced Soul"
Commentator @ Chicago Sun Times[10]

"He is not operating on the same plane as ordinary politicians....the agent of transformation in an age of revolution, as a figure uniquely qualified to open the door to the 21st century."
Gary Hart[11]

"This is bigger than Kennedy....This is the New Testament...I felt this thrill going up my leg. I mean, I don't have that too often. No, seriously. It's a dramatic event."
Chris Matthews[12]

"[Obama is] creative imagination which coupled with brilliance equals wisdom … [He is] the man for this time."

Toni Morrison[13]

"Obama has the capacity to summon heroic forces from the spiritual depths of ordinary citizens and to unleash therefrom a symphonic chorus of unique creative acts whose common purpose is to tame the soul and alleviate the great challenges facing mankind."

Gerald Campbell[14]

From the website ManifestObama.com:

Between now and November 4...
Let's spend one minute a day...
Envisioning Barack Obama...
As our President...
Prepare your heart to fill with hope...
Prepare your mind to embrace the change...
Envision Barack victorious on election night...
...Taking the oath of office...
On Inauguration Day...
Believe that this great moment in American history is already
a reality...
Say the words to yourself...
To your family...
To your friends and neighbors...
Say it to the world...
Your vision is a sacred trust...
You are a sanctuary of a sacred vision for a renewed
America...
Envision it...
Say it...
Feel it...
Believe it...
Make it our reality...
Manifest Obama, America![15]

For such [are] false apostles, deceitful workers, transforming themselves into the apostles of Christ. And no marvel; for Satan himself is transformed into an angel of light.

2 Corinthians 11:13-14

PART V

ON THE HORIZON

"The powers of human skill will be in the hands of the devil ..... Satan may attempt to seduce us in little things, and so to move the Church ... little by little from her true position ...It is his policy ...to divide us, to dislodge us gradually from off our rock of strength. And if there is to be a bloody persecution, perhaps it will be then; ...when ... all parts of Christendom are so full of schism, so close upon heresy. When we have cast ourselves upon the world and depend for protection upon it, and have given up our independence and our strength to World Government, then he may bust upon us in fury ... using Antichrist and barbarous nations."

John Henry Newman
English prelate and theologian
In Tract Eighty-Five (1838)[1]

"The United Nations is the greatest fraud
in all History. Its purpose is to destroy the United States."
Representative John E. Rankin (1945)[2]

THE COMING
NEW WORLD ORDER

There is little doubt that Barack Obama's vision includes more of than just our piece of the pie. An article in the Sioux City Journal says:

Barack Obama's secret dangers include: His infatuation with the U.N. He believes the U.N. is the solution to all the world's problems and our sovereignty must be subjected to their control, then the world would become a heaven...

His defense of the Treaty of the Seas. The treaty would grant the U.N. absolute control of 70 percent of the earth's surface located under the oceans. They would control and regulate all activity on, in and below the water's surface..

The United Nations has more than a few troubling ideas, some of the most dangerous include:

Pubic Distribution Land:

"Land . . . cannot be treated as an ordinary asset, controlled by individuals and subject to the pressures and inefficiencies of the market. Private land ownership is also a principal instrument of accumulation and concentration of wealth and therefore contributes to social injustice; Public control of land use is therefore indispensable. . . ."

Agenda Item 10 of the Conference Report for the United Nations Conference on Human Settlements (1976)[4]

Selective Population Reduction:

"The United Nation's goal is to reduce population selectively by encouraging abortion, forced sterilization, and control human reproduction, and regards two-thirds of the human population as excess baggage, with 350,000 people to be eliminated per day…. It's terrible to have to say this. World Population must be stabilized and to do that we have to eliminate 350,000 people per day. In one year that would equal 128 million people."

Jacques-Yves Cousteau
French oceanographer
Filmmaker and Environmentalist (1991)[5]

Children's rights:

"Every child is our child."
Chilling motto of the United Nations
Children's Fund, UNICEF (1946)

Article 2: Parents are not to punish their child in any way for actions or words contrary to their beliefs or standards.

Article 6: The government is to have the final say in everything concerning the child.

Article 13: Parents are not to place any restrictions on what a child sees, hears, or is taught, or experiences in any way.

Article 14: Parents may not determine medical treatment for their children, nor may they refuse State-mandated treatment.

Article 28: Parents may not educate their children at home.

Excerpts from the articles of the
"Charter of the Rights of The Child"
passed at the United Nations...following
the "World Summit on Children" (1990)[6]

DISARMAMENT:

"The first stage would significantly reduce the capabilities of nations to wage war by reducing the armed forced of the nations ... nuclear capabilities would be reduced by treaties ... and UN peace-keeping powers would be strengthened ..."

State Department document #7277; Freedom From War: The United States'
Program for General and Complete Disarmament in a Peaceful World (1961)

According to a report, Joe Biden recently made a speech entitled, "On the Threshold of the New World Order: A Rebirth for the United Nations," he said:

> "Collective security today must encompass not only the security of nations," he said, "but also mankind's security in a global environment that has proven vulnerable to debilitating changes wrought by man's own endeavors.

> "Thus, in setting an American agenda for a new world order, we must begin with a profound alteration in traditional thought," he said.

> He said the START treaty ratified by the Senate early in October limits Russia and the United States to possessing no more than 9,000 nuclear warheads each, but said "more dramatic progress" could be made to reduce the nuclear threat.

> "We should seek a steady, mutual draw-down to a ceiling of no more than 500 warheads (per side)," he said.

> Representatives of the United Nations should be used to monitor the dismantling of the weapons, he said. "We should cut the Gordian knot of difficult dismantlement by acting immediately to sequester all warheads to be eliminated," he suggested.

> Biden also advocated a global ban on the production of weapons-grade missile material and a comprehensive test ban treaty for all countries with nuclear capabilities. He said the

United States and other countries should commit military forces to exclusive use by the United Nations' Security Council, which would enforce nuclear agreements.[7]

"You just wait and see. The lily-livered bastards in Washington will demobilize. They'll say they've made the world safe for democracy again. The Russians are not such damned fools. They'll rebuild; and with modern weapons."

George S. Patton (1945)[8]

"When the existing governments and ruling theories of life, the decaying religious and the decaying political forms of today, have sufficiently lost prestige through failure and catastrophe, then and then only will world-wide reconstruction be possible ... Although world government had been plainly coming for some years, although it had been endlessly feared and murmured against, it found no opposition prepared anywhere."

H.G. Wells (1933)[9]

For the Lord himself shall descend from heaven with a shout,
with the voice of the archangel, and with the trump of God: and
the dead in Christ shall rise first: Then we which are alive and
remain shall be caught up together with them in the clouds, to
meet the Lord in the air: and so shall we ever be with the Lord."

1 Thessalonians 4:16-17

THE RETURN OF THE KING

The most anticipated event in world history is on the horizon. No man knows the day or hour, but all the signs point to our Lord's imminent return.

All who have accepted the Lord Jesus Christ are feeling the stirrings that are reminiscent of a child waiting for Christmas morning, but we know there is nothing that we could imagine, that will come close to what we will experience on that day.

The only reason we can actually have joy, in times of trouble, such as these... is in knowing that we will miss the worst part of this brewing storm.

Christ Jesus provides us the "peace that passeth all understanding." How true those word are....when others see us and marvel that we are not fretting about the up and down stock market, we have to explain it is not our doing, but rather a gift from God.

The time is now, to make sure that our hearts are right and that we've done everything possible to see that our loved ones are ready.

There are many who say that we can't and shouldn't try to predict His Second Coming, and to a degree they are correct. Even the angels don't know.

However; the Bible does give us clear signs to look for, there's even a crown waiting for those who watch and anticipate with longing.

The events are unfolding at an alarming pace, and according to the Bible once the process starts, the whole thing will unravel at a rapid pace.

So likewise ye, when ye shall see all these things, know that it is near, even at the doors.

Matthew 24:33

Watch therefore:

for ye know not what hour

your Lord doth come.

Matthew 24:42

"WHO IS A LIAR BUT HE

THAT DENIETH THAT

JESUS IS THE CHRIST?

HE IS ANTICHRIST,

THAT DENIETH THE

FATHER AND THE SON"

I John 2:22

Let no man deceive you by any means: for that day shall not come,
except there come a falling away first, and that man of sin be revealed,
the son of perdition;

II Thessalonians 2:3

THE BEAST

John Hagee, Pastor of Cornerstone Church in San Antonio, Texas
was interviewed recently on the Glenn Beck Show:

BECK: Pastor Hagee, here we go. Yes or no. You ready? Lightning
round.

HAGEE: I hope I`m ready.

BECK: Is the anti-Christ alive today?

HAGEE: I believe he is.[1]

An article by Tim Sexton reports:

"…. the one common element that binds the world's major
religions together is the expectation of the arrival of a holy
man. From the messiah still expected by the Jews to the second
coming of Jesus that has been predicted more often than the

the end of reality TV to Imam Mahdi of Islam and the arrival of Krishna awaited by the Hindus, the purpose of this holy man may differ, but the wait continues. But what if these various personages turned out to be the very same messenger?

A follower of Theosophy - a belief system based primarily upon Buddhist and Hindu teachings that also subscribes to the belief in an alien-based supernatural overseer of humanity-named Benjamin Creme has spent his life promoting the idea that this figure is, in fact, a single individual; a teacher whose appearance will guide the people of earth to the long sought world peace. He called this holiest of holy men Maitreya. Critics say that Benjamin Creme fashioned himself as a contemporary John the Baptist, essentially endowing himself with the role of announcing the arrival of Maitreya. Creme created Share International to spread the word of Maitreya.

Lest you think that Creme and Share International are dismissed as a bunch of kooks, you might be interested to know that the **United Nations** has officially recognized it as a non-governmental organization. Even more impressive is the list of people who have contributed articles to Share International Magazine: Kofi Annan, the Dalai Lama and even Prince Charles have been published within its pages.[2]

The Share International website says:

> Many now expect the return of their awaited Teacher, whether they call him the Christ, Messiah, the fifth Buddha, Krishna, or the Imam Mahdi. Millions now know that the Teacher who fulfills all these expectations is already living among us.

> Maitreya is not a religious leader, but an educator in the broadest sense.

He is here to inspire us to create a new era based on sharing and justice, so that all may have the basic necessities of life: food, shelter, health care, and education.

His open mission in the world is about to begin. As Maitreya himself has said: 'Soon, now very soon, you will see my face and hear my words.'

"The present chaotic conditions, especially in the economic and financial fields, have tipped the scales and made possible a decision on a period which men themselves would welcome as 'soon'. It will not be long, therefore, until the Great Lord begins His open mission, albeit undeclared. Watch and wait with a sure understanding of His priorities, and so miss Him not."

Among Maitreya's recommendations will be a shift in social priorities so that adequate...medical care become universal rights.

He will appear as in fact He is, in the self-created body in which He manifests now in the world.

His acceptance by countless millions in the world as a spiritual teacher and guide will make it easier for the most fanatical Israeli Jew or Palestinian Muslim to accept the necessity of living together side by side. This can only take place when justice is given to the Palestinians.

Maitreya is in the world, but once He emerges openly, every action that we take in the right direction – that is towards oneness, justice, freedom for all people – will invoke His help and energy. He will potentize our actions and the changes will proceed with enormous speed and order.

Maitreya's coming is about world change:...The true understanding that humanity is one will show the absolute necessity for this profound transformation. It is the making of a new world.

"What is the Plan?...the installation of a new world order government and new world religion under Maitreya."[3]

Going back to the Glenn Beck interview with John Hagee, discussing some of the signs that we are living in the last days:

HAGEE: ...Second Peter says, "There will come in the last days scoffers saying where's the sign of his coming, the coming of Christ?"

The very fact that there's skepticism, so much skepticism, saying you people are crazy, believing in this, is a literal sign that Christ is going to appear.

BECK: Everybody's looking for the antichrist. Everybody says, "OK, end of times, is this going to be it? Well, then who's the antichrist? Is he alive, et cetera, et cetera?"

I have been struck by President Ahmadinejad and how many times -- and we'll get into this later -- he refers to the promised one.

BECK: He's looking for the 12th imam to return.

HAGEE: He is indeed.

BECK: There is an army of the Mahdi. They -- one of the

things that made hair stand up on the back of my neck is when
I heard that the 12th Imam was going to come out of a well and
then he was going to go to ancient Babylon and conquer in ancient
Babylon and rule from the world in ancient Babylon.

HAGEE: . The Bible says that the antichrist is going to come as a
man of peace. It says he will destroy wondrously with peace. That
means he`s going to make peace treaties with lots of people but
never intend to keep it.

HAGEE: He promises peace, but he will, in fact, lead the world
into bloody war.

BECK: OK. He will be the vice regent leader of Muslims
worldwide. He will be the supreme political and religious leader
for all Muslims. However, he will also then go to unite the
Muslim world and the non-Muslim world and create one-world
government.

HAGEE: There is a -- there is a very strong teaching that the
antichrist will produce a one-world government.

BECK: This is what -- this is what President Ahmadinejad believes
of the Mahdi, the 12th imam returning, and this is also in the Bible
as the antichrist?

HAGEE: Absolutely.

BECK: He will conquer Israel for Islam and lead the faithful
Muslims in a final slaughter or battle against the Jews.

BECK: He will establish a new Islamic world headquarters from
Jerusalem.

HAGEE: He`s going to set up an eternal kingdom in Jerusalem.

BECK: He will appear riding a **white horse.**

HAGEE: ...The sixth chapter of Revelation, the first seal is the rider on the white horse. That is the antichrist. That`s exactly right. He does come on a white horse.

HAGEE: The Rapture of the Church happens where all of the people who believe in Jesus Christ are taken into heaven.

Then the next thing that happens immediately is the appearance of the antichrist. The appearance of the antichrist, he comes as a man of peace, as the prince of peace to the whole world.

Daniel says he will destroy wondrously with peace. That means he`s going to make peace treaties, never intending to keep them, but he has the world in a state of peace. He will create a one-world government. We see something of that going on in the United Nations. He will bring about a one-world currency.

BECK: He`ll do this all in seven years?

HAGEE: All in seven years. He`ll do it quicker than seven years. Every person will have to receive his mark in their right hand or forehead, without which they cannot buy nor sell. You cannot buy a loaf of bread...

BECK: How freaked out were you when you saw the chips now that we can implant that are RFID chips that will do that very

very thing? And they're even making them, I understand, to fuse with the body because they're afraid of theft.

HAGEE: Yes.

HAGEE: All of the technology is just in place. There will be you a one-world government, a one-world currency, a one-world religion. This lines up with what your researchers are talking about.

The Bible then says he will understand dark sentences, which means he will have a demonic anointing to know the unknown.

BECK: What really -- what really convinces people, though, is when he's killed and then rises again?

HAGEE: He's going to make a seven-year treaty with Israel and set up his image to be worshiped in Israel. And that is where I'm convinced that a Jewish person who understands who he is shoots him, because the Bible says he's wounded in the head and recovers wondrously, emulating the death and the resurrection of Jesus Christ.

HAGEE: At this point in time when he comes back to life he has the personality of a Hitler. He now pursues the Jewish people.

HAGEE: ...as he gets ready to pursue him, the Bible says that he, the antichrist, hears tidings from the east that disturb him. The tidings from the east is that there are -- the Chinese army is marching up the Euphrates River, 200 million of them, and they're moving toward the battle of Armageddon, because they want the oil that will make them a superpower.

BECK: Condoleezza Rice said something, I think it was last year or the year before. She said what we`re witnessing here in the Middle East are birth pangs, and that word stuck out to me. For one reason, it clearly means, if anybody who`s had children, birth pangs get stronger and closer together, and then there`s a nasty little event there at the end. In human life, it ends with something nice, but there is that extraordinary pain at the end. Does birth pangs play a role, the word "birth pangs" play a role in the Bible?

HAGEE: The birth pangs are in the scripture. And your analysis is absolutely accurate...Now, in this case, the child is the new era, or the new world order..[4]

Todd Strandberg has studied this subject in-depth and gives further clarification on this subject and what to expect:

The antichrist will ride across the pages of history on a white horse, a symbol of conquest. His sweet-sounding words of peace will not match his terrible acts of war. This fictitious christ will present himself as a lamb, but he will really be a wolf in sheep's clothing.

A crown is worn by people who earn or inherit the right to wear one, but the antichrist will not earn or inherit the right to wear his crown. It will be a gift from the wicked power brokers of the world. What a terrible mistake! The world's gullible politicians will empower a leader without doing the all-important background check. Some will think they are crowning a godly man, but they will be elevating a fake with a very dark side. The Bible says this fake will "ascend out of the bottomless pit."[5]

And now ye know what withholdeth that he might be revealed in his time.

For the mystery of iniquity doth already work: only he who now letteth will let, until he be taken out of the way.

And then shall that Wicked be revealed, whom the Lord shall consume with the spirit of his mouth, and shall destroy with the brightness of his coming:

Even him, whose coming is after the working of Satan with all power and signs and lying wonders,

And with all deceivableness of unrighteousness in them that perish; because they received not the love of the truth, that they might be saved.

And for this cause God shall send them strong delusion, that they should believe a lie:

That they all might be damned who believed not the truth, but had pleasure in unrighteousness.

2 Thessalonians 2: 6-12

PART VI
CHOOSE THIS DAY

Who

will rise up for me
against the evildoers?

Who

will stand up for me

against the

workers of iniquity?

PSALM 94:16

"The true danger is when liberty is nibbled away, for expedients, and by parts ... the only thing necessary for evil to triumph is for good men to do nothing ... Nobody made a greater mistake than he who did nothing because he could only do a little ... The people never give up their liberties but under some delusion"
Edmund Burke (1729–97)[1]

SLOW FADE

Michael Bresciani writes:

More than at any time in history the emphasis on the gospel message is now prophetic in nature. Although the love of Christ can never be eliminated from the message the warning and call to repentance becomes the main thrust of the message as the judgment and the second coming of Christ approaches. Those emphasizing this hard aspect of the gospel will not be well received and fewer people will respond; but that too is prophetic.

The meteoric rise of an inexperienced Senator from Illinois who represents the opposite of everything the founders of this country first brought forth is sad but it is prophecy fully underway.

America should take warning from the well used adage "take heed what you ask for because you just might get it."[2]

Where are our pastors in this fight? Many churches have been taken over by men who refuse to preach the full gospel.

Is it too old-fashioned to preach the full truth, not just the loving God, the God who prospers us; but, the God who also demands righteousness?

Ellis Washington with WorldNet Daily recently wrote a column on one well-known pastor, who has shown a different side by the comments he's made regarding Barack Obama:

> For me it was almost déjà vu as I sat with my son. I remembered a little over 40 years ago watching the famous King speech with my dad. Similarly, I watched with my youngest son last night as a historical moment unfolded. He and I saw the dreams of slaves come true as the sons of slaves and the slave owners clapped their hands in one progressive sweep.
>
> *Bishop T.D. Jakes*[3]

He also said, "...I like most Americans of all stripes, watched with visible goose bumps as history was made."[4]

Washington says:

> Why would Jakes last Saturday get "goose bumps" of awe-inspiring emotion listening to Obama's speech claiming the Democratic Party presidential nomination? Obama, a certified Marxist, an enemy of the Christian evangelical movement and a unapologetic friend of the most reactionary forces in American society. Could Jakes and I be talking about the same man?

Because I knew that Jakes is a true stalwart of the faith...Bishop T.D. Jakes wouldn't sacrifice moral truth on the altar of political expediency, or exchange the priceless gifts of God for filthy lucre and for the capricious applause of mere men. No, no, no, not Bishop Jakes!

...I quickly pulled it up on the Internet and saw that the story was indeed true, that none other than the great Bishop T.D. Jakes had fallen prey to the intoxicating siren call of Identity Politics – blacks for blacks, whites for whites, white women for white women, homosexuals for homosexuals, one-legged, transgendered midgets for one-legged, transgendered midgets, etc.

It greatly pains me that Jakes has tarnished his reputation by joining his great name to Obama, but I am not in utter despair. Why? If it's Martin Luther, MLK Jr., Jerry Falwell, or Pat Robertson, while I admire the man, I try not to be a sycophant to any man.[5]

There are a small group of pastors who have decided that they will speak out from their pulpit, naming names; and if needed, endorsing a candidate, if God lays it on their heart, regardless of the consequences.

What consequences?

For one, it's not a popular thing to do among their peers.

Two, the IRS prohibits such endorsements, by a 1954 amendment to the Internal Revenue Code that says nonprofit, tax-exempt entities may not "participate in, or intervene in . . . any political campaign on behalf of any candidate for public office."

This is the reason that we are not hearing more public outcry from pulpits. According to National Public Radio:

> A group of pastors around the country are angling to weigh in on
> the presidential election from an unlikely platform — their pulpits.
> Although elections have long been linked to faith issues such as
> aiding the poor, denouncing abortion, etc., churches were banned
> from direct involvement in political campaigns because of their tax-
> exempt status.

> Now a group of pastors is out to change that. Late last month, 33
> pastors from around the country banded together to openly violate
> the law, an effort called "The Pulpit Initiative," organized by the
> conservative legal group Alliance Defense Fund.[6]

NPR gave a more in-depth look at this subject in a separate article:

> Among the pastors expected to violate the ban is Pastor Gus
> Booth.

> Booth will endorse Republican nominee John McCain — four
> months after delivering a sermon opposing the two main candidates
> seeking the Democratic presidential nomination.

> In May, Booth told his 150 congregants of the Warroad Community
> Church in Warroad, Minn., that the next president will determine
> policy on issues like same-sex marriage and abortion.

> "If you're a Christian, you cannot support a candidate like Barack
> Obama or Hillary Clinton," Booth said.

> With that, Booth gleefully zipped by the line barring ministers from
> engaging in political campaigns. The IRS bars people

from endorsing or opposing specific candidates from the pulpit. Booth sent an article about his sermon to the IRS so the agency wouldn't miss it. He and his elders knew he would be jeopardizing the church's tax-exempt status.

But, he says, it's his job to evaluate candidates in light of biblical teachings.

"Bottom line is, I'm a spiritual leader in this community, and spiritual leaders need to make decisions. We need to lead spiritually, and we need to be able to speak about the moral issues of the day. And right now, the moral issues of today are also the political issues of today," he said.

So what will happen if Booth's church in Minnesota loses its tax-exempt status?

"Big deal," he said. He added that he can get it back the next day because churches are automatically tax-exempt.

Besides, he said, electing **"Godly people is more important than money."**[7]

Wow! A simple statement, maybe, but what a true heart!

Why wouldn't the pastors, leaders of their flock...call evil - EVIL, and defy the chains of bondage through silence that the world places on them, knowing the very reason that they accepted their honored occupation, was to lead the fight for their God.

"Now I beseech you,

brethren,

MARK THEM

which cause
divisions
and offenses
**contrary to the doctrine
which ye have learned;**
and avoid them.

Romans 16:17

The gospel of Jesus wasn't weak or intimidated by important men or poll numbers. It demands more of our leaders and more of us.

Sir Alex Fraser Tyler (1742-1813) Scottish jurist and professor at the University of Edinburgh from his book, *The Fall of a Republic*, a study of the fall of the Athenian empire. Humans are organisms and follow a life-cycle:

> From Bondage to spiritual faith:
> From spiritual faith to great courage;
> From courage to liberty;
> From liberty to abundance;
> From abundance to complacency;
> From complacency to apathy;
> From apathy to dependence;
> From dependence back into bondage.[8]

Martin Niemoller, the son of a pastor and a U-Boat Captain in World War I said:

> In Germany the Nazis came for the communists,
> and I did not speak up because I was not a communist.
> Then they came for the Jews,
> and I did not speak up because I was not a Jew.
> Then they came for the trade unionists,
> and I did not speak up because I was not a trade unionist.
> Then they came for the Catholics,
> and I did not speak up because I was Protestant.
> Then they came for me.
> By that time there was no one left to speak up for anyone."[9]

Martin Niemoller in the 1930s became a pastor in a comfortable Berlin Suburb. Niemoller initially supported Hitler but become disillusioned with the direction of Germany under the Nazis. He was arrested by the Gestapo in 1937 for his open opposition to Hitler, charged with treason and imprisoned in Sachsenhausen and Dachau concentration camps.

However, he reproofed himself for not doing more sooner, as in the quote above, which is of course the perennial cry of people throughout the ages when faced with evil.

Thus throughout history the majority have found it more comfortable to ignore or take a neutral position in times of moral crises, which begs the perennial questions concerning the facing down and defeating of Evil...

"If not you, who? If not now, when?"

It is on this most crucial of things that Dante Alighieri (1265-1321) in *The Inferno* warned that:

"The hottest places in Hell are reserved for those who, in time of moral crisis, maintain their neutrality."[10]

Open thy mouth
for the dumb in the cause of all
such as are appointed to destruction.
Open thy mouth,
judge righteously, and plead
the cause of the poor and needy .
Proverbs 31:8-9

An end, the end is come upon the four corners of the land.

Now is the end come upon thee, and I will send mine anger upon thee, and will judge thee according to thy ways, and will recompense upon thee all thine abominations.

And mine eye shall not spare thee, neither will I have pity: but I will recompense thy ways upon thee, and thine abominations shall be in the midst of thee: and ye shall know that I am the LORD.

Thus saith the Lord GOD; An evil, an only evil, behold, is come.

An end is come, the end is come: it watcheth for thee; behold, it is come.

The morning is come unto thee, O thou that dwellest in the land: the time is come, the day of trouble is near...

Now will I shortly pour out my fury upon thee, and accomplish mine anger upon thee: and I will judge thee according to thy ways, and will recompense thee for all thine abominations.

And mine eye shall not spare, neither will I have pity: I will recompense thee according to thy ways and thine abominations that are in the midst of thee; and ye shall know that I am the LORD that smiteth.

Ezekiel 7:2-9

"... yet you have not returned unto me."
Amos 4:9

A RIGHTEOUS GOD'S FURY

This is not the first time a nation has faced God's judgement.

Author Bonnie Willis writes about another time in history and a man who came was willing to speak out. Here's are portions of her article:

A farmer from a small town south of Bethlehem in Judah, Amos was an unlikely candidate for a prophet of the people of Israel. Not only was he not a well known "man of God" nor even from a line of prophets, Amos was not even from the Kingdom of Israel. What he had to say was not the pleasant, uplifting word that they wanted to hear. Everyone knew what he was saying was true, but they didn't want to hear about it; it hurt too much. The truth has a way of doing that.

Amos comes on the scene during a very troubled time in the history of Israel. It has been about 170 years since the kingdom split and most of the members of the Northern tribes were no longer worshipping Adonai at His temple in Jerusalem. They were instead worshipping at one of the false altars set up in Israel.

Amos, unlike most prophets of old, had a very short ministry. According to most sources, it only lasted about 2 days before he was kicked out of Bethel because , "The land cannot bear all his words." (Amos 7:10) Between you and me, I don't think it was the land that couldn't bear the words, I think it was the people who couldn't bear to hear the words of the Lord.

He said: **"The LORD roars from Zion and thunders from Jerusalem; the pastures of the shepherds dry up, and the top of Carmel withers."** *Amos 1:2*

...what Amos is saying is that Adonai was going to rise up from His dwelling among the people and bring Judgment upon the false worshippers of Israel. These are His own people that He is going to wipe out so that these false shepherd will have no sheep to pasture. He is fed up with the false worship "in His Name" and He is going to do away with those who do not repent of this sin. He wants His people to repent and turn back to following Him the way He prescribed. He has sent Amos to warn these people before the judgment falls.

No wonder the people didn't want to hear from Amos. He was telling them that they were wrong, and no one wants to hear they are wrong. That is a "slap in the face" of everything they ever believed in. They had adapted to the people around them, instead of inspiring others to reach to God in the way He intended. This was just the beginning of what Amos had to say to the people of Israel, but before he continues, he talks about the countries surrounding Israel.

Because of all of this, the Lord is ready to crush His own people and there is no one who will be able to save them selves from the wrath to come. No matter how strong or smart or rich the person may be, it will not do him any good. There is no escaping the judgment of the Lord. This is a very important message that we, the children of Israel, need even today.

In chapter 3 verse 3 we read: Do two walk together unless they have agreed to do so? The word translated as "agreed" is the same word used for "betrothal." Adonai wants to remind the people of Israel that they are "engaged" to Him, and have been since Mt. Sinai. There they made an agreement, a covenant, that they would walk together in this life and that Israel would be a light unto the world, drawing others into this same relationship. He is reminding them that they agreed to do exactly what He said to do, exactly as He told them to do it. They were not living up to their end of the agreement.

Verse 6 also contains a little reminder that most people don't want to hear about, even today.

> **When a trumpet sounds in a city, do not the people tremble?**
> **When disaster comes to a city, has not the LORD caused it?**
> *Amos 3:6*

This is the kind of message that people today are afraid to give, especially in light of 9/11....We still need to remember that He is in control of everything, and nothing can happen outside of His will. There is a reason that God allows certain things to happen, and that is to have us turn back to Him.

Let's be honest with ourselves, have we really turned back to Him, as a nation, as the result of any of the disasters that have come our way in recent years? No, we haven't… and neither did the Israelites.

> *Surely the Sovereign LORD does nothing without revealing his plan to his servants the prophets.*
> *Amos 3:7*

Once again, nothing is new under the sun. The end was foretold from the beginning. Moses told them this would happen. They didn't listen then, we aren't listening now. Like the Israelites, we would rather listen to soothing words even if they don't fully match up with scripture. If it doesn't line up, it must be tossed out before we find ourselves guilty of worshipping a false god without even realizing that it has happened.

> **"They do not know how to do right," declares the LORD, "who hoard plunder and loot in their fortresses." Therefore this is what the Sovereign LORD says: "An enemy will overrun the land; he will pull down your strongholds and plunder your fortresses."**
> *Amos 3:10-11*

Did this ignorance save them from the wrath to come? No, it did not. The truth is, we are held accountable for the knowledge presented to us. Whether we take hold of that knowledge is up to us, but we are still held responsible. In this case, ignorance is not bliss!

Even in the midst of this, the Lord reminds us that He will not utterly destroy His people. This is what the LORD says:

"As a shepherd saves from the lion's mouth only two leg bones or a piece of an ear, so will the Israelites be saved,"

Amos 3:12

Yes, some will survive what is to come, but most will not. It seems to me that those who have tried to stay faithful to the covenant would be those who are able to "make it through." These are the people often referred to as "the remnant."

Amos found the same self-centeredness that we find today. The well-to-do people of Samaria couldn't care less about those who are orphaned or widowed. This was not pleasing God.

These same people would sacrifice daily and tithe regularly, but their hearts were without pity. The Lord has made it plain to them, and us, that He desires mercy, not sacrifice. (Hosea 6:6) So why are they doing it? Why bother sacrificing and tithing if it's not going to bless the Lord? Because they like doing it. They are not doing all of this for Him, but for themselves. They enjoy the process of worshipping, not the One they were worshipping.

As a parent trying to reason with a child, Adonai continues to remind Israel of all the things He has done for them. But this is a parent trying to teach the child about the love of discipline. So, He reminds of all of the things He did to try and bring about repentance.

So, what does Adonai say through Amos to these people who would not return? The following is one of the most widely paraphrased scriptures in the world, yet few know it's found in Amos.

"Therefore this is what I will *do to you, Israel, and because I will do this to you,* **prepare to meet your God***, O Israel.*"

Amos 4:12

...This phrase brings with it visions of the final judgment of God.... This is that "time's up" we all dread, because we all know it is coming....Obviously, the Israelites were going to be taken by surprise because they wouldn't listen to the prophets of God. Many of us will be taken by surprise as well because we won't listen either.

This is the God who made the universe and created the order of the day. He also brought justice to the earth once before and He will do it again. There is nothing that can stand in the face of His mighty hand.

Unfortunately they will not, so God will punish them by taking away those things they hold most dear...But those who are wise will listen to the Lord's advice:

Therefore the prudent man keeps quiet in such times, for the times are evil. Seek good, not evil, that you may live. Then the LORD God Almighty will be with you, just as you say he is. Hate evil, love good; maintain justice in the courts. Perhaps the LORD God Almighty will have mercy on the remnant of Joseph.

Amos 5:13-15

The phrase "in such times" can be literally translated as "that time," which usually indicates they are referring to "the end times." There is a time for speaking the truth, and a time for keeping quiet. When we see injustice, we are to do every thing within our power to "right the wrong", but there comes a time when just opening your mouth can get you killed. A wise man knows the difference and that knowledge will be a key to whether or not he is included within the remnant of Israel.

"I hate, I despise your religious feasts; I cannot stand your assemblies. Even though you bring me burnt offerings and grain offerings, I will not accept them. Though you bring choice fellowship offerings, I will have no regard for them. Away with the noise of your songs! I will not listen to the music of your harps."

Amos 5:21-23

These are tough words for those who feel that they are just following the Lord as best as they know how, don't you think? It may seem that way to us, but we don't see things the same way as the Lord.

"For my thoughts are not your thoughts, neither are your ways my ways," declares the LORD.

Isaiah 55:8

Remember, these are the people who treat the poor and needy with contempt. These are religious folks who did not care about anyone outside of their own circle of friends. There is only one thing that God wants from these people:

But let justice roll on like a river, righteousness like a never-failing stream!

Amos 5:24

Once again the Lord does not leave us without hope.

This is what the Sovereign LORD showed me: The Sovereign LORD was calling for judgment by fire; it dried up the great deep and devoured the land. Then I cried out, "Sovereign LORD, I beg you, stop! How can Jacob survive? He is so small!" So the LORD relented. "This will not happen either," the Sovereign LORD said.

Amos 7:1-6

This is a wonderful example of how the fervent prayers of a righteous man can do much good. Amos cried out to the Lord on behalf of the people, and the Lord relented.

Although Adonai relented of the plagues He had intended to send, He was still ready to say, "enough is enough!"

This is what he showed me: The Lord was standing by a wall that had been built true to plumb, with a plumb line in his hand. And the LORD asked me, "What do you see, Amos?" "A plumb line," I replied. Then the Lord said, "Look, I am setting a plumb line among my people Israel; I will spare them no longer.

Amos 7:7-8

He will draw a line in the midst of His people. Only those of His people who are truly following the Lord, those who are "true to plumb," will be saved. This is clearly an indication that God wants His people to worship Him according to His plan, not their (or our) own plan. If they don't line up with the word, they will not be spared.

"The high places of Isaac will be destroyed and the sanctuaries of Israel will be ruined; with my sword I will rise against the house of Jeroboam."

Amos 7:9

What does he mean by the high places of Isaac?....All we know is that these sanctuaries would become ruins at the hand on a Mighty God.

Well, that was all the high priest could handle hearing.

Then Amaziah the priest of Bethel sent a message to Jeroboam king of Israel: "Amos is raising a conspiracy against you in the very heart of Israel. The land cannot bear all his words. For this is what Amos is saying: `Jeroboam will die by the sword, and Israel will surely go into exile, away from their native land.'"

Amos 7:10-11

Now then, hear the word of the LORD. You say, "Do not prophesy against Israel, and stop preaching against the house of Isaac." Therefore this is what the LORD says: "Your wife will become a prostitute in the city, and your sons and daughters will fall by the sword. Your land will be measured and divided up, and you yourself will die in a pagan country.

And Israel will certainly go into exile, away from their native land."
Amos 7:16-17

Because they would not listen to the word of the Lord, things are going to go from bad to worse. Those women who were once so high and mighty will be reduced to the lowest of the low. Everything will be taken from them. But worst of all, they will die in an unclean land. They will not be able to be buried in the Promised Land. They will never see their native land ever again. They should have listened.

Amos now goes back to relaying to us what the Lord has shown him. This time it is a basket of ripe fruit.

Then the LORD said to me, "The time is ripe for my people Israel; I will spare them no longer."
Amos 8:2

The clock has been ticking and the time has run out. There will be no more delays. God can stand them no longer.

"In that day," declares the Sovereign LORD, "the songs in the temple will turn to wailing. Many, many bodies—flung everywhere! Silence!"
Amos 8:3

"In that day" refers to judgment day. The songs in the temple will turn to wailing.

This goes hand-in-hand with 1 Peter 4:17: **For it is time for judgment to begin with the family of God;** The first thing we are told by the Lord is that the singing in the temple will stop. Many people felt that they would be safe within the temple when judgment came.

"In that day," declares the Sovereign LORD, "I will make the sun go down at noon and darken the earth in broad daylight. *Amos 8:9*

Darkness comes upon them in the daytime; at noon they grope as in the night.
Job 5:14

All of these men were writing about the Great and Horrible Day of the Lord; Judgment Day. In the midst of warning of judgment against Israel, Adonai reminds us that this is not the final judgment. There is still a much bigger judgment to come.

I will turn your religious feasts into mourning and all your singing into weeping. I will make all of you wear sackcloth and shave your heads. I will make that time like mourning for an only son and the end of it like a bitter day.
Amos 8:10

We must look at our own beliefs and the way we live them out. We might just be in for a big surprise in that day. Are you going to be one of those who Amos would preach to, and be caught up in the coming judgment, or will you be an overcomer? The choice is yours.[1]

Return unto me, and I will return unto you...

Malachi 3:7

RETURN TO ME

John did baptize in the wilderness, and preach the baptism of repentance for the remission of sins.

And straightway coming up out of the water, he saw the heavens opened, and the Spirit like a dove descending upon him:

And there came a voice from heaven, saying, Thou art my beloved Son, in whom I am well pleased.

Mark 1:4,10-11

Verily I say unto you, Among them that are born of women there hath not risen a greater than John the Baptist: notwithstanding he that is least in the kingdom of heaven is greater than he.

Matthew 11:11

"there hath not risen a greater than John the Baptist:"

The greatest compliment ever given by anyone!

John the Baptist was, in every sense of the word, pleasing to the Lord Jesus Christ.

To "return to the Lord," we could emulate this man whom the Lord so loved.

The steps and characteristics of this lifestyle include:

1. Salvation
2. Baptism
3. Holiness
4. Sacrifice
5. Courage
6. Boldness
7. Purity
8. Passion
9. Purpose

Rose Weiner, of Weiner Ministries International says, "**The Cross is a Radical Thing**," excerpts include:

He asks for everything that men and women hold dear asking that they forsake all and obediently follow Him. He makes no concessions.

Thousands have turned from Him because they will not meet His conditions. He will admit no one by compromise. Everyone must decide if he will take Christ as Lord now or meet Him as Judge then. Every man, every woman holds their future in their hand. Everyone is a man or a woman of destiny. Everyone chooses which way his soul shall go and, as he chooses, destiny waits on the nod of his head. As he chooses hell enlarges itself or heaven prepares another mansion.

Silently, terribly the work goes on. Each one decides whether he will hear or ignore the Voice of invitation. Unknown to the world, perhaps unknown even to the individual, the work of separation takes place. He will not argue, nor put Himself on trial again. But the morning of the Judgment will confirm what each man and woman has decided in the twilight.

Most people are apathetic to matters of heart and conscience. The person in whom God has begun a work has become sensitive to matters of good and evil, displaying a moral discontent. While most of mankind has struck a truce with their conscience and are living it up in sin, the one that God is concerned with has turned sour on the world and the pleasure of sin. When this is accompanied by a consuming spiritual hunger, salvation stands at the door and makes ready to knock.

It is unto those that Christ stands knocking at the door, issuing an invitation. But it is not an invitation without conditions. What are the conditions of discipleship? Jesus said, "If any man will come after me, let him deny himself, and take up his cross, and follow me."

Can this be right? Would Jesus lay down such severe conditions for those who would follow Him? He not only can, He does. Self denial - if anyone would be saved he must be delivered from the chains by which self has bound him - and cross bearing.

The cross that Jesus spoke of was not some pretty thing to

hang around your neck or to use to make a nice pair of earrings. It was not some beautiful ornament to adorn the top of a steeple or the front of an altar. It was rather a place where men were slain. It was an instrument of death which was its only function, for no one was ever taken off a cross alive. It was on a cross that a living man was fastened to groan and writhe in pain until death silenced him. The cross cared not for peace. Its only purpose was to end its opposition as fast as possible. It won by defeating its opponent. That is the cross and it is nothing less.

When the apostles went out and preached after Christ was raised from the dead, they went out and preached His message, and what they preached was the cross. Wherever they went revolutionary power went with them. Their message upset the whole life of the individual and made him into another person altogether. It laid hold of the life and brought it under obedience to Jesus. Its aim was that the individual, through the power of God, would be wholly transformed into the image of Another.

This and nothing less is true Christianity. The Bible teaches in the last days men will be "haters of the cross." As Tozer observed, "A shallow and worldly leadership would modify the cross to please the entertainment mad saintlings who will have their fun even within the very sanctuary; but to do so is to court spiritual disaster and risk the anger of the Lamb turned Lion.

To submit to the cross is to submit the whole pattern of our lives to be destroyed and built again in the power of an Endless Life. The cross will cut into our lives where it hurts worst, sparing neither us nor our carefully cultivated reputations. It will defeat us and bring our selfish lives to an end. Only then can we rise in fullness of life to establish a pattern of living wholly new and free and full of good works.[1]

Greg Gambles, Christian blogger asked these questions that require true reflection:

Are your own paths straight?

Do you know that you are not in charge, that you can't call the shots, that you cannot have your own way?

Have you said to God, "I turn my back on my way of running my life, and I let you be in charge?"

Do you know who you are? Do you see your life as a mission, a preparation for God's activity in you and in the world?

Have you said to God, "I will boldly follow you! I will point people to you. I will stand in the wilderness and I will come against the mountains and hills of injustice and wrong in our world, as a way of preparing for you to come?"

Because our world is a mess, and it needs the people of God to stand up.

We will not make the paths straight on our own. God is calling us to a wholehearted and holistic repentance, both personally and as a society.

When we follow the Baptist model, we know we are not the focus. We are not in charge.

When we follow the Baptist model, we know our job. We prepare the way for Jesus, and we point people to follow him for themselves, without making ourselves the focus.

When we follow the Baptist model, we stand as Isaiah 40 people, willing to stand outside of and at times even against polite religion to be radical followers of Jesus Christ.

We recognize it is both our personal lives that need salvation and that God cares about justice in our world, as well.

We need the people of God to stand straight in the wilderness, preparing the way of the Lord!

How will you prepare the way for Jesus?[2]

I know that my Redeemer lives, and that in the end he will stand upon the earth.

And after my skin has been destroyed, yet in my flesh I will see God;

Job 19: 25-26

I will not fear the tens of thousands drawn up against me on every side.

Psalms 3:6

Though an army besiege me, my heart will not fear; though war break out against me, even then will I be confident.

Psalms 27:3

Why are you downcast, O my soul?

Why so disturbed within me?

Put your hope in God,

for I will yet praise him,

my Savior and my God.

Psalms 42:11

So teach us to
number our days,
that we may apply
our hearts unto
wisdom.

Psalms 90:12

Amos answered Amaziah, "I was neither a prophet nor a prophet's son, but I was a shepherd, and I also took care of sycamore-fig trees. But the LORD took me from tending the flock and said to me, `Go, prophesy to my people Israel.'"

Amos 7:14-15

AFTERWORD

You might ask, "Who are you? We've never heard of Kaelyn Hart."

It doesn't matter who I am. I am insignificant, just one person touched by God, for one minute in history. But just as surely as He has spoken throughout the history of the Bible to His people, He has spoken to me.

I have no personal agenda, not part of a political group, not worried about a non-profit status.

Just an awesome reverence for my God and a burden to fulfill what I was born to do.

As God chose Amos, a lowly farmer, not a typical prophet; He has chosen me to be a voice. Although not one who would normally feel adequate to take on such a task, I trusted in His Word, when

He said:

> "My grace is sufficient for you, for my power is made perfect in weakness." Therefore I will boast all the more gladly of my weaknesses, so that the power of Christ may rest upon me.

> For the sake of Christ, then, I am content with weaknesses, insults, hardships, persecutions, and calamities. For when I am weak, then I am strong.

> *2 Corinthians 12:9-10*

And so, I say in thanksgiving:

> "Thank You Heavenly Father, for giving me this insight, revealing yourself, and allowing me to feel your comforting and gentle caress as I was gathering this information. The focus, the strength when I felt I was too weary to go on, the prayers of the faithful group you have given me, to pray over me; it is all overwhelming, as the Bible says, it is too awesome, to great for me to imagine.

> I finish with a prayer for our nation, your people...that they hear the word, open their eyes, return to you and that we once more feel your mercy.

> Amen.

However, as Jesus said in the garden:

O my Father, if it be possible,

let this cup pass from me:

nevertheless not as I will,

but as thou wilt.

Matthew 26:39

For my brethren and companions' sake,

I will now ask,

Peace be with thee.

Psalms 122:8

BIBLIOGRAPHY

Source articles and quotations are included in accordance with the Fair Use Doctrine.

Opinions are exclusively those of the author and in no way reflect opinions of the sources cited.

CHAPTER ONE

1. Overlords of Chaos. <http://www.overlordsofchaos.com/html/1945-49.html>.
2. Ibid.
3. Ibid.
5. Ibid.
6. Ibid.
7. Ibid
8. Overlords of Chaos. <http://www.overlordsofchaos.com/html/1935-39.html>.
9. Overlords of Chaos. <http://www.overlordsofchaos.com/html/1950-54.html>.
10. Overlords of Chaos. <http://www.overlordsofchaos.com/html/1960-64.html>.
11. Overlords of Chaos. <http://www.overlordsofchaos.com/html/1975-79.html>.
12. Overlords of Chaos. <http://www.overlordsofchaos.com/html/1990-94.html>
13. Ibid.
14. Ibid.
15. Ibid.
16. Overlords of Chaos. <http://www.overlordsofchaos.com/html/1985-89.html>

CHAPTER TWO

1. "Obama's Global Tax." IBD Editorials. 29 July 2008. <http://www.ibdeditorials.com/ibdarticles.aspx?id=302222641317480>.
2. Ibid.
3. A Clockwork Obama. <http://aclockworkobama.com/>.
4. "Barack Obama's Stealth Socialism." IBD Editorials. 28 July 2008. <http://www.ibdeditorials.com/ibdarticles.aspx?id=302137342405551>.
5. Ibid.
6. "Like Father, Like Son." IBD Editorials. 18 Aug. 2008. <http://www.ibdeditorials.com/ibdarticles.aspx?id=303952499910291>.
7. A Clockwork Obama. <http://aclockworkobama.com/>.
8. "Obama to Plumber." Fox News.com. 13 Oct. 2008. <http://elections.foxnews.com/2008/10/13/obama-plumber-plan-spread-wealth/>.
9. Overlords of Chaos. <http://www.overlordsofchaos.com/html/1930-34.html>.
10. Overlords of Chaos. <http://www.overlordsofchaos.com/html/1910-19.html>.
11. Overlords of Chaos. <http://www.overlordsofchaos.com/html/2004.html>.
12. Overlords of Chaos. <http://www.overlordsofchaos.com/html/1955-59.html>.
13. Overlords of Chaos. <http://www.overlordsofchaos.com/html/1985-89.html>.

CHAPTER THREE

1. "Senate Liberal Scores." National Journal. <http://www.nationaljournal.com/voteratings/sen/lib.htm>.
2. "Barack Obama, Doubting Thomas." IBD Editorials. 19 Aug. 2008. <http://www.ibdeditorials.com/ibdarticles.aspx?id=304039300920692>
3. Ibid.
4. "Barack Obama." Govtrak.us. <http://www.govtrack.us/congress/person.xpd?id=400629>.
5. Bettelheim, Adriel. "Obama's "present" tension." PolitiFact.com. 13 Feb. 2008. <http://www.politifact.com/truth-o-meter/article/2008/feb/13/obamas-present-tension/>.
6. The Candidates on the Death Penalty." The Pew Forum. <http://pewforum.org/religion08/compare.php?issue=death_penalty>.
7. "Obama promises universal health care by end of first term." Chicago SunTimes. 14 May 2007. <http://www.gopusa.com/forum/showthread.php?t=46726>.
8. Holmes, Shona. "Mother's Tragic Tale Underscores Big Flaws Of Canadian Health Care." IBD Editorials. 9 July 2008. <http://www.ibdeditorials.com/ibdarticles.aspx?id=300495064758477>.
9. "Barack Obama on Civil Rights." Obama Statement on Flag Burning Amendment. <http://obama.senate.gov/press/060627-obama_statement_29/>.

10. Brady, Patrick. "It's Not the Flag; It's the Constitution." Military.com. 2 Oct. 2008. <http://www.military.com/opinion/0,15202,176558,00.html>.

11. Ibid.

12. "Obama's Plan To Disarm The U.S." IBD Editorials. 6 June 2008. <http://www.ibdeditorials.com/ibdarticles.aspx?id=297645696465868>.

13. Ibid.

14. "On the Second Amendment, Don't Believe Obama." Gun Ban Obama. <http://www.gunbanobama.com/default.aspx?navguid=530ecfa4-ae4e-4819-97e6-892463d99f08&siteguid=c63367a2-996a-422c-9afd-0d6f49a0ca86>.

15. Ponte, Lowell. "NRA to Fight Obama Over Gun Rights Flip-Flops." Newsmax.com. 29 Sept. 2008. <http://www.newsmax.com/lowell_ponte/nra_obama/2008/09/29/135501.html>.

16. Tucker, William. "Secret dangers about Obama." Sioux City Journal. <http://www.siouxcityjournal.com/articles/2008/10/07/news_opinion/letters/573a7c16c595a292862574da0077d32f.txt>.

17. "The Candidates on Gay Marriage." The Pew Forum. <http://pewforum.org/religion08/compare.php?issue=gay_marriage>.

18. Wulfhorst, Ellen. "Michelle Obama speaks to gay Democrats." Reuters. 26 June 2008. <http://blogs.reuters.com/trail08/2008/06/26/michelle-obama-speaks-to-gay-democrats/>.

19. "Barack Obama on Civil Rights." On The Issues. <http://www.ontheissues.org/domestic/barack_obama_civil_rights.htm>.

20. "Vice presidential debate quotes from Biden, Palin." Associated Press. 2 Oct. 2008. <http://ap.google.com/article/aleqm5hsda2vvx_nahx3rkhndmi4maafaad93ipef00>.

21. Brody, David. "Obama's Pro-Gay Flyers." CBNNews.com. 1 July 2008. <http://www.cbn.com/cbnnews/401969.aspx>.

22. "Barack Obama on Education." On The Issues. <http://www.ontheissues.org/social/barack_obama_education.htm>.

23. Dreher, Rod. "Obama and the kindergarten sex ed bill." Beliefnet. 16 Sept. 2008. <http://blog.beliefnet.com/crunchycon/2008/09/obama-and-the-kindergarten-sex.html>.

24. Ibid.

25. "The Candidates on Education." The Pew Forum. <http://pewforum.org/religion08/compare.php?issue=education>.

26. "School takes 1st-graders to see lesbian teacher wed." WorldNet Daily. 11 Oct. 2008. <http://www.worldnetdaily.com/index.php?fa=page.view&pageid=77734>.

27. "School textbook promotes Obama." WorldNet Daily. 14 Oct. 2008. <http://www.worldnetdaily.com/index.php?fa=page.view&pageid=77957>.

28. Overlords of Chaos. <http://www.overlordsofchaos.com/html/1995-99.html>.

29. Overlords of Chaos. <http://www.overlordsofchaos.com/html/1930-34.html>.

30. Overlords of Chaos. <http://www.overlordsofchaos.com/html/1970-74.html>.

31. Overlords of Chaos. <http://www.overlordsofchaos.com/html/1990-94.html>.

32. Overlords of Chaos. <http://www.overlordsofchaos.com/html/1980-84.html>.

33. "Human Life & Bioethics." Family Research Council. <http://www.frc.org/life--bioethics>.

34. "Death with Dignity Act." Oregon.gov. <http://www.oregon.gov/dhs/ph/pas/>.

35. "He favors long-term timber-payments solution." Mail Tribune. 23 Mar. 2008. <http://www.mailtribune.com/apps/pbcs.dll/article?aid=/20080323/news/803230336>.

36. Ertelt, Steven. "Barack Obama Would Take Back Vote Helping Terri Schiavo Avoid Euthanasia." Free Republic. 26 Feb. 2008. <http://www.freerepublic.com/focus/f-news/1977276/posts>.

37. Ibid.

38. "The Candidates on Abortion." The Pew Forum. <http://pewforum.org/religion08/compare.php?issue=abortion>.

39. "Barack Obama on Abortion." On The Issues. <http://www.ontheissues.org/social/barack_obama_abortion.htm>.

40. Smith, Peter. "Obama's Abortion Bombshell:." LifeSiteNews.com. 10 June 2008. <http://www. lifesitenews.com/ldn/2008/jun/08061010.html>.

41. Gerson, Michael. "Obama's Abortion Extremism." WashingtonPost.co. 2 Apr. 2008.<http://www. washingtonpost.com/wp-dyn/content/article/2008/04/01/ar2008040102197.html>.

42. "Partial-Birth Abortion Ban Act." Wikipedia. <http://en.wikipedia.org/wiki/partial-birth_abortion_ ban_act>.

43. Stanek, Jill. "Why Jesus would not vote for Barack Obama." WorldNet Daily. 19 July 2006. <http:// www.worldnetdaily.com/news/article.asp?article_id=51121>.

44. "Frequently Asked Questions." BornAliveTruth.org. <http://www.bornalivetruth.org/faq.aspx>.

45. "Senator Obama's Voting Record." BornAliveTruth.org. <http://www.bornalivetruth.org/ obamarecord.aspx>.

46. Stanek, Jill. "Obama's 10 reasons for supporting infanticide." WorldNet Daily. 16 Jan. 2008. <http:// www.wnd.com/index.php?fa=page.view&pageid=45553>.

47. Willke, Dr. and Mrs. JC. "WHY CAN'T WE LOVE THEM BOTH." AbortionFacts.com.<http:// www.abortionfacts.com/online_books/love_them_both/why_cant_we_love_them_both_37. asp#can%20you%20draw%20a%20parallel%20between%20today's%20abortionists%20and%20the%20 nazi%20doctors?>.

48. "Political positions of Barack Obama." Wikipedia. <http://en.wikipedia.org/wiki/political_ positions_of_barack_obama#sex_education>.

CHAPTER FOUR

1. A Clockwork Obama. <http://aclockworkobama.com/>.

2. "Barack Obama on Abortion." On The Issues. <http://www.ontheissues.org/social/barack_obama_ abortion.htm>.

3. Brody, David. "Constitution: Living Document or Original Intent?" CBN News. <http://www.cbn. com/cbnnews/news/050801a.aspx>.

4. Hell Nobama 08. <http://www.hellnobama.com/quotes.html>.

5. "Obama Wants You." IBD Editorials. 31 July 2008. <http://www.ibdeditorials.com/ibdarticles. aspx?id=302396723240343>.

6. Ibid.

7. Farah, Joseph. "Obama's 'civilian national security force'" WorldNet Daily. 15 July 2008. <http://www. worldnetdaily.com/index.php?fa=page.view&pageid=69601>.

8. "Hitler, Obama, Socialism." America vs Obama. 5 June 2008. http://fredshelm.wordpress. com/2008/06/05/barack-the-black-hitler/.

9. "Biden to Supporters: "Gird Your Loins", For the Next President "It's Like Cleaning Augean Stables"" ABC News. 20 Oct. 2008. <http://blogs.abcnews.com/politicalradar/2008/10/biden-to-suppor.html>.

CHAPTER FIVE

1. Hollyfield, Amy. "Obama's birth certificate: Final chapter." Politifact.com. 27 June 2008. St. Petersburg Times.

2. "Barack Obama on Principles & Values." On The Issues. <http://www.ontheissues.org/social/ barack_obama_principles_+_values.htm>.

3. "Barrack Obama: The Early Years." Associated Content. 27 Aug. 2007. <http://www.associatedcontent. com/article/353635/barrack_obama_the_early_years.html?cat=9>.

4. "Family of Barack Obama." Wikipedia. <http://en.wikipedia.org/wiki/onyango_obama#hussein_ onyango_obama>.

5. Obama, Barack. Dreams from My Father : A Story of Race and Inheritance. New York: Three Rivers P, 2004. 9.

6. Powell, Kimberly. "Ancestry of Barack Obama." About.com. <http://genealogy.about.com/od/ aframertrees/p/barack_obama.htm>.

7. "Madelyn and Stanley Dunham." Wikipedia. <http://en.wikipedia.org/wiki/madelyn_and_stanley_ dunham>.

8. Obama, Barack. Dreams from My Father : A Story of Race and Inheritance. New York: Three Rivers P, 2004. 12

9. "Madelyn and Stanley Dunham." Wikipedia. <http://en.wikipedia.org/wiki/madelyn_and_stanley_dunham>.

10. Ibid.

11. Obama, Barack. Dreams from My Father : A Story of Race and Inheritance. New York: Three Rivers P, 2004. 17.

12. Kincaid, Cliff. "Obama's Red Mentor Was a Pervert." Accuracy In Media. 24 Aug. 2008. <http://www.aim.org/aim-column/obamas-red-mentor-was-a-pervert>.

13. Obama, Barack. Dreams from My Father : A Story of Race and Inheritance. New York: Three Rivers P, 2004. 77.

14. Ibid.

15. "Barack Obama, Sr." Wikipedia. <http://en.wikipedia.org/wiki/barack_obama_sr.>. 5.

16. "Barack Obama, Sr." Wikipedia. <http://en.wikipedia.org/wiki/barack_obama_sr.>.

17. Ibid.

18. Ripley, Amanda. "The Story of Barack Obama's Mother." Time Magazine. 9 Apr. 2008. <http://www.time.com/time/nation/article/0,8599,1729524-1,00.html>.

19. Corsi, Jerome. "What Obama didn't dispute in my book." WorldNetDaily.com. 16 Sept. 2008. <http://www.wnd.com/index.php?fa=page.view&pageid=75478>.

8. Ibid.

20. Obama, Barack. Dreams from My Father : A Story of Race and Inheritance. New York: Three Rivers P, 2004. 26.

21. "Barack Obama, Sr." Wikipedia. <http://en.wikipedia.org/wiki/barack_obama_sr.>.

22. Ibid.

23. Ibid.

24. Ripley, Amanda. "The Story of Barack Obama's Mother." Time Magazine. 9 Apr. 2008. <http://www.time.com/time/nation/article/0,8599,1729524-1,00.html>.

25. Ibid.

26. Ibid.

27. "Ann Dunham." Wikipedia. <http://en.wikipedia.org/wiki/ann_dunham>.

28. Ibid.

29. Scott, Janny. "The Story of Barack Obama's Mother." A Free-Spirited Wanderer Who Set Obama's Path. 14 Mar. 2008. <http://www.nytimes.com/2008/03/14/us/politics/14obama.html?pagewanted=3&_r=1&fta=y>.

30. Corsi, Jerome. "What Obama didn't dispute in my book." WorldNetDaily.com. 16 Sept. 2008. <http://www.wnd.com/index.php?fa=page.view&pageid=75478>.

30. Ibid.

31. "Ann Dunham." Wikipedia. <http://en.wikipedia.org/wiki/ann_dunham>.

32. Ibid.

33. Scott, Janny. "The Story of Barack Obama's Mother." A Free-Spirited Wanderer Who Set Obama's Path. 14 Mar. 2008. <http://www.nytimes.com/2008/03/14/us/politics/14obama.html?pagewanted=3&_r=1&fta=y>.

34. Obama, Barack. Dreams from My Father : A Story of Race and Inheritance. New York: Three Rivers P, 2004. 46-47.

35. "Ann Dunham." Wikipedia. <http://en.wikipedia.org/wiki/ann_dunham>.

36. Ripley, Amanda. "The Story of Barack Obama's Mother." Time Magazine. 9 Apr. 2008. <http://www.time.com/time/nation/article/0,8599,1729524-7,00.html>.

37. Ripley, Amanda. "The Story of Barack Obama's Mother." Time Magazine. 9 Apr. 2008. <http://www.time.com/time/nation/article/0,8599,1729524-6,00.html>.

38. Scott, Janny. "The Story of Barack Obama's Mother." A Free-Spirited Wanderer Who Set Obama's Path. 14 Mar. 2008. <http://www.nytimes.com/2008/03/14/us/politics/14obama.html?pagewanted=3&_r=1&fta=y>.

39. Ibid.

40. Obama, Barack. Dreams from My Father : A Story of Race and Inheritance. New York: Three Rivers P, 2004. 43.

41. Obama, Barack. Dreams from My Father : A Story of Race and Inheritance. New York: Three Rivers P, 2004. 47-48.

42. Obama, Barack. Dreams from My Father : A Story of Race and Inheritance. New York: Three Rivers P, 2004. 10.

43. Obama, Barack. Dreams from My Father : A Story of Race and Inheritance. New York: Three Rivers P, 2004. 32.

44. Ripley, Amanda. "The Story of Barack Obama's Mother." Time Magazine. 9 Apr. 2008. <http://www.time.com/time/nation/article/0,8599,1729524-7,00.html>.

45. "Keris." Pitt Rivers Museum. <http://webprojects.prm.ox.ac.uk/arms-and-armour/o/swords,-knives-and-daggers/1884.24.232/>.

46. "Ann Dunham." Wikipedia. <http://en.wikipedia.org/wiki/ann_dunham>.

47. Ibid.

48. Tarpley, Webster G. "Behind The Copied Speeches -." Rense.com. 19 Feb. 2008. <http://www.rense.com/general80/s0pa.htm>.

49. "Obama's Lost Years." Wall Street Journal. 11 Sept. 2008. <http://online.wsj.com/public/article_print/sb122108881386721289.html>.

50. Klein, Aaron. "Barry Obama - We Keep Finding Your Muslim Ties." Daily Musings. <http://dailymusings.spaces.live.com/blog/cns!ebab74da8f94c559!5448.entry>.

51. "Obama Visits Pakistan When All Non-Muslim Vistors Unwelcome." <http://dailymusings.spaces.live.com/blog/cns!ebab74da8f94c559!5351.entry>.

52. Lamb, Kenneth. "Barack Obama: Washington Post, Chicago Tribune investigations confirm autobiography lies; now asking: Is "African-American" a lie too?" Weblog post. Reading Between the Lines. 14 Feb. 2008. <http://kennethelamb.blogspot.com/2008/02/barak-obama-questions-about-ethnic.html>.

53. Klein, Aaron. "Barry Obama - We Keep Finding Your Muslim Ties." Daily Musings. <http://dailymusings.spaces.live.com/blog/cns!ebab74da8f94c559!5448.entry>.

54. "Michelle's speech inspired by radical socialist?" WorldNet Daily. 26 Aug. 2008. <http://www.worldnetdaily.com/index.php?fa=page.view&pageid=73533>.

CHAPTER SIX

1. Geller, Pamela. "FALLACI!" Atlas Shrugs. 29 Nov. 2005. http://atlasshrugs2000.typepad.com/atlas_shrugs/2005/11/i_leave_shreds_.html.

2. A Clockwork Obama. <http://aclockworkobama.com/>.

3. Johnson, Alex. "Powell endorses Obama for president." MSNBC. 19 Oct. 2008. <http://www.msnbc.msn.com/id/27265369/>.

4. Fallaci, Oriana. "A Sermon For The West." FrontPageMag.com. Jan. 2003. <http://www.frontpagemagazine.com/articles/read.aspx?guid=4f1caf59-13a5-44bb-8ff9-bdde5571becb>.

5. Geller, Pamela. "FALLACI!" Atlas Shrugs. 29 Nov. 2005. http://atlasshrugs2000.typepad.com/atlas_shrugs/2005/11/i_leave_shreds_.html.

6. "Oriana Fallaci." Wikipedia. <http://en.wikipedia.org/wiki/oriana_fallaci>.

7. "Islam, conquering Americans from within?" Right Truth. 9 Aug. 2006. <http://righttruth.typepad.com/right_truth/2006/08/islam.html>.

8. Koret, Reuven. "Is Barack Obama a Muslim wolf in Christian wool?" Israel Insider. 27 Mar. 2008. <http://web.israelinsider.com/articles/politics/12745.htm>.

9. Ibid.

10. Ibid.

11. Warner, Bill. "Barack Obama and Slavery." American Thinker. 26 Sept. 2008. <http://www.americanthinker.com/2008/09/barack_obama_and_slavery.html>.

12. Sammon, Bill. "Can a past of Islam change the path to president for Obama?" Examiner.com. 29 Jan. 2007. <http://www.examiner.com/a-534540~can_a_past_of_islam_change_the_path_to__president_.html>.

13. "Obama recited the Muslim call to prayer NYT." DanielPipes.org. <http://www.danielpipes.org/comments/137991>.

14. Nickerson, Matt. "Oops! Barack Obama says 'my Muslim faith' in interview with ABC's George Stephanopoulos." Chicago SunTimes. 8 Sept. 2008. <http://www.suntimes.com/news/politics/obama/1150540,cst-nws-faith08.article>.

15. Schlussel, Debbie. "Obama's Nation of Islam Staffers." DebbieSchlussel.com. <http://www.debbieschlussel.com/archives/2008/01/obamas_nation_o.html>.

16. "Obama's Muslim Brotherhood-linked aide hasn't really quit." Jihad Watch. 10 Sept. 2008. <http://www.jihadwatch.org/archives/022629.php>.

17. Jay, Dr, and Nathan Lerman. "Obama, The Reborn Zionist? [incl. Rashid Khalidi]." Campus Watch. 24 July 2008. <http://www.campus-watch.org/article/id/5410>.

18. Lasky, Ed. "Obama plans to organize a Muslim summit." American Thinker. 30 Jan. 2008. <http://www.americanthinker.com/blog/2008/01/obama_plans_to_organize_a_musl.html>.

19. "Fitzgerald: How the Islamic world views Obama." Jihad Watch. 8 Sept. 2008. <http://www.jihadwatch.org/archives/022601.php>.

20. "Iranians Hoping for 'Muslim' Obama Victory." Newsmax.com. <http://news.newsmax.com/?z64r.id3wi4a7rm97wzwd3rzdxykxjuaz>.

21. Pipes, Daniel. "Barack Obama through Muslim Eyes." Militant Islam Monitor. 25 Aug. 2008. http://www.militantislammonitor.org/article/id/3576.

22. Klein, Aaron. "Racists endorse Obama on candidate's website." WorldNet Daily. http://www.wnd.com/index.php?fa=page.view&pageid=59326.

23. "Obama, Be Proud of His Muslim." AOL News. <http://video.aol.com/video-detail/muammar-al-qadhafi-obama-be-proud-of-his-muslim-identity/1430316196/?icid=vidurvnws04>.

24. "Fitzgerald: How the Islamic world views Obama." Jihad Watch. 8 Sept. 2008. <http://www.jihadwatch.org/archives/022601.php>.

CHAPTER SEVEN

1. Overlords of Chaos. <http://www.overlordsofchaos.com/html/1990-94.html>.

2. Sater, Terry. "The Sweet Illusion Of Socialism." IBD Editorials. 22 July 2008. <http://www.ibdeditorials.com/ibdarticles.aspx?id=301616451833130>.

3. Alden, Diane. "Saul Alinsky and DNC Corruption." Newsmax.com. 7 Jan. 2003. <http://www.tysknews.com/articles/dnc_corruption.htm>.

4. "Obama's Radical Roots And Rules." IBD Editorials. 14 Aug. 2008. <http://www.ibdeditorials.com/ibdarticles.aspx?id=303605575673142>.

5. Kincaid, Cliff. "OBAMA'S COMMUNIST MENTOR." News With Views. 21 Feb. 2008. <http://www.newswithviews.com/kincaid/cliff209.htm>.

6. Scarborough, Melanie. "Obama scorns founders' vision of freedom." Dcexaminer.com. 25 Aug. 2008. <http://www.dcexaminer.com/opinion/columns/melaniescarborough/obama_scorns_founders_vision_of_freedom.html>.

7. "Michelle's speech inspired by radical socialist?" WorldNet Daily. 26 Aug. 2008. <http://www.worldnetdaily.com/index.php?fa=page.view&pageid=73533>.

8. Shiver, Kyle-Ann. "Obama's Alinsky Jujitsu." American Thinker. 8 Jan. 2008. <http://www.americanthinker.com/2008/01/obamas_alinsky_jujitsu.html>.

9. "Son sees father's handiwork in convention." Boston.com. 31 Aug. 2008. <http://www.boston.com/bostonglobe/editorial_opinion/letters/articles/2008/08/31/son_sees_fathers_handiwork_in_convention/>.

CHAPTER EIGHT

1. Hell Nobama 08. <http://www.hellnobama.com/therealobama.html>.

2. "Obama's Rapid Response Backfires." IBD Editorials. <http://www.ibdeditorials.com/ibdarticles.aspx?id=303953050138122>.

3. Finch, Scout. "Barack Obama Speech." Daily Kos. 18 Mar. 2008. <http://www.dailykos.com/story/2 008/3/18/105356/186/915/479103>.

4. Obama, Barack. Dreams from My Father : A Story of Race and Inheritance. New York: Three Rivers P, 2004. 198-99.

5. Bradley, Anthony B. "The Marxist Roots of Black Liberation Theology." Action Institute. <http://www.acton.org/commentary/443_marxist_roots_of_black_liberation_theology.php>.

6. Tarpley, Webster. "The men behind Obama." Interview with Daan De Wit. Deep Journal. 11 May 2008. http://www.deepjournal.com/p/7/a/en/1497.html

7. Obama, Barack. Dreams from My Father : A Story of Race and Inheritance. New York: Three Rivers P, 2004. 283.

8. Obama, Barack. Dreams from My Father : A Story of Race and Inheritance. New York: Three Rivers P, 2004. 284.

9. "The Oppression of Black Liberation Theology." Let Us Reason Ministries. <http://letusreason.org/cult25.htm>.

10. Ibid.

11. Ibid.

12. Smith, Ben. "Obama's Wright: 'White folks' greed'" Politico. 14 Mar. 2008. <http://www.politico.com/blogs/bensmith/0308/obamas_wright_white_folks_greed.html>.

13. Obama, Barack. Dreams from My Father : A Story of Race and Inheritance. New York: Three Rivers P, 2004. 86.

14. Obama, Barack. Dreams from My Father : A Story of Race and Inheritance. New York: Three Rivers P, 2004. 98.

15. Obama, Barack. Dreams from My Father : A Story of Race and Inheritance. New York: Three Rivers P, 2004. 124.

16. Obama, Barack. Dreams from My Father : A Story of Race and Inheritance. New York: Three Rivers P, 2004. 85.

17. Obama, Barack. Dreams from My Father : A Story of Race and Inheritance. New York: Three Rivers P, 2004. 134.

18. Obama, Barack. Dreams from My Father : A Story of Race and Inheritance. New York: Three Rivers P, 2004. 156.

19. Obama, Barack. Dreams from My Father : A Story of Race and Inheritance. New York: Three Rivers P, 2004. 155.

20. Obama, Barack. Dreams from My Father : A Story of Race and Inheritance. New York: Three Rivers P, 2004. 133.

21. Obama, Barack. Dreams from My Father : A Story of Race and Inheritance. New York: Three Rivers P, 2004. 103.

22. Obama, Barack. Dreams from My Father : A Story of Race and Inheritance. New York: Three Rivers P, 2004. 91.

23. "STOKELY CARMICHAEL Biography." Notable Biographies. <http://www.notablebiographies.com/ca-ch/carmichael-stokely.html>.

24. Kurtz, Stanley. "Barack Obama's Lost Years." The Weekly Standard. <http://www.weeklystandard.com/content/public/articles/000/000/015/386abhgm.asp>.

25. "New Black Panther's Shabazz and Oprah say Obama's "The One"" Rezko Watch. <http://rezkowatch.blogspot.com/2008/05/rezkowatch-factchecker-new-black.html>.

26. "Glenn Beck." CNN.com. 20 Mar. 2008. <http://transcripts.cnn.com/transcripts/0803/20/gb.01.html>.

27. "New Black Panther's Shabazz and Oprah say Obama's "The One"" Rezko Watch. <http://rezkowatch.blogspot.com/2008/05/rezkowatch-factchecker-new-black.html>.

CHAPTER NINE

1. Kincaid, Cliff. "OBAMA'S COMMUNIST MENTOR." News With Views. 21 Feb. 2008. <http://www.newswithviews.com/kincaid/cliff209.htm>.

2. Harnden, Toby. "Frank Marshall Davis, alleged Communist, was early influence on Barack Obama." Telegraph.co.uk. 24 Aug. 2008. <http://www.telegraph.co.uk/news/newstopics/uselection2008/barackobama/2601914/frank-marshall-davis-alleged-communist-was-early-influence-on-barack-obama.html>.
3. Kincaid, Cliff. "OBAMA'S RED MENTOR PRAISES RED ARMY." News With Views. 9 Apr. 2008. <http://www.newswithviews.com/kincaid/cliff216.htm>.
4. . "Edward Said." Wikipedia. <http://en.wikipedia.org/wiki/edward_said>.
5. Barsamian, David. "Interview with Edward W. Said." The Progressive. Nov. 2001. http://www.progressive.org/0901/intv1101.html.
6. Wallsten, Peter. "Rashid Khalidi." Los Angeles Times. 10 Apr. 2008. <http://www.latimes.com/news/politics/la-na-obamamideast10apr10,0,1780231,full.story>.
7. Barsamian, David. "Interview with Edward W. Said." The Progressive. Nov. 2001. http://www.progressive.org/0901/intv1101.html.
8. "Tony Rezko." Wikipedia. http://en.wikipedia.org/wiki/tony_rezko.
9. "Sweet Home Obama." IBD Editorials. 22 Aug. 2008. <http://www.ibdeditorials.com/ibdarticles.aspx?id=304297980806710>.
10. "AliAbunimah." DiscovertheNetworks.org. 10 Sept. 2008. http://www.discoverthenetworks.org/individualprofile.asp?indid=1426.
11. Jay, Dr, and Nathan Lerman. "Obama, The Reborn Zionist? [incl. Rashid Khalidi]." Campus Watch. 24 July 2008. <http://www.campus-watch.org/article/id/5410>.
12. Timmerman, Ken. "Obama Had Close Ties to Top Saudi Adviser at Early Age." Newsmax.com. 3 Sept. 2008. <http://www.newsmax.com/newsfront/obama_sutton_saudi/2008/09/03/127490.html>.
13. Ibid.
14. "Bill Ayers." Wikipedia. <http://en.wikipedia.org/wiki/bill_ayers>.
15. Kurtz, Stanley. "Chicago Annenberg Challenge Shutdown?" National Review Online. 18 Aug. 2008. <http://article.nationalreview.com/?q=mtgwztvmn2qynzk2mmuxmza5otg0odzlm2y2ogi0ndm=>.
16. "Annenberg Papers: Putting On Ayers?" IBD Editorials. 27 Aug. 2008. <http://www.ibdeditorials.com/ibdarticles.aspx?id=304729375940845>.
17. Hell Nobama 08. <http://www.hellnobama.com/quotes.html>.
18. Ibid.
19. Ibid.
20. "Michael Pfleger." Wikipedia. <http://en.wikipedia.org/wiki/michael_pfleger>.
21. Lewis, James. "The demonic Father Pfleger." American Thinker. 30 May 2008. <http://www.americanthinker.com/blog/2008/05/the_demonic_father_pfleger.html>.
22. "Zbigniew Brzezinski." Wikipedia. <http://en.wikipedia.org/wiki/zbigniew_brzezinski>.
23. "The Brzezinski/Obama Axis: Aiming For A World Without Israel*." Jewish Indy. 25 Feb. 2008. <http://www.jewishindy.com/modules.php?name=news&file=article&sid=7697>.
24. "Zbigniew Brzezinski to Jihadists: Your cause is right!" YouTube. <http://www.youtube.com/watch?v=ojtv2nfjmbk>.
25. Lorimer, Doug. "Afghanistan: Taliban continue growing in strength." Green Left Online. 3 May 2008. <http://www.greenleft.org.au/2008/749/38726>.
26. Hillier, Ben. "How the US created Osama bin Laden." The Socialist Alternative. May 2007. <http://www.sa.org.au/index.php?option=com_content&task=view&id=1148>.
27. "Seven Questions: A Conversation with Zbigniew Brzezinski." Foreign Policy. <http://www.foreignpolicy.com/story/cms.php?story_id=4034>.
28. Lake, Eli. "Obama Adviser Leads Delegation to Damascus." New York The Sun. 12 Feb. 2008. <http://www.nysun.com/foreign/obama-adviser-leads-delegation-to-damascus/71123/>.
29. Warner, Bill. "Barack Obama and Slavery." American Thinker. 26 Sept. 2008. <http://www.americanthinker.com/2008/09/barack_obama_and_slavery.html>.
30. MacGillis, Alec. "Brzezinski Backs Obama." The Washington Post. 25 Aug. 2007. <http://www.washingtonpost.com/wp-dyn/content/article/2007/08/24/ar2007082402127.html>.

31. "Finding Friends On Far, Far Left." IBD Editorials. 20 Aug. 2008. <http://www.ibdeditorials.com/ibdarticles.aspx?id=304124899839152>.

32. Saul, Micchael. "Major Barack Obama supporter slams Jewish groups." NY Daily News. 29 May 2008. <http://www.nydailynews.com/news/politics/2008/05/29/2008-05-29_major_barack_obama_supporter_slams_jewis.html>.

33. Sweeton, Lynn. "Sweet column: Before Jewish group, Obama distances himself from Brzezinski; says Farrakhan fan Rev. Wright like an "old uncle."" Chicago SunTimes. 25 Feb. 2008. <sweet column: before jewish group, obama distances himself from brzezinski; says farrakhan fan rev. wright like an "old uncle.">.

34. "The Art of Ostracism." National Review Online. 6 June 2008. <http://corner.nationalreview.com/post/?q=m2qwndaynzazmmjkzgrjnjk0odhiyjizntllzty5ymi>.

Chapter Ten

1. Christian, Ernest. "Will Democrats Ever Recover From Obama?" IBD Editorials. 17 Sept. 2008. <http://www.ibdeditorials.com/ibdarticles.aspx?id=306538589280393>.

2. Obama, Barack. Dreams from My Father : A Story of Race and Inheritance. New York: Three Rivers P, 2004. 141

3. Obama, Barack. Dreams from My Father : A Story of Race and Inheritance. New York: Three Rivers P, 2004. 193.

4. Obama, Barack. Dreams from My Father : A Story of Race and Inheritance. New York: Three Rivers P, 2004. 94-95.

5. Obama, Barack. Dreams from My Father : A Story of Race and Inheritance. New York: Three Rivers P, 2004. 158-59.

6. Obama, Barack. Dreams from My Father : A Story of Race and Inheritance. New York: Three Rivers P, 2004. 96.

7. Obama, Barack. Dreams from My Father : A Story of Race and Inheritance. New York: Three Rivers P, 2004. 135.

8. Hanscom, Aaron. "Obama Does Offer Hope — to America's Foes." Pajamas Media. 24 July 2008. http://pajamasmedia.com/blog/obama-offers-hope-%e2%80%94-to-americas-foes/2/.

9. Wehner, Peter. "Off-the-Record Obama." National Review Online. 14 Apr. 2008. http://article.nationalreview.com/?q=mtlinjljytu2ndzinwe3zwe2ntdjntrmzgi0zwi3yzu=

10. Ibid.

11. Kristol, William. "The Mask Slips." The New York Times. 14 Apr. 2008. http://www.nytimes.com/2008/04/14/opinion/14kristol.html?_r=3&ref=opinion&oref=slogin&oref=slogin&oref=slogin.

12. Weblog post. OBAMA TO SUPPORTERS: Argue With Your Neighbors, Get In Their Face. <http://www.freerepublic.com/focus/news/2084874/posts>.

13. Ibid.

14. Koret, Reuven. "Is Barack Obama a Muslim wolf in Christian wool?" Israel Insider. 27 Mar. 2008. http://web.israelinsider.com/articles/politics/12745.htm.

15. Walden, Andrew. ""There is only the Fight"." FrontPageMag.com. 21 Aug. 2007. <http://frontpagemag.com/articles/read.aspx?guid=39595ecb-c0ad-4e37-a093-a2e510fe3a60>.

Chapter Eleven

1. Eberle, Bobby. "Hands up! You're under arrest for saying 'Hussein Obama!'" The Loft. 9 Oct. 2008. <http://www.gopusa.com/theloft/?p=795>.

2. Livengood, Chad. "Blunt, GOP say Obama 'truth squad' seeks to squash free speech with police power." NewsLeader.com. 27 Sept. 2008.

3. "Gov. Blunt Statement on Obama Campaign's Abusive Use of Missouri Law Enforcement." Missouri Governor's Office. 27 Sept. 2008. <http://governor.mo.gov/cgi-bin/coranto/viewnews.cgi?id=ekkkvfulkpozxqgmaj>.

4. Lowry, Rich. "The Obama Rules." Real Clear Politics. 13 May 2008. <http://www.realclearpolitics.com/articles/2008/05/the_obama_rules.html>.

CHAPTER TWELVE

1. Richardson, Joel. "Obama And Hitler." Weblog post. Joels Trumpet. 27 Aug. 2008. <http://www. joelstrumpet.com/?p=1439#comments>.
2. Ibid.
3. 13. West, Chelsie. "Obama says, 'Believe.' In what?" Free Republic. 2 June 2008. <http://www. freerepublic.com/focus/f-news/2024977/posts>.
4. Richardson, Joel. "Obama And Hitler." Weblog post. Joels Trumpet. 27 Aug. 2008. <http://www. joelstrumpet.com/?p=1439#comments>.
5. Ibid.
6. Vaknin, Sam. "Narcissistic and Psychopathic Leaders." <http://samvak.tripod.com/15.html>.
7. "Obama blasts Bush, McCain over 'attacks'" CNNPolitics.com. 16 May 2008. <http://www.cnn. com/2008/politics/05/16/obama.bush.mccain/index.html>.
8. "I'm not Bush, McCain tells Obama." The Times of India. 16 Oct. 2008. <http://timesofindia. indiatimes.com/im_not_bush_mccain_tells_obama/rssarticleshow/3601685.cms>.
9. "Joseph Goebbels." Wikipedia. <http://en.wikipedia.org/wiki/joseph_goebbels>.
10. Goebbels, Dr. Joseph. "German Propaganda Archive." Calvin.edu. http://www.calvin.edu/academic/cas/gpa/ahspeak.htm.
11. Kershaw, Ian. "How Hitler Won Over the German People." Speigel Online International. <http://www.spiegel.de/international/germany/0,1518,531909-2,00.html>.
12. Wehner, Peter. "Off-the-Record Obama." National Review Online. 14 Apr. 2008. http://article. nationalreview.com/?q=mtlinjljytu2ndzinwe3zwe2ntdjntrmzgi0zwi3yzu=
13. "The Rise Of The Fourth Reich." WhatReallyHappened.com. <http://whatreallyhappened.com/wrharticles/reich.html>.
14. "Man of The Year." Time Magazine. 2 Jan. 1939. <http://www.time.com/time/magazine/article/0,9171,760539-1,00.html>.
15. Ibid.
16. Overlords of Chaos. <http://www.overlordsofchaos.com/html/2007.html>.
17. Ibid.
18. "The Rise Of The Fourth Reich." WhatReallyHappened.com. <http://whatreallyhappened.com/wrharticles/reich.html>.
19. 13. A Clockwork Obama. http://aclockworkobama.com/

CHAPTER THIRTEEN

1. Sammon, Bill. "Can a past of Islam change the path to president for Obama?" Examiner.com. 29 Jan. 2007. http://www.examiner.com/a-534540~can_a_past_of_islam_change_the_path_to__president_.html.
2. "Barack Obama on Principles & Values." On The Issues. <http://www.ontheissues.org/social/barack_obama_principles_+_values.htm>.
3. Ripley, Amanda. "The Story of Barack Obama's Mother." Time Magazine. 9 Apr. 2008. http://www.time.com/time/nation/article/0,8599,1729524-6,00.html.
4. Obama, Barack. Dreams from My Father : A Story of Race and Inheritance. New York: Three Rivers P, 2004. 37.
5. Obama, Barack. Dreams from My Father : A Story of Race and Inheritance. New York: Three Rivers P, 2004. 33.
6. Earle, Geoff. "BARACK'S A 'CHARMER'" New York Post. 24 June 2008. http://www.nypost.com/seven/06242008/news/nationalnews/baracks_a_charmer_116926.htm.
7. "Is Obama devotee of monkey-god idol?" WorldNet Daily. 27 June 2008. <http://www.worldnetdaily.com/index.php?fa=page.view&pageid=68156>.
8. Johnson, Jr., Robert. "The Real Obama is the Obama Oprah Knows." HumanEvents.com. 5 Sept. 2008. <http://www.humanevents.com/article.php?print=yes&id=28408>.
9. Obama, Barack. Dreams from My Father : A Story of Race and Inheritance. New York: Three Rivers P, 2004. 141

10. Obama, Barack. Dreams from My Father : A Story of Race and Inheritance. New York: Three Rivers P, 2004. 274.

11. Obama, Barack. Dreams from My Father : A Story of Race and Inheritance. New York: Three Rivers P, 2004. 163.

12. De Zutter, Hank. "What Makes Obama Run?" Chicago Reader. 8 Dec. 1995. http://www.chicagoreader.com/features/stories/archive/barackobama/.

13. "TV ad features Obama mocking Bible." WorldNet Daily. 10 Oct. 2008. http://www.worldnetdaily.com/index.php?fa=page.view&pageid=77629.

14. "Obama Denies Christ in His Own Words." Christian Anti-Defamation Commission. <http://christianadc.org/pages/page.asp?page_id=38840>.

15. Ibid.

16. Ibid.

17. Ibid.

18. Ibid.

19. Ibid.

20. Ibid.

CHAPTER FOURTEEN

1. "Oprah Winfrey touted as Barack Obama's top ambassador." Herald Sun. 25 Oct. 2008. <http://www.news.com.au/heraldsun/story/0,21985,24547603-663,00.html>.

2. "Nothing Funny About Obama Losing." Breitbart.com. <http://www.breitbart.com/article.php?id=080919193927.ite7zfed&show_article=1>.

3. "Top 10 Celebrity Obama Supporters." Huffington Post. 20 Apr. 2008. <http://www.huffingtonpost.com/2008/04/20/top-10-celebrity-obama-su_n_96313.html>.

4. "Black Leaders, Celebrities in Denver for Obama Camp 'Unity' Breakfast on MLK Anniversary." ABC News. 28 Aug. 2008. <http://blogs.abcnews.com/politicalradar/2008/08/black-leaders-c.html>.

5. Bozell III, L. Brent. "Celebrities Embarrass Obama." Culture and Media Institute. 29 Aug. 2008. <http://www.cultureandmediainstitute.org/articles/2008/20080829164506.aspx>.

6. "Is Barack Obama the Messiah." <http://obamamessiah.blogspot.com/2007/12/oprah-winfrey-obama-has-tongue-dipped.html>.

CHAPTER FIFTEEN

1. "Barack Obama's Speech in Berlin." BarackObama.com. 24 July 2008. <http://my.barackobama.com/page/content/berlinvideo/>.

2. Allen, Mike. "Obama promises to 'remake the world'" Politico. 24 July 2008. <http://dyn.politico.com/printstory.cfm?uuid=565916c4-3048-5c12-0064d5c4f73a4411>.

3. DeWeese, Tom. "BARAK OBAMA & THE UN's DRIVE FOR GLOBAL GOVERNANCE." NewsWithViews.com. 20 July 2008. <http://www.newswithviews.com/deweese/tom114.htm>.

4. "McCain vs Obama: Who's better for India?" The Times of India. 8 June 2008. http://timesofindia.indiatimes.com/opinion/sunday_specials/special_report/mccain_vs_obama_whos_better_for_india/articleshow/msid-3110215,curpg-1.cms

5. "Barack Obama on Principles & Values." On The Issues. <http://www.ontheissues.org/social/barack_obama_principles_+_values.htm>.

6. Ibid.

7. Freedland, Jonathan. "The world's verdict will be harsh if the US rejects the man it yearns for." The Guardian. 10 Sept. 2008. <http://www.guardian.co.uk/commentisfree/2008/sep/10/uselections2008.barackobama>.

CHAPTER SIXTEEN

1. "Barack Obama: More Popular Than Jesus, Angelina Jolie." Gawker.com. 25 June 2008. <http://gawker.com/tag/magazines/?i=5019689&t=barack-obama-more-popular-than-jesus-angelina-jolie#cbarack-obama-more-popular-than-jesus-angelina-jolie>.

2. "THE YEAR THE MEDIA DIED." WorldNet Daily. 2 Oct. 2008. <http://www.worldnetdaily.com/index.php?fa=page.view&pageid=76890>.

3. Ibid.

4. Huston, Warner T. "Obama's Propagandistic Iconography: the Making of a Messiah." NewBusters. 22 June 2008. <http://newsbusters.org/blogs/warner-todd-huston/2008/06/22/obamas-propagandistic-iconography-making-messiah>.

5. Huston, Warner T. "Obama's Propagandistic Iconography: the Making of a Messiah." NewBusters. 22 June 2008. <http://newsbusters.org/blogs/warner-todd-huston/2008/06/22/obamas-propagandistic-iconography-making-messiah>.

CHAPTER SEVENTEEN

1. Baker, Gerard. "Times Online." He ventured forth to bring light to the world. 25 July 2008. <http://www.timesonline.co.uk/tol/comment/columnists/gerard_baker/article4392846.ece>.

2. Morford, Mark. "Is Obama an enlightened being?" SG Gate. 6 June 2008. http://www.sfgate.com/cgi-bin/article.cgi?f=/g/a/2008/06/06/notes060608.dtl.

3. "Farrakhan on Obama: The Messiah is absolutely speaking'" WorldNet Daily. 9 Oct. 2008. <http://www.worldnetdaily.com/index.php?fa=page.view&pageid=77539>.

4. Shiver, Kyle-Ann. "Obama, the Closer." National Review Online. 27 Mar. 2008. <http://article.nationalreview.com/print/?q=ntnkntu5mje2mjuwnmq2mwq3ywrlyjhmnzq4otqyogu>.

5. Ibid.

6. Duigon, Lee. "Obama, the World Teacher." ChronWatch. 18 July 2008. <http://www.chronwatch-america.com/articles/3241/1/obama-the-world-teacher/page1.html>.

7. "Is Barack Obama the Messiah." <http://obamamessiah.blogspot.com/2008/10/prepare-me-sanctuary-pure-and-holy.html>.

8. Ibid.

9. Ibid.

10. Ibid.

11. Ibid.

12. Ibid.

13. Ibid.

14. Ibid.

15. Ibid.

CHAPTER EIGHTEEN

1. Overlords of Chaos. <http://www.overlordsofchaos.com/html/1800-49.html>.

2. Overlords of Chaos. <http://www.overlordsofchaos.com/html/1945-49.html>.

3. Tucker, William. "Secret dangers about Obama." Sioux City Journal. <http://www.siouxcityjournal.com/articles/2008/10/07/news_opinion/letters/573a7c16c595a292862574da0077d32f.txt>.

4. Overlords of Chaos. <http://www.overlordsofchaos.com/html/1975-79.html>.

5. Overlords of Chaos. <http://www.overlordsofchaos.com/html/1990-94.html>.

6. Ibid.

7. "Joe Biden's New World Order Speech." BlackListedNews.com. 25 Aug. 2008. <http://www.blacklistednews.com/?news_id=1226>.

8. Overlords of Chaos. <http://www.overlordsofchaos.com/html/1945-49.html>.

9. Overlords of Chaos. <http://www.overlordsofchaos.com/html/1930-34.html>.

CHAPTER TWENTY

1. "Glen Beck." CNN.com. 12 Oct. 2007. <http://transcripts.cnn.com/transcripts/0710/12/gb.01.html>.

2. Sexton, Timothy. "Maitreya: The Messenger of Peace Expected by Believers in Christianity, Judaism, Islam, Hinduism, Buddhism...." Associated Content. 24 Mar. 2007. <http://www.associatedcontent.com/article/180760/maitreya_the_messenger_of_peace_expected.html?cat=34>.

3. . http://www.share-international.org/maitreya/ma_main.htm.

4. "Glen Beck." CNN.com. 12 Oct. 2007. <http://transcripts.cnn.com/transcripts/0710/12/gb.01.html>.

5. "Antichrist (Beast)." Rapture Ready. <http://www.raptureready.com/abc/antichrist.html>.

CHAPTER TWENTY-ONE

1. Overlords of Chaos. <http://www.overlordsofchaos.com/html/nwo_quotes.html>.
2. Bresciani, Michael. "Mesmerizing Obama." CrossAction News. 11 June 2008. <http://www.crossactionnews.com/articles/view/mesmerizing-obama>.
3. Washington, Ellis. "Obama, Bishop T.D. Jakes and me." WorldNet Daily. 12 June 2008. http://www.worldnetdaily.com/index.php?fa=page.view&pageid=66833.
4. "Commentary: Obama nomination gives 'goose bumps'" CNNPolitics.com. <http://www.cnn.com/2008/politics/06/04/jakes/index.html>.
5. Washington, Ellis. "Obama, Bishop T.D. Jakes and me." WorldNet Daily. 12 June 2008. http://www.worldnetdaily.com/index.php?fa=page.view&pageid=66833.
6. "Political Endorsement From The Pulpit." NPR. 10 Oct. 2008. <http://www.npr.org/templates/story/story.php?storyid=95594731>.
7. Hagerty, Barbara B. "Pastors To Preach Politics From The Pulpit." 24 Sept. 2008. <http://www.npr.org/templates/story/story.php?storyid=95594731>.
8. Overlords of Chaos. <http://www.overlordsofchaos.com/html/nwo_quotes.html>.
9. Overlords of Chaos. <http://www.overlordsofchaos.com/html/1945-49.html>.
10. Ibid.

CHAPTER TWENTY-TWO

1. Willis, Bonnie. "A Study of Amos." It's Time. <http://its-time.info/articles/amos/3/>.

CHAPTER TWENTY-THREE

1. Weiner, Rose. "The Cross is a Radical Thing." Weiner Ministries International. <http://www.bobweinerministries.com/site/index.php?option=com_content&task=view&id=31&itemid=60>.
2. Gregg's Gambles.com. <http://greggsgambles.com/messages/06-01-15blog.htm>.